Alvey

Alvey: Britain's Strategic Computing Initiative

Brian Oakley and Kenneth Owen

The MIT Press
Cambridge, Massachusetts
London, England

© 1989 Massachusetts Institute of Technology

All rights reserved. No part of this book may be reproduced in any form or by any electronic or mechanical means (including photocopying, recording, or information storage and retrieval) without permission in writing from the publisher.

This book was set in Baskerville by Compset, Inc.
and printed and bound in the United States of America.

Library of Congress Cataloging-in-Publication Data

Oakley, Brian.
 Alvey, Britain's strategic computing initiative / Brian Oakley and Kenneth Owen.
   p.   cm.
 Bibliography: p.
 Includes index.
 ISBN 0-262-15038-7
 1. Computers—Great Britain.   I. Owen, Kenneth.   II. Title.
QA76.0225   1990
338.4′7004′0941—dc20   89-35121
                                                                CIP

Contents

Preface x
List of Characters xii

I
INTRODUCING ALVEY

1
What Was Alvey? 3

2
Origins 7

A Coordinated Program. The Roberts Panel. Ministering to IT. A Universal Project. The Artificial Intelligentsia. Collaboration with Japan? The Clarke Initiative. From Tokyo to Number Ten.

3
A Call for Action 22

The Team's Report. Cosener's House. Project IT87. Lord's Cricket Ground.

4
Committee Time 34

The Alvey Committee. Points of Principle. Size and Shape of the Program. Alvey's People. The Alvey Report. AI Revisited. Consultation. Action.

II
DIRECTING THE PROGRAMME

5
Birth of the Programme 57

The Part Played by Kenneth Baker. Sir Keith Joseph Plays his Part. The Alvey Decision in Whitehall. Changes from the Alvey Committee's Recommendations. The Choice of Director. Qualifications for the Director Post? To Accept or Not to Accept?

6
The Directorate Moves into Action 68

The Deputy Director. The Key Administrator. Secondments from Industry. Directors from the MoD and SERC. Directors from Industry. Delegation. Preparation of the Strategies. The VLSI Strategy. Software Engineering Strategy. IKBS Strategy. An Operating System Standard for Alvey. MMI Strategy.

7
The Directorate Process in Action 86

Board Meetings. The Large-Demonstrator Projects. Evaluation of Project Proposals. Advisory Committees. The Alvey Programme Steering Committee. Cooperation. Cooperation with Universities.

8
Problems and Other Issues 102

Where the Responsibility Lay. Funding Problems. Support of the U.K. Industry Through Capital Purchases. Small Firms. Collaboration with ESPRIT. Communications. Skill Shortages and Training. In the Eye of the Press. Monitoring and Evaluation.

Contents   vii

III
VIEWS FOR AND AGAINST

9
Alvey Observed   127

Shape of the Programme. Role of the Steering Committee. Assorted Technologies. Administration.

10
Errors and Additions   147

Architectures are Added. Large-Scale Demonstrators. Speech Input, Confused Output. The Series 63 Mistake. A U.S. Critic. The MMI Scene. Individual Views. Search for Surgeons.

11
Breaking the Mold   169

Collaboration. The AI Scene. Industrial Views. Defense Interests. New Mechanisms. Breaking the Mold. Expats Return. Baker's Baby. The Second Wave.

12
The Evaluators   190

Evaluation—Official. No Audit Plaudit. Most Monitored Program. Evaluating the Evaluators. VLSE: Very Large-Scale Evaluation. Academic-Flavored IKBS. IT Users' Views. Cabinet Office Critic. The Alvey Ethos.

IV
ALVEY AND AFTER

13
Meanwhile, in Other Places   213

Precedents for Cooperative Research. The Japanese 5G Announcement. The U.S. Response. An Industrial Research

Cooperative in the United States. The European Response—
ESPRIT. The Japanese 5G Program. The Cost and the Staff.
The Initial Phase. The Japanese User Language. The Value of the
Japanese Program.

14
A Son of Alvey?   229

First and Future Task. Academic Action. Edinburgh 85 and
IT86. Workshop Time. Research and Applications. The Bide
Report. The Long Silence. Enter Enterprise.

15
The New Era   245

Responses to the Response. A Political View. The New Era. The
Oakley View. The Persuader. After-Alvey Directions. Exit Alvey,
Rather Quietly.

16
Was it All Worthwhile?   265

Evaluation of Research. Scale of the Programme. Progress
Toward the Goal of AI. Human Interface in AI. Parallel
Architecture Work in Japan. Parallel Architecture Work in the U.K.
Small Firms. Market Penetration of Knowledge-Based Systems.
Achievement in VLSI. Integrated Circuit CAD. Integrated Circuit
Instrument Industry. Software Engineering. Speech Technology in
Alvey. The Wheel Turns. The Lessons that Remain.

Appendix 1
A Program for Advanced Information Technology   295
Appendix 2
U.K. Government Approves Alvey Plan   299
Appendix 3
Academics Favor After-Alvey Program   302
Appendix 4
A Plan for Concerted Action   304
Appendix 5
Evaluators Report on Alvey Programme   307

Appendix 6
U.K. Government Responds to IT86   313
Appendix 7
National Audit Office Audits Alvey   316
Abbreviations   322
References   326
Further Reading   328
Name Index   330
Subject Index   333

Preface

This book is an inside story of the Alvey Programme, a collective—and selective—personal memoir based largely on the recollections of many of those involved. It is *not* an official history or a research report. It aims to provide an album of snapshots of important issues and events, drawing on contemporary material to set the 1988 views in context. Individuals' opinions and attitudes differ on some topics; these contrasting perspectives help to illuminate the human story of what was a unique, exciting, and successful experiment. We hope this book conveys the flavor of Alvey; sources of more detailed information on the Programme and its projects are listed under References and Further Reading at the end of the book.

We should declare our interests. Brian Oakley was Director of the Alvey Programme from 1983 to 1987, and his personal account of the Alvey years and of parallel programs and his overall conclusions appear in chapters 5 through 8, 13, and 16.

Kenneth Owen is a freelance writer who was an editorial consultant to the Alvey Directorate from 1983 to 1988; his role here, in chapters 1 through 4, 9 through 12, 14, and 15, has been to sketch the factual background and report the views of participants and others. The book includes the personal views of members of the Alvey Directorate and its successor, the Information Engineering Directorate, but does not represent the official view of the Department of Trade and Industry or of any other agency.

We should mention that, as is normal practice for retired British civil servants writing about their work, Brian Oakley discussed the draft of his chapters with officials of the government departments involved, and made certain changes to the original text as a result.

In the Alvey tradition this book is a collaborative effort, and we acknowledge the help of many members of the Alvey community (notably those identified in the List of Characters). Many are quoted here, and others provided valuable interpretative guidance. Where they are quoted in the present tense, their words come from special interviews with Kenneth Owen (or in a few cases from letters, electronic mail, or telephone conversations) during the summer of 1988, in the course of research for the book. The sources of other quotations are indicated.

Brian Oakley thanks Pat Tibbles for word-processing assistance, and Kenneth Owen thanks his partner Suzette Owen for research and word-processing assistance. In seeking background information, we were helped by John Head-Rapson, Bernard Tan, and Linda Prior at the Information Engineering Directorate; John Cooper at the Institution of Electrical Engineers; staff at the SERC headquarters and the Rutherford Appleton Laboratory; Ken Howe of ICL; Janet Tomlinson at the IEE/BCS Library; and staff at the University of Surrey Library and the Lyon Playfair Library of Imperial College, London. We appreciate Polly Read's kind help in letting us see the late Charles Read's papers. Extracts from HM Government publications are Crown Copyright and are reproduced with the permission of the Controller of Her Majesty's Stationery Office.

October 1988

List of Characters

Contributors to the Research for this Book

John Alvey, Chairman, Alvey Committee

Professor Eric Ash, Rector, Imperial College, London; Alvey Programme Steering Committee; and Chairman, SERC After-Alvey Working Party

Reay Atkinson, Head, DoI Japan Mission, 1981

Kenneth Baker, MP, Minister of State for Industry and Information Technology, 1981–1984

Iann Barron, Alvey Committee

Alan Bagshaw, Alvey Directorate (Architectures)

Derek Barber, Alvey Directorate (I & C)

Chris Barrow, Alvey Directorate (MMI)

Keith Bartlett, Alvey Directorate (I & C)

Alan Benjamin, Chairman, IT82 Year

Sir Austin Bide, Chairman, IT86 Committee

Professor Michael Brady, University of Oxford

Professor Alec Broers, University of Cambridge; IT86 Committee

Professor Alan Bundy, University of Edinburgh

Laurence Clarke, Alvey Directorate

Dr. John Dowell, University College, London

Professor Michael Duff, University College, London

Tony Egginton, SERC; IT86 Committee

Owen Etoe, Confederation of British Industry

John Fairclough, Chief Scientific Adviser, Cabinet Office

Dr. Bill Fawcett, Alvey Directorate (VLSI)

Dr. Alan Fox, DoI Japan Mission

Dr. Peter Gray, University of Aberdeen

Colin Haley, Alvey Committee

Dr. John Holmes, Consultant

Dr. Nigel Horne, IT86 Committee

Sir John Hoskyns, Institute of Directors

Professor Jim Howe, University of Edinburgh; IT86 Committee

Philip Hughes, Alvey Committee; Alvey Programme Steering Committee

Professor Frank Land, London Business School

Professor John Laver, University of Edinburgh

Professor Simon Lavington, University of Essex

Cameron Low, IT86 Committee

Alastair Macdonald, DTI; Alvey Committee; Alvey Programme Steering Committee

James Merriman, Chairman, DoI seminar, January 1982

Professor Donald Michie, The Turing Institute

David Morgan, Alvey Directorate (Software Engineering)

Robert Morland, Alvey Directorate (VLSI)

Brian Murphy, PITCOM

Professor Roger Needham, University of Cambridge; DoI Japan Mission; Alvey Committee

Adrian Norman, Cabinet Office IT Unit, 1981–1983

Professor Graham Nudd, University of Warwick

Brian Oakley, Director, Alvey Programme, 1983–1987

Kenneth Owen, freelance writer

List of Characters

Sir Geoffrey Pattie, MP, Minister for Information Technology, 1984–1987

Professor Brian Randell, University of Newcastle-upon-Tyne; DoI Japan Mission

Patrick Raymont, National Computing Centre

Derek Roberts, Alvey Committee

Professor Brian Shackel, Loughborough University

Bill Sharpe, SERC and Alvey Directorate (IKBS)

David Shorter, Alvey Directorate (IKBS)

Professor Derek Sleeman, University of Aberdeen

Professor Aaron Sloman, University of Sussex

Colin Southgate, Alvey Programme Steering Committee

Dr. Mike Tainsh, Alvey Directorate (HI)

Bill Talbot, Alvey ANSA Project, Cambridge

David Talbot, Alvey Directorate (Software Engineering)

Dr. Austin Tate, AIAI, University of Edinburgh

Dr. John Taylor, Chairman, SERC/DoI IKBS Architecture Study

Sir Robert Telford, Chairman, Alvey Programme Steering Committee

Dr. David Thomas, SERC and Alvey Directorate (IKBS)

Dr. Timothy Walker, Alvey Directorate (Administration), 1983–1985; Head of Information Engineering Directorate, 1987–1989

Professor David Warren, University of Bristol

Dr. Keith Warren, Alvey Committee; Alvey Programme Steering Committee

Dr. Robb Wilmot, Managing Director, ICL, 1981–1985

Dr. Rob Witty, SERC and Alvey Directorate (Software Engineering)

Dr. Robert Worden, Logica

Dr. David Worsnip, SERC

Others Whose Views are Quoted

John Aris, Director, NCC; Chairman, Alvey IT Users Panel

Kenneth Clarke, MP, Minister of Trade and Industry, 1987–1988

Professor Edward Feigenbaum, Stanford University

Sir Colin Fielding, Ministry of Defence

Ken Guy, Science Policy Research Unit, University of Sussex

Sir Brian Hayes, Permanent Secretary, DTI

Dr. Andrew Herbert, Alvey ANSA project, Cambridge

Roger Hird, Alvey Directorate (Administration)

Patrick Jenkin, Secretary of State for Industry, 1981–1983

Dr. Leo Keliher, London School of Economics, 1986–1987

Charles Read, DoI Japan Mission; Alvey Committee; Information Technology Advisory Panel

Dr. Mike Watson, Alvey Programme Steering Committee; IT86 Committee

I
Introducing Alvey

1
What Was Alvey?

In the decade of the 1980s the organization of computing research and technology in Britain was transformed. A combination of forces—political, technical, international—came together to reshape the pattern of industrial and university research and development in this all-pervasive and fast-moving technology. A unique experiment known as the Alvey Programme revolutionized traditional attitudes and mechanisms. In its five-year lifetime a new information technology community was born and rapidly matured; at the end of that period new concepts pioneered in Alvey became a continuing feature of science and technology policy in the United Kingdom. What then was the Alvey Programme? Kenneth Owen gives a nine-point summary.

Alvey was John

The original Alvey is John Alvey, now retired, who in 1982 was senior director, technology, at British Telecom. He chaired a committee that recommended that a national program in advanced information technology (IT) research should be launched. Such a program, bearing his name, was indeed launched; otherwise this book could not have been written.

Alvey was Research

The area chosen for the Alvey experiment was that of precompetitive, advanced information technology research. "Precompetitive research" meant that the research concentrated on so-called enabling technologies—broad areas identified as vital to the subsequent development of competitive IT products and systems. Examples of these technologies appear in advanced microelectronics, software engineering, knowledge-based systems stemming from the world of artificial intelligence, and the complex interaction between human beings and computer-based systems. The Alvey research in part resembled the type of IT research associated with Japan's national program to develop fifth-generation computer systems, launched internationally at a historic conference in Tokyo in October 1981—and was in part a direct response to that program.

Alvey was Collaboration

Above all else the keynote of the Alvey Programme was collaboration. The Programme persuaded universities and industry to talk and work together, which in Britain was quite an achievement. It persuaded different companies to talk and work together, an even greater achievement. It even persuaded three separate government departments to talk and work together, which many would regard as an altogether unprecedented achievement. Over 200 research projects were mounted, each involving a group of participants from various firms, government establishments, universities, and polytechnics. This project collaboration was extended into a research community activity with the formation of research clubs and special interest groups that focused on relevant scientific topics.

Alvey was Innovation

Beyond the emphasis on collaborative research, the Alvey Programme was innovative in many other respects. Projects were assessed not only on their research quality and extent of collaboration but also on their relevance to the Programme's overall objective—to mobilize the United Kingdom's technical strengths in IT to improve the country's competitive position in world markets—and hence on their potential for the exploitation of results. A small central directorate was created to lead the Programme, staffed by a mixture of industrial secondees, government officials, and academics. New mechanisms for research were set up, including distributed projects, single-site project centers, and centers devoted to the general advancement of particular disciplines. New approaches to education and training also were developed, including distance-learning techniques and a "journeyman" scheme for high-level apprenticeship in artificial intelligence. In addition to research, effort went into increasing industrial awareness of the potential of the Alvey technologies; as part of this effort expert-system community clubs brought groups of organizations together to share the costs of system development.

Alvey was Controversy

Politically, technically, and internationally the Alvey Programme was controversial throughout its life. Why should the U.K. government provide the substantial public funding that was required? Why ape the Japanese, if that was what the Programme was doing? Was more research needed, anyway? What was the point, if most of the money was going to the big, rich electronics firms? What was the route to exploitation? Why not put all our eggs into the European basket? Why not leave it all to private industry? Why that particular choice of technologies? Why the bureaucratic delays in launching projects? What hope was there for the smaller firms to participate?

Alvey was Investment

The Alvey Programme was expected to cost a total of about £350 million over five years, of which about £200 million was to come from public funds administered by the three government departments involved. University work was expected to total about £50 million, fully paid for from public funds; while industry was to pay 50 percent toward the cost of the joint projects making up the remaining £300 million. In the event the academic share was more than expected.

Alvey was Cultural Revolution

Though there were many examples of contact between Britain's academic ivory towers and industry's dark satanic mills in the years before Alvey, the cultural change brought about by the Alvey Programme has made those weary clichés even more abstract. Both academic researchers and industrial developers found that those on the other side had much to contribute to their joint projects, and could be quite pleasant individuals. This realization came as even more of a shock to staff members of rival companies who "precompetitively" came together in Alvey projects. Government research laboratories also found collaboration could be stimulating. This cultural revolution had a twofold implication: Britain's academic/industrial complex, so to speak, has been immensely strengthened in the IT field; and Britain's companies are better placed to collaborate in the broader arena of Europe.

Alvey was Achievement

Perhaps this cultural change will prove to be the outstanding achievement of the Alvey Programme. At £350 million it is arguably quite cheap, not that that argument would convince governments or companies. But the British taxpayers who paid their £200 million have a fair bargain. The technology transfer is there. The technical achievements have yet to be proven, though there have been notable advances in many areas of research. Alvey's impact on U.K. government research organization is a further specific achievement—generally, in the closer relationships between the three departments involved, and specifically, in the joint IT research framework introduced by the Department of Trade and Industry and the Science and Engineering Research Council.

Alvey was Community

Alvey brought Britain's IT research community together and made known to a wider community what advanced IT could offer. At annual conferences and at countless workshops and seminars, by electronic mail, facsimile and telephone the community communed to good effect. In 1988 the government decided against an "Alvey 2" program as such. The signs are that the Alvey community has survived that blow and is alive and well.

2
Origins

Many tributaries flowed into the river that became the Alvey Programme—from the Science and Engineering Research Council, from the Ministry of Defence, from the Department of Industry, from a backbench Member of Parliament, and from a conference in Tokyo. The artificial intelligence community thought of a new name for their subject in the interests of respectability and funding. A mission was sent to Japan to find out what was going on there. When the group got back, a fast-talking professor tried to tell the prime minister all about it. Kenneth Owen outlines these origins.

A Coordinated Program

In September 1974 Iann Barron, an individualistic computer scientist who at that time was a consultant and visiting professor at Westfield College, London, was appointed to the Computing Science Committee of the Science Research Council (SRC). Barron went on in 1978 to cofound Inmos, the semiconductor company that later developed the revolutionary transputer; and the SRC, renamed the Science and Engineering Research Council (SERC) in April 1981, went on to play a major role in the Alvey Programme. But Barron's 1974 appointment led to a significant SRC initiative that paved the way toward Alvey. This initiative was known as the Distributed Computing Systems (DCS) Programme.

The Science and Engineering Research Council is one of five U.K. research councils that, using public funds provided by the Department of Education and Science, sponsor research in U.K. universities and polytechnics. Traditionally the council responds to research proposals by subjecting them to peer review by committees (of which it has many) of experts. The Computing Science Committee and the later Information Engineering

Committee, which features prominently in the Alvey story, came under the Engineering banner in the SERC organization.

Barron's introduction to this organization was not auspicious. At the committee he recalls:

> I was absolutely appalled by what went on there, in terms of inefficiency and lack of drive. I wrote a letter to the then chairman, Professor Tom Kilburn, saying this is dreadful, and in reply he invited me to do something about it by making a positive proposal. So I did. I proposed that instead of what they were doing, which was peer review of arbitrary programs, there should be some directed research. There should be a specific goal, and the research should be directed by the SRC with specific targets. People should be requested to do particular items of research, rather than coming up and saying "We'd like to play in this area."

Or, as an official account[1] published in 1984 puts it, "The Computer (sic) Science Committee, recognizing the importance of distributed computing as a research area, appointed a panel in June 1976 under the chairmanship of Prof. I. Barron, to consider what action was necessary to encourage, coordinate, or direct research in distributed computing."

The resulting Distributed Computing Systems Programme was the first attempt by the SRC to establish a substantial coordinated program of research in information technology. The key word was "coordinated"—it was in effect a halfway house between the random style of peer review and the directed (or more directed) style that was to be a feature of Alvey. It brought distinguished individual scientists together into an organized and communicating community, with coordinating staff based at the Council's Rutherford Appleton Laboratory at Didcot in Oxfordshire.

It also involved industry. Rob Witty, an SERC scientist who worked on the DCS and other programs at Rutherford and later at the Alvey Directorate, says: "When Barron put together DCS, one of its objectives was to link it into industry. It was totally funded by SRC, funding university people to do the research, but industrial relevance was a criterion. We made sure that it was linked into industry in the social sense of inviting industrialists to workshops; we had industrial members on the DCS panel, and we were looking to do technology transfer."

The DCS Programme started in 1977 and ended in 1984.

The phrase "distributed computing systems" covered a spectrum of research that embraced networks of conventional computers, systems containing sets of microprocessors, and novel forms of highly parallel computer architecture. DCS-funded projects that were to be pursued further in Alvey included the Manchester University Dataflow parallel computing system and Imperial College's ALICE graph-reduction multiprocessor machine.

The Roberts Panel

Another SRC initiative was mounted in October 1977, when a special panel was appointed to formulate a new national program of collaborative research in computing science and computer applications (the panel excluded networks and distributed computing, not wishing to duplicate the DCS work, but went beyond its terms of reference in proposing new initiatives in education and training). Chairman of the panel was Derek Roberts of Plessey. Panel members included Iann Barron, Alan Benjamin of the Computing Services Association, Colin Haley of ICL, and Philip Hughes of Logica.

In their report[2] the panel recommended a national program involving education and training, new computer applications, and new computer technology. In applications the focus was to be on industrial robotics, measurement and instrumentation, microprocessor workbench/teaching aids, and the man/machine interface. Members had been unable to define a program of academic research in robotics, commenting, "The panel has no doubt that the reluctance of the present community to take up the challenge is due at least in part to the general discouragement of artificial intelligence which took place in this country several years ago, and that it is now up to SRC to take steps to remedy the situation." (This point is developed further in subsequent chapters.)

The panel also urged greater effort in four areas of new technology: silicon chip design, software technology, database utilization, and resilient systems. But these areas should not be tackled in isolation; there were significant relationships between them.

Though the Science Research Council accepted these recommendations in principle, no "Roberts Programme" as such was implemented. But the panel's report was significant, as Tony Egginton, SERC Engineering Director for most of the Alvey period, notes:

> It was the start of a considerable debate which I suppose ended up with the Alvey Programme. The report triggered quite a lot of things, including a considerable build-up of funding and a much more programmatic approach to things, which coincided with the development of a much broader program. The Engineering Board began to realize that a way of generating the kind of things they believed were necessary was to have a very much more active approach to the community. In 1976 the SERC Polymer Engineering Directorate was the start, and Alvey represents the ultimate in that sense.

Specific actions resulting from the Roberts report included industrially relevant research initiatives in software technology, database utilization, systems reliability and man/machine interaction, and new graduate-level courses in integrated circuit design.

Britain missed a big opportunity in not mounting a total Roberts-type program, says Rob Witty: "The Roberts Panel was excellent. If only we had adopted their program, we would be ten years further on than we are now. It was an enormous missed opportunity. One or two little bits and pieces came out, but the whole thrust was thrown away."

Ministering to IT

The British government's attitude to information technology took a positive step forward in 1981 (though it could be argued that it retreated several steps backward again in 1987). A leading role in the 1981 events was played by Kenneth Baker, a Conservative Member of Parliament who had been Minister for the Civil Service (responsible for the Central Computer Agency) under Edward Heath from 1972 to 1974. Banished to the back benches as a Heath man when Margaret Thatcher's government was returned in 1979, Baker took an interest in IT and was a consultant to Logica, a software house set up by Philip Hughes and colleagues in 1969.

In June 1980 Baker, with a little help from Hughes, prepared a paper "A National Strategy for Information Technology." He presented it publicly at an Online conference on business telecommunications and circulated it widely. The prime minister was among the recipients.

"I wish to argue for the development in a very short space of time of a national strategy in which the government has to take the lead," Baker declared. "Its role should be that of coordinator and catalyst. I am not arguing for a national-plan type of intervention with vast state intervention and direction of investment. The opportunity for Britain in this industry is immense, and we must not let it slip between our fingers. I propose a ten-point program." Baker's ten points were

1. A Minister for Information Technology should be appointed within the Department of Industry.

2. The government should prepare and issue a policy document, "Information Technology in the U.K. in the 1980s."

3. The Departments of Industry and of Trade should initiate a strong program to sell the products of Britain's information technology abroad.

4. The government should announce a new procurement policy replacing the ICL-oriented policy with one concerned with national interest.

5. The government should identify a number of applications for advanced systems within its own activities and procure them from the British information technology industry.

6. Corporation tax should be changed so that the discrimination against service industry companies is reduced or eliminated.

7. The new minister should take the lead in setting up technology agreements.

8. The government's research-and-development program in information technology, almost exclusively a preserve of universities and the government research establishments, should be put on a wider basis.

9. The Enterprise Zones should be the subject of a major government initiative in promoting information technology in small firms.

10. The government should ensure that more people are trained at all levels in these new skills.

(Computer service firms, compared with manufacturers, paid a much higher proportion of their earnings in taxes, hence point 6. The technology agreements of point 7 were intended to ease the introduction of new technology by agreement between trade unions and employers.)

Such a program would cost money, Baker admitted. At the time of his paper, he said, the total annual expenditure of the Department of Industry on information technology was about £17 million—"roughly equivalent to three weeks' running losses of British Steel." Britain should get its industrial priorities straight and provide more for the wealth creators of the future.

It was essential to have a focal point in government for this diverse IT industry, Baker argued, hence point 1, the need for a Minister for Information Technology. "This appointment is not a gimmick," he insisted. (The same recommendation was made three months later in a report[3] by the government's Advisory Council for Applied Research and Development [ACARD].) Five months after Baker and two months after ACARD, in November 1980, Thatcher did indeed appoint a Minister for Information Technology ("The first such appointment in any country", the DoI later claimed[4].) He was Adam Butler, and he lasted two months in the job. In January 1981, to the relief of many, Butler was replaced by Kenneth Baker.

Commenting in 1988 on his 1980 ten-point plan, Baker, now Secretary of State for Education and Science, says: "It was a program which I set about implementing when I became Minister of State for Industry and Information Technology in January 1981. There had been various DoI initiatives in the whole area of computers and information technology. What I did was to start pulling these together and to develop a cohesive policy." Among these initiatives Baker cites the microcomputers-in-schools scheme, launched in 1981, which "really ensured that, toward the end of the 1980s, we have a world lead in computing in the classroom."

A good basis for Baker's cohesive policy in 1981 had been prepared from 1979 to 1980 by a team in the Information Technology Division of the DoI. At that time the Secretary of State for Industry in the new Conservative government was Sir Keith Joseph. Reay Atkinson, then Head of IT Division, recalls: "In 1979 Keith Joseph asked me and my division to produce a report on information technology. I had four superb assistant secretaries: Jonathon Solomon, John Thynne, Robin Lingard, and Don Harrison. We put the report together which, infelicitously, we had headed 'A strategy for information technology.' I remember Lord Trenchard, the Industry minister, responding: 'Atkinson, what's this bloody nonsense? We don't have strategies in this government.'"

In another initiative, 1982 was designated Information Technology Year (IT82) and a £4 million national IT awareness campaign was mounted. The idea for such a campaign was suggested to backbencher Baker and to members of the IT industry in October 1980 by Alan Benjamin (then with ICL); after Baker was appointed IT minister and the idea was approved by the prime minister, Benjamin (then with the CAP software house) became chairman of the IT82 Committee, which organized the event.

In introducing IT82 Baker gave the nation this message:

Information technology is the fastest-developing area of industrial and business activity in the western world. Its markets are huge, its applications multitudinous, and its potential for increasing efficiency immense. Without doubt it will be the engine of economic growth for at least the rest of the century. Britain's economic prosperity depends on the success with which we manufacture its products and provide and exploit its services. This is the message that must be got over to everyone in this country—the general public, school children, as well as industry, trade, and commerce.

It was against this general consciousness-raising scene that the U.K. IT research initiatives got under way.

A Universal Project

In discussing the precursors to the Alvey Programme, experts point to Project Universe as perhaps the first example of collaboration between U.K. academia, industry, and government on a major IT research project. In many ways the pattern of collaboration pioneered in Universe was followed through in the Alvey Programme. Universe aimed to explore the linking of a number of local area networks of computers by satellite to form a high-speed, wide-area computer network. The name Universe, the participants decreed, stood for UNIVersity Expanded Ring and Satellite Experiment.

14   *Introducing Alvey*

The project was conceived in the summer of 1980 as a university/SERC initiative involving Cambridge University Computer Laboratory (developers of the Cambridge Ring local-area network); University College, London; and the networking group at the SERC Rutherford Appleton Laboratory. The Electrical and Electronic Engineering Department of Loughborough University joined the team to add satellite communications experience. A proposal for a three-year program costing £1.6 million was presented to the SRC Engineering Board through the Information Engineering Committee in October 1980. An unusual feature of the proposal was its "now or never" aspect; the European Space Agency's Orbital Test Satellite (OTS), which was to be used for intersite communications, was not expected to remain operational beyond the end of 1983.

The response of the Engineering Board was favorable but accompanied (in the board's go-ahead recommendation to the SRC Council) by a suggestion that other bodies, including industry, might help fund the project because of its potential industrial relevance. By the end of March 1981 a collaborative deal had been reached; British Telecom, GEC, and Logica would join the original four partners to implement the project, with the DTI funding 50 percent of the SRC, GEC, and Logica costs. British Telecom was to fund its own participation and pay the satellite charges.

The Universe network was built during the latter half of 1981 and throughout the following year, and a comprehensive set of experiments and demonstrations was conducted during 1983. The network linked seven research laboratories: Rutherford, Cambridge, UCL, Loughborough, GEC's Marconi Research Centre, British Telecom Research Laboratories, and Logica London. About 200 computers were interconnected via the 13 local-area networks installed at these sites. Though a proposal for an extension of the Universe program was not accepted, the partners were to mount two smaller projects, known as Admiral and Unison (standing for "son of Universe") as part of the Alvey Programme. Laurence Clarke, IEC Chairman at the time, describes Project Universe as "quite definitely the prototype" for the trilateral collaboration that became the keynote of Alvey. The Universe partners worked out a collaboration agreement, he recalls—"and one acceptable to the GEC lawyers, which is saying a lot." That agreement, he suggests, could have formed a model for Alvey projects.

The Artificial Intelligentsia

The branch of computer science known as artificial intelligence (AI) has suffered much over the years from the claims of over-enthusiastic advocates at one extreme and from the dismissive scorn of unbelievers at the other. Meanwhile steady progress has been made by researchers in the field, notably in the United States[5] but also in Britain. In SRC circles the subject came up for special attention in 1973, when a damning review[6] of AI prospects by Sir James Lighthill, then Lucasian Professor of Applied Mathematics in the University of Cambridge, led to a major cutback in SRC funding for the subject. This dealt a heavy blow to AI research in Britain from which, in 1981, it had yet to recover.

In the summer of that year Britain's artificial intelligentsia struck back. "A bunch of us had felt for quite a time that we really ought to try to do something about rehabilitating AI in the U.K. after Lighthill," says John Taylor, at that time Head of the Command Systems Division of the Admiralty Surface Weapons Establishment (ASWE) and also Chairman of the Computing and Communications Subcommittee (CCSC) of the SERC IEC. The aim was to set up an SERC "specially promoted program" (SPP) in AI, along the lines of the Distributed Computing Systems project. Discussion papers were written, and meetings were held. At an early meeting in London a group including Donald Michie, a pioneer of AI research at Edinburgh University, and Robert Kowalski of Imperial College discussed strategy. "We were sitting around a table wondering what to call this new area," says John Taylor. "Should we call it artificial intelligence? We didn't want to call it artificial intelligence because of all the Lighthill connotations, and we didn't want to call it expert systems, and we came up with this awful phrase 'intelligent knowledge-based systems' or IKBS."

Plans for a special IKBS program within the SERC later merged into plans for the Alvey activity in this area, but more immediately, in the autumn of 1981, attention switched to events in Japan, where artificial intelligence had assumed a key role in the fifth-generation computer project.

Collaboration with Japan?

In October 1981 a Department of Industry mission to Japan set in train the events that were to lead directly to the Alvey Programme. The mission was led by Reay Atkinson. Earlier Atkinson had participated in a number of DoI visits that had established contacts with the Japanese consumer electronics industry, computer companies, and semiconductor companies. Kenneth Baker had first visited Japan with Philip Hughes of Logica in 1978, and when he was appointed Information Technology Minister in January 1981 he was keen to explore the possibilities of joint ventures between the two countries.

But one of Baker's more immediate concerns early in 1981 was to ensure the survival of ICL, Britain's major computer company. Takeovers by some of the major U.S. computer firms were discussed but not consummated. In the new ICL that emerged, with Dr. Robb Wilmot as managing director, an important element in corporate strategy was a link with Fujitsu on integrated circuit technology and large computers. Wilmot of ICL and Shiro Yoshikawa of Fujitsu had forged the link, the first major example of collaboration between U.K. and Japanese computer companies.

After an official visit by Baker to Japan in April 1981 the minister instructed Atkinson to explore further the possibilities of industrial collaboration on IT with Japan. Arrangements for a DoI-led mission were negotiated, initially for June or July, but MITI officials made it clear that they were not interested in industrial joint ventures. Industrial participation would be inappropriate, they indicated, but academic researchers would be welcome. The date of the visit was changed to 14–23 October so that the team could attend the international fifth-generation conference in Tokyo.

With a little help from his friends Atkinson assembled the team he would take to Japan: from academia, professors Brian Randell of Newcastle-upon-Tyne and Roger Needham of Cambridge (Professor Mike Rogers of Bristol, SERC IEC ex-Chairman, would be in Japan at that time on other business and was to support the team as an adviser); from the government service, Dr. Alan Fox, communications head of the Royal Signals and Radar Establishment (RSRE) at Malvern; from the real world, so to speak, Charles Read of the Inter-Bank Research Organization. Invaluable local support was to come from Dr.

Graham Marshall, Science and Technology Counsellor at the British Embassy and a former RSRE man. (Atkinson was urged to add to his team but in August 1981 noted that the trip threatened to exhaust his division's total travel budget.)

Thus the mission to Japan had a two-part program: in essence, a week devoted to discussions and visits with MITI, industry, academics, and government laboratories; followed by a week at the fifth-generation conference. In the first week the emphasis was on explaining Japanese plans to the British visitors; where collaboration was discussed it was in the context of the fifth-generation program. Professor Needham was not able to stay beyond the first week.

On arrival in Tokyo team members were fascinated to discover a completely alien culture, with strange customs, exotic behavior, ancient traditions, and quaint patterns of speech. And that, they recall, was just the British Embassy. As for their Japanese hosts at the Ministry of International Trade and Industry (MITI), the Japan Information Processing Development Center (JIPDEC), and the Electro-Technical Laboratory (ETL), they proved remarkably frank and open in discussing prospects and problems. "All the time we were probing, on Baker's insistence, the scope for joint industrial ventures," Atkinson comments. "But the Japanese fended us off all the time. They really did not want a joint academic/industrial team going out to talk to their companies about collaboration."

On the fifth-generation program the former DoI official comments, "They were on a great international brain-picking exercise. They would have loved for our academics to go out and join up with them on particular aspects of the fifth generation. They made it clear that they were totally self-sufficient in hardware terms, but they were clearly very impressed by the quality of the Needhams and the Randells, and of course they had their eyes on the Donald Michies back at the ranch here."

Professor Michie has described[7] collaboration with Japan as "rather like cooperating with a vacuum cleaner," and the vacuum-cleaner point was not lost on the members of the team as they discussed their impressions of the visit and their likely recommendations. "This was a very important point to get over in our report to Baker," Atkinson recalls. "There was no scope for trading our academic excellence for joint ventures in the commercial field; the Japanese were not interested at all."

But the team had no doubt that the fifth-generation effort signaled a major, and expensive, thrust in informatics. If Britain was to participate, then, far from collaborating with Japan she should emulate the Japanese approach in bringing together industry, academia, and government research in a substantial national project. The team's visit to Japan, coupled with the ICL experience, convinced Reay Atkinson that only in very specific areas agreed upon by individual companies could Anglo-Japanese industrial collaboration work. The main thrust of Japanese companies' interest in Britain was to set up their own operations in order to gain a European base.

Since leaving the IT division in November 1981 Reay Atkinson has had much contact with Japanese companies in his work in northeast England. They are honorable people, he says, but they fight hard for their national interests, strike the hardest bargains, play to their strengths, and exploit the other side's weaknesses. "Unless you approach them in a totally hard, realistic way, you're lost."

This was brought home to Atkinson by a significant incident during the visit to Japan:

I had a day out with Fujitsu during the fifth-generation conference. We were still negotiating terms with them for the ICL/Fujitsu deal. Wilmot had suggested ICL could give up its design capability in components, as an economy, and rely on Fujitsu technology. I expressed some concern about this to Yoshikawa during a car journey. He was very fond of Robb Wilmot, indeed it was their mutual empathy that led to the agreements between their companies. But he said firmly: "Tell Lobb not do this."

What he was saying was that Fujitsu had reached a very specific agreement with ICL on a particular project—but was competing with them ruthlessly in every other way. There's nothing wrong with that; that's how the Japanese companies treat each other. There are no cosy relationships. I think it was that aside in the car that reinforced what the other lads were saying.

Kenneth Baker comments:

I was always in favor of some form of collaboration with Japan, and not just on research and development. I was very much behind the ICL/Fujitsu collaboration, which was part of Robb Wilmot's recovery program for ICL in the spring of 1981. After the group led by Reay Atkinson returned from Japan, their message was we had to do something, we had to put our act together. My main interest was to ensure that we didn't lose out. It was the team's visit that made me believe a national IT program was needed. Also, I was aware that hardware was going to be less important in the future than software. We in Britain were and are good at software; I was looking for an area where we could build on our strengths.

The Clarke Initiative

As the team flew back from Tokyo, Reay Atkinson stopped off to attend to other official business in Hong Kong—and to dictate from the team's notes a first draft of their report. Returning to Britain, Atkinson sent the draft out to his team members for their comments on 27 October 1981. In his incoming mail on the same day was a letter from Laurence Clarke, Technical Director (Automation) of GEC-Marconi Electronics and Chairman of the SERC Information Engineering Committee, that was to prove another Alvey tributary.

Clarke was writing in his capacity as IEC chairman to alert Atkinson to a serious problem that the committee and the SERC Engineering Board were facing. This problem was that SERC "forward look" plans included no provision for the increased funding that would be needed to mount a number of planned initiatives in information engineering that were regarded as "vital to restore our ailing position" in information engineering.

In the light of the Japanese fifth-generation program, he suggested, there was an urgent need for the U.K. to form its own fifth-generation computing strategy. The Department of Industry, industry, the SERC, and the universities should have some form of guiding light or rallying standard, so that the U.K. could exploit the inventiveness that was one of the country's strengths. As a first step the DoI should consider commissioning a task force to undertake a special study. The DoI could base its strategy to stimulate and support the IT user, manufacturer, and service industries on the results of this study; and the SERC could design a larger Universe-type project.

Clarke suggested that a group of about five carefully chosen individuals should work on this study for about four weeks, spread over a period of two months. Initially they would establish the scope of the project, after which they would lead short, sharp investigations in major areas of R & D with a second tier of experts. The task force would then review the investigations, define a direction for U.K. research in IT, and list the university and industrial groups most likely to contribute.

Clarke sent copies of this letter to Sir Robert Telford, Chairman of the DoI's Electronics and Avionics Requirements Board, and to Brian Oakley, Secretary of the SERC. Though initiated independently of the DoI visit to Japan, Clarke's proposal converged with the conclusion of the Atkinson team that the U.K. should, as a matter of urgency, try to set its IT house in order. And, though his specific proposal was overtaken by events, Clarke was to go on to play a key role in the pre-Alvey discussions that occupied much of December 1981 and January 1982. In particular, he organized the crucial workshop held at Cosener's House, Abingdon, early in the new year.

From Tokyo to Number Ten

Among individual comments made by members of the Atkinson team following their return, Professor Randell wrote a comprehensive report[8] of his impressions of the fifth-generation project. "The Japanese conference presentations were an amazingly well-orchestrated series of vague accounts of various parts of an ambitious and wide-ranging plan," he began. "Everybody made respectful references, at least, to logic programming and knowledge engineering, and some of them obviously believed, and perhaps even understood, what they were saying. It came over to me as a very skillful plan which filled MITI's wish for a very ambitious goal that sounded very plausible and which could be presented to a layman in such a way as to seem socially beneficial. . . ."

Randell went on to amplify his doubts about the long-term fifth-generation plan—and about its dependence on logic programming and knowledge engineering in particular. But he stressed that, from the British point of view, such doubts were largely irrelevant. The project would build up the Japanese pool of software and architectural expertise and would give Japanese industry significant additional funding and potential products.

The Newcastle professor urged that developments in Japan should be closely monitored. Collaboration between the U.K. and Japan was clearly inappropriate in the current government/industrial environment. "In the meantime," he concluded, "I see Japan gradually turning various European computer companies into sales agents and dominating various other industries by their greater financial and technological strength and aggressiveness. It seems a whole series of miracles is called for if our research is to be fully exploited to our own commercial benefit."

On his return from Japan Randell had been surprised to find an invitation to attend an information technology seminar to be held by the prime minister at 10 Downing Street on 2 November 1981. The event was being organized in connection with the IT82 campaign to enable Thatcher and her senior ministers to hear the views of selected members of the IT community. On that occasion Randell seized the opportunity to bring the team's message from Tokyo to the highest political level.

In a brief contribution to the seminar he outlined the Japanese fifth-generation program and stressed the contrast between the strengths of Japan and the weaknesses of Britain in developing, organizing, and focusing their respective national IT efforts. It would be folly for Britain to collaborate with Japan in fifth-generation R & D, he said, until and unless the U.K. government and industry got their act together and were in a position to gain benefits comparable to those that Japan would reap.

After the seminar the group adjourned to another room for drinks and further informal discussion. Professor Randell was talking to Kenneth Baker when he was told that the prime minister desired a word with him. Alas, it transpired that Thatcher was pursuing not fifth-generation computing but a Newcastle Science Park.

3
A Call for Action

The mission to Japan brought back the message that the fifth-generation program was real, that collaboration with Japan posed dangers, and that Britain must get organized in IT. Eventually, as Kenneth Owen reports in this chapter, IT research and industrial leaders came together to call for action on a national scale to stimulate research and improve Britain's competitive position. They sought inspiration by meeting within sight of an important British national institution—Lord's Cricket Ground.

The Team's Report

In its formal report to Kenneth Baker, submitted in November 1981, the Atkinson team began by defining the broad objectives of its visit to Japan:

• To identify the objectives of the fifth-generation program and how these objectives were to be achieved

• To determine the prospects for effective collaboration with Japan in particular aspects of the fifth-generation program— or, indeed, more generally in electronics.

The fifth-generation program was just one of a number of MITI initiatives to promote Japanese electronics, the team pointed out. Other areas covered in this way included supercomputers and optoelectronics. Japanese industry and its R & D projects were staffed by large numbers of graduate scientists and engineers and a generally well-educated workforce. But the visit had confirmed that the Japanese effort in electronics was characterized not only by the substantial financial resources and intellectual effort but by the effective way in which this effort was organized.

The MITI's own R & D was primarily concentrated at its Electro-Technical Laboratory and through industrial contracts let by its Agency of Industrial Science and Technology. The Japan Information Processing Development Center, funded half by industry and half by the MITI, provided a neutral focal point for formal consultations between industry, government, and universities. But the regular informal discussions that took place between senior executives, officials, and professors out of normal working hours were probably even more important.

Against this background, Japan's R & D and manufacturing effort was marked by two key factors: first, what might be termed "competitive cooperation" in research by different groups working in parallel; second, outright competition between companies in bringing the fruits of this research through to production and the world marketplace. Any collaboration between the U.K. and Japan in electronics must recognize this fact, the team warned. The exchange of information between researchers would in no way inhibit Japanese industry from competing actively with British industry. On the contrary, such information would swiftly be turned to competitive advantage.

At the time of the team's visit the fifth-generation program was not yet fully defined or planned in detail. But the team believed that the program would move forward rapidly, mainly because Japanese industry had already recognized that the program would enable companies to bring innovative products to the marketplace much sooner than would otherwise be possible.

In the view of the British team—and, they believed, in the view of most of the foreign delegates at the Tokyo fifth-generation conference—the fifth-generation program was an ambitious and wide-ranging set of ideas for the development of revolutionary computers, which in turn would open up many new areas of computer application. The total program contained some questionable technical aspects, the team opined. But it presaged important advances in VLSI/CAD systems, personal computers, speech input/output devices, image processing, and expert systems. Whether or not the full fifth-generation program was completed in ten years, as planned, Japanese industry would be well placed to exploit developments in these areas throughout the period. Primary objectives of the fifth-generation program, the team judged, were:

- To improve productivity and efficiency in Japanese offices, factories, and new areas for automation such as agriculture; and to develop systems such as those for health and welfare that would benefit the international community
- To establish Japan's IT industries at the top of the world league as producers of advanced systems
- To share some of the resource costs and risks involved in such an ambitious program
- Once and for all to achieve victory over IBM.

Japan's greatest relevant strength was in its VLSI capability, and its other strengths included particular subsystem areas such as speech and character recognition, facsimile, and peripheral equipment. Japan aimed to implement basic parts of the fifth-generation design in terms of VLSI. Main relative weaknesses in the fifth-generation program, as perceived by the U.K. team, concerned systems and software issues. There was uncertainty over the appropriate software and programming strategy to be adopted. There was uncertainty over the internal computer organization to be used to achieve the required level of parallel processing. And there was confusion about the true significance of distributed processing and networks. In these areas British R & D expertise was recognized by the Japanese.

The team then turned to discuss the prospects for fifth-generation collaboration between Britain and Japan. Japan's publicly stated reasons for seeking such collaboration were:

- To establish that Japan was now prepared to take a lead role in promoting future technological development in the interests of the world community
- To promote the general internationalization of Japan through international collaboration

Underlying these reasons, the team believed, was an understandable wish to counter the then growing opposition to Japan in world trading communities, which, it was feared, might lead to quotas and embargoes. Also, the Japanese made no secret of the fact that through the open exchange of ideas they hoped to obtain information that would enable Japanese industry to steal a march on the competition. Finally, the MITI was fighting an internal battle with the Ministry of Finance and believed that a favorable international response to its plans would help it to obtain more funds.

Initially the MITI envisaged that the main thrust of fifth-generation basic research would come from Japan, with first-phase collaboration in the form of research projects undertaken by separate national teams exchanging information on progress through exchanges of researchers and two-way secondments. Whatever the theoretical possibility of international industrial collaboration, the team noted, it was clear that in practice the MITI expected this to be achieved by individual companies in accordance with their own commercial interests. Japanese companies would certainly be reluctant to trade information on key elements in base technology such as VLSI, where they held a significant lead.

Collaboration would be easiest to achieve in wider issues such as data protection, social and economic consequences of information technology, and IT awareness, though these aspects were strictly speaking not part of the fifth-generation program. Beyond this it was possible that Japan might invite U.K. researchers' involvement in a number of fifth-generation topics. More extensive collaboration would clearly require the full agreement of participating U.K. industry.

The team noted the preliminary responses of representatives from other countries at the Tokyo conference. From the United States, academics welcomed collaboration while industrialists remained silent. From the French government research institute INRIA, delegates believed that France could gain from research collaboration with Japan. From West Germany, delegates said that their country could not contemplate releasing key researchers for work in Japan but might join a European collaborative program. From the European Commission, a senior official was anxious that Japan should not be in a position to play off one European country against another.

One of the most useful results of their visit, the team concluded, lay in the lessons that the team members learned of the ways in which Japan was organizing its IT developments for the 1990s. In many important respects the Japanese approach could be taken as a model for what any country would need to do if it was to be credible and competitive in IT over the next ten years or so. If the United Kingdom was to maintain a presence in this vital technology—with or without collaboration with Japan—four things were needed:

1. Generally, the U.K. effort must be more effectively organized. It would be useful to try to achieve the informal consensus-forming arrangements used in Japan.
2. There must be rapid concentration of the financial and other resources that were essential if the U.K. was ever to catch up on Japan in key areas such as advanced VLSI design.
3. To achieve this concentration a selective approach must be adopted toward promoting key technologies in key industrial sectors and exploiting the results of research.
4. The competitive edge so prominent in Japan from the R & D stage onward must be further developed as an integral part of this process.

Finally, the team warned, full-scale research collaboration with Japan should not be undertaken unless and until the U.K. had urgently improved its internal arrangements so that it could benefit fully from such collaboration.

Cosener's House

The report of the Japan mission was to be Reay Atkinson's swansong as head of the IT Division before moving to the North-Eastern Regional Office of the DoI. Alastair Macdonald took over at IT Division on Monday, 16 November 1981, and it was during his first week in the job that things began to move. Brian Oakley, Secretary of the SERC, telephoned early in the week to suggest a meeting, and that Friday Oakley together with two colleagues—David Thomas, Associate Engineering Director at Rutherford and David Worsnip, Secretary of the Information Engineering Committee—called on Macdonald and his colleague Robin Lingard at the DoI. Macdonald remembers the date because he read an article[9] in *The Times* that morning on approaches by Professor Tohru Moto-aka to three U.K. academics—Robert Kowalski, Donald Michie, and John Gurd—exploring possible collaboration on fifth-generation research in Japan. The article also reported an approach to the SERC earlier that year by a group of British AI scientists urging action following the Japanese fifth-generation initiative, an approach that had met with no reply.

The article injected some urgency into the group's discussion, and they began to develop plans (as recommended by the

Atkinson team) for a "town meeting" of the U.K. IT community, in particular the IT industrial community, at which the Japan team would report back and possible U.K. responses would be discussed. A small planning team was organized, and, as a basis for discussion at the planned industry briefing, the DoI accepted an SERC offer to prepare working papers outlining the content and organization of a possible unified national IT research program.

To take preparation for the industry briefing a stage further Laurence Clarke, as IEC chairman, organized a one-week workshop for January 4–8 at Cosener's House, a historic town house in Abingdon owned by the SERC and used by the nearby laboratories for residential meetings. (And, indeed, there had been a pre-workshop meeting in Burlington House, London on December 16.) Leading academics (including the members of the Atkinson mission) and SERC, DoI, MoD, and British Telecom officials attended at Abingdon, with the aim of thrashing out a draft of a national IT research plan as a basis for further discussion.

Sessions covered specific technologies (including VLSI, computer-aided design and manufacture, the man/machine interface, networks and distributed computing systems, novel computer configurations, software engineering, and IKBS) and general discussion. An illuminating view of envisaged problems in cooperation between industry and academia was presented in a viewfoil diagram reproduced as table 3.1.

TABLE 3.1.
Problems in Cooperation

Universities	Industry
Publication	Secrecy* (national)
Academic freedom	Autonomy
Distributed geography:	
Lack of management	Lack of inspiration
Intellectual arrogance	Intellectual poverty
Professional jealousy	Commercial suspicion
NIH:	
Teaching conflict	Profit *now*

*Government labs problem

The NIH shown in table 3.1 is of course the notorious "Not Invented Here" syndrome.

An early appreciation of a topic that was to emerge in Alvey as a major problem was shown in the general discussion at the workshop. This concerned the question of property rights. Workshop participants split into opposing groups on this. One view was that all detailed discussion should be shelved until after the program was launched in order to avoid becoming bogged down in legal wrangling from the outset. The underlying assumption here was that if industry was really committed to a nationally coordinated program, it would find a way of solving the property-rights problems. The second, diametrically opposed view was that the question of property rights was so important and central to the project that it should be resolutely tackled as an urgent matter.

Discussion at Cosener's during the week was quite heated at times. The climate cooled down on Saturday morning, when those present found themselves snowed in and unable to escape.

Project IT87

The name "IT87" was attached to the proposed national IT research program that emerged from the Cosener's House workshop. This implied a five-year program starting in 1982. Documents outlining the proposal were prepared by Clarke, Thomas, and colleagues for presentation at the industry meeting to be held in London on the weekend of January 29–30.

The main conclusion of the workshop had been that a major U.K. research initiative in information technology should be launched immediately, directed at the single focus of intelligent knowledge-based systems. On a preliminary estimate, the program would cost £250 million over five years, divided between government and industry. Long-range research and items of urgently needed infrastructure should be funded 100 percent by government, while other parts of the program—those closest to commercial exploitation—should be jointly funded by government and industry.

Intelligent knowledge-based systems, the workshop believed, would be applied on a major scale in most areas of industrial and domestic life over the coming decade. New products and services were expected significantly to improve performance, reliability, and cost effectiveness over the whole range of commerce and manufacturing. Specialized systems would be used in the office and factory for command and control, for automatic software production, and for the next generation of intelligent robots. IKBS applications would be found increasingly in defense systems, and consumer mass-market items were also anticipated. Influencing the workshop's choice of the IKBS focus was Britain's prominent international position in several highly relevant areas of research, including functional and relational programming languages, novel computer architectures, and certain areas of knowledge engineering. The importance of IKBS was clearly recognized in the Japanese fifth-generation program.

The proposed U.K. program would consist of two parallel activities. First, the IKBS research program itself, which would culminate in the construction of about ten demonstration projects that could lead directly to significant commercial products. Second, development of the supporting infrastructure, including VLSI design and fabrication facilities for one-micron feature-size circuits and software tools. Some infrastructure items would be needed at the outset: a data communications network, a "common base" of software development tools running on standardized computer hardware, and a "silicon brokerage." These items would cost an estimated £40 million.

TABLE 3.2.
Project IT87—Summary of Costs

Sub-project	Cost over 5 years (£m)
IKBS research	30
Demonstration experiments	30
VLSI enhancements	65
CAD for VLSI	45
Silicon brokerage	2
Software engineering	30
Distributed computing	10
Network	8
Man/machine interaction	5
Project management and coordination	25
Total	250

Though the plan represented initial thinking rather than a firm and detailed proposal, the breakdown of costs envisaged (table 3.2) makes interesting reading. Note that a figure of 10 percent of total cost was assumed for technical coordination and program management.

This broad proposal for the IT87 program, the workshop recommended, should be followed up by a substantial design study that would confirm or modify the overall concept and produce detailed plans. A ten-man design study team should work full-time for about three months on this, under the supervision of a steering group.

Lord's Cricket Ground

On 11 January, the Monday after the Cosener's House workshop ended in a snowdrift, Alastair Macdonald sent out invitations to senior IT industrialists and researchers to attend a meeting in London on 29–30 January to hear the findings of the Atkinson mission to Japan and to discuss the proposed U.K. response.

The occasion was described as a seminar on the future organization and scope of Britain's R & D in microelectronics and computing. It had resulted from consideration of the possible effects on the U.K. industry of the Japanese approach to developments in these areas, in particular the need to review whether the U.K. should participate in the Japanese fifth-generation proposals—and whether this could be done from a position of strength. Though the meeting would be focused on the report of the U.K. mission to Japan, it would provide an opportunity to explore wider issues.

Thus, at the time the London meeting was being planned, the prime emphasis was still on the issue of Anglo-Japanese collaboration. Before too long this was to be forgotten in driving forward the focused national effort that became the Alvey Programme. And Reay Atkinson's sharp comment at the Tokyo conference to Jean-Marie Cadiou, head of the European Community's embryonic ESPRIT program, that Britain was not prepared to see her bilateral arrangements with the Japanese founder in a morass of prolonged European discussion, was to appear ironic indeed, as ESPRIT got under way and gathered momentum.

Macdonald's invitations were to the London Holiday Inn, Chelsea, but in the event the meeting was held at the Ladbroke Westmoreland Hotel, St. John's Wood, overlooking Lord's Cricket Ground, home of the Marylebone Cricket Club. To this day some of those present refer to the occasion as the Lord's Cricket Ground meeting. (To add to the confusion, because the meeting originally was to have been held at the Civil Service Staff College at Sunningdale, some of those involved continued to call the event the Sunningdale meeting, even after they had attended it at the Westmoreland. Thus does Britain essay to confuse her enemies—and those researching books on information technology research programs.)

A week before the meeting, participants received the Atkinson team's report and the SERC IT87 proposals among their seminar papers. IT87 was a starting point for discussion, Macdonald told them in his covering letter. Chairman of the seminar was Dr. James Merriman, Chairman of the National Computing Centre, Chairman of the Project Universe Steering Committee, and former Technology Director of Post Office Telecommunications.

Kenneth Baker set the scene in his opening speech to the meeting—a meeting that was quite unique, he said. There had been a number of collaborative ventures in the past, but never had such a joint attempt been made to come together to try to determine a common policy. The U.K. mission to Japan had recommended that Britain should arrange national collaboration and put her own house in order before embarking on any research collaboration with Japan. The main question for the meeting was: should the U.K. follow that recommendation? Indeed, could Britain's IT industry survive without collaboration? Was the time right for a major change in attitude to collaboration between firms and in government?

The minister went on to outline his government's position. Collaboration must be a partnership between government and industry, private and public sectors, and universities and research establishments. If Britain were to develop fifth-generation computing, there would be enormous benefits to hardware, software, and IT-using companies. The government would play its part, but industry would be expected also to play its part by providing money and skills.

Industry should not think that it was merely going to devise an elaborate system of sharing in a very substantial government

R & D program, Baker warned. The government was prepared to commit significant funds but was looking to industry also to commit substantial funds, either in cash or people. It was not a question of deciding how best companies could spend among themselves the resources made available by the government, because this would not achieve the true purpose of collaboration. This was one of the most crucial initiatives that Britain had taken, the minister concluded; he would welcome specific recommendations.

Reay Atkinson introduced the topic of his team's visit to Japan, reporting the main points of the team's formal report and sketching in the background. Next, team members outlined specific aspects of their visit: Randell on fifth-generation computing; Needham on knowledge information processing systems; Rogers on VLSI; Fox on IT in Japan; and Read on the Japanese model for collaboration. After questions Macdonald spoke briefly on the DoI approach; and Clarke previewed the SERC working party's findings. These findings were described in detail when the meeting resumed the next morning: Clarke, Randell, Needham, Clive Foxall of British Telecom, and John Taylor spoke on the technical proposals and David Thomas on the management proposals. A general discussion period concluded the meeting.

The Westmoreland meeting was without doubt a key event in Alvey prehistory. But opinions differ as to the general atmosphere that it generated and the overall response of the senior industrialists present. Certainly the meeting attracted a top-level audience. And, though those present stopped short of formally endorsing the IT87 proposal, there appeared to be general agreement that Britain should put its own IT house in order and take a step toward a national initiative of some kind. At the final session the chairman posed two questions: was the issue sufficiently important to be taken further and, if so, should a joint task force be set up involving industry, academia, and government? The answer to both questions was yes.

Macdonald recalls: "The first thing that Kenneth Baker said to me, as he was leaving the conference, was that he had been struck by the seniority of the audience there. In effect, he invited the community to go away from that meeting to see whether they could put flesh upon the bones of the proposals which had been tabled."

Merriman, chairman of the meeting, has three strong recollections of the meeting and the IT research scene at that time, two of them positive and one negative. First, a coordinated university view of IT had emerged, including Universe and the IT87 proposals. Second—a point made also by others—a catalytic role was played by Sir Robert Telford in urging action and in harmonizing the academic and defense strands of IT research. Third, the head of Britain's main computer company, though present, showed no interest in participating in the Westmoreland discussions. The chairman found this gentleman's front-row preoccupation with a briefcase full of other business disconcerting, to say the least.

Thus the foundations for the Alvey edifice were laid. The base was a number of separate initiatives, brought together in an academic plan that was then submitted for industry approval. The plan was in part an original design, in part a defensive response to the Japanese fifth-generation program. The catalyst was Kenneth Baker, Member of Parliament, Her Majesty's Minister of State for Industry and Information Technology.

4

Committee Time

Relatively rapidly for a U.K. government process, but agonizingly slowly for those concerned, the Westmoreland Hotel consensus was translated into action. Britain is rather good at committees, and so a committee was duly set up to advise the minister. In this chapter Kenneth Owen describes how the committee discussed, argued, and reported back. Unusually, the committee's recommendations were accepted. By April 1983 the stage was set for the Alvey Programme to get under way.

The Alvey Committee

The message of the Westmoreland Hotel meeting was taken back to Whitehall, discussed further with industry, and discussed in Cabinet. On 6 April 1982 the Department of Industry announced that Kenneth Baker had invited John Alvey, at that time Senior Director for Technology at British Telecom, the national telecommunications utility, to be chairman of a study group to advise on the scope for a collaborative research program in information technology. The group had held its first meeting on 25 March, the announcement disclosed.

John Alvey had not been present at the Westmoreland, but his name had been put forward informally at the end of that meeting to Alastair Macdonald. In a sense he straddled the gap between industry and government; he had a broad technical knowledge of the field and was not tied to any industrial company. (British Telecom lost its "neutral" status when the corporation was privatized in November 1984; it would now be regarded by much of the IT industry as a direct competitor.)

Initially the committee members came from industry and Whitehall. Representing industry were Iann Barron, by then Managing Director of Inmos; Colin Haley, Director of Product

Line Planning at ICL; Philip Hughes, Chairman of Logica; Charles Read; Derek Roberts, by then Research Director of GEC; and Dr. Keith Warren, Director of Technology and Strategic Planning for Plessey. Representing the Civil Service were Brian Oakley, Secretary of the SERC; Dr. Hywel Davies, Deputy Controller of Research Programmes at the MoD; and the under-secretaries in charge of the two relevant parts of the DoI, Alastair Macdonald of the Information Technology Division and John Major of the Electronics Applications Division. At its first meeting the committee decided to recruit an eminent academic to its ranks: Professor Roger Needham, Director of the Computer Laboratory at the University of Cambridge and member of the DoI Japan mission.

It was in the Alvey Committee that a significant change was made in the thrust of the proposed program. At the Westmoreland the SERC plan had been for a fifth-generation style, IKBS-led program supported by infrastructure elements such as VLSI and software tools. In the Alvey deliberations the pattern that emerged was for a broader-based program giving equal importance to the four "enabling" technologies of IKBS, VLSI, software engineering, and what at that time was known as the man/machine interface or MMI (the phrase "human/computer interaction" or HCI has since become socially more acceptable).

"We started with a blank sheet of paper," says John Alvey, "though I was aware of the Westmoreland proposals. I began by thinking that we ought to consider what the market was, to present something that looked like a business case, otherwise we wouldn't be credible. I flogged that for about an hour at the first meeting but very quickly got disillusioned. I was told that there were no useful answers down that route and that we would have to talk enabling technologies. So I gave up and agreed that we should talk enabling technologies." The resulting choice of technologies was totally arbitrary, says John Alvey, though it did draw on the earlier discussions.

The work of drafting the four technology plans was delegated to four members of the committee: Derek Roberts on VLSI, Philip Hughes on software engineering, Charles Read on IKBS, and Colin Haley on MMI. Supported by working groups, they adopted different approaches to the task.

Derek Roberts had the benefit of earlier work on possible

VLSI programs prepared for the U.K. Ministry of Defence and for the European industrial round-table discussions that led to ESPRIT. "I used the draft that I already had of the ESPRIT silicon program," he says, "but edited to conform to the needs of the U.K. There were two phases in producing the Alvey VLSI plan. First, draft copies of the ESPRIT proposals were discussed by GEC, Plessey (who had also been involved in the European work), and Ferranti, and the three companies together produced an edited version for the U.K. This was then circulated to a lot of other people for comment, and then the three met again to produce the final version."

Some years earlier, as chairman of the Solid-State Physics and Devices Committee of the Electronics Research Council, an MoD advisory group, Roberts had initiated a study in response to the national VLSI program mounted by the Ministry of International Trade and Industry (MITI) in Japan. Not only was the Japanese plan highly ambitious, he noted, but, significantly, it involved research collaboration between such companies as Hitachi, Fujitsu, and NEC. The SSPDC submitted an action plan to the MoD which, says Roberts, received universal acclaim but no action.

Delayed action was in prospect in the proposed Very High-Performance Integrated Circuit (VHPIC) program that the MoD was considering in the pre-Alvey period. In effect this was envisaged as a response to the U.S. Defense Department's Very High-Speed Integrated Circuit (VHSIC) program, which itself was a response to the Japanese VLSI plan. Roberts was caustic in the Alvey Committee in noting these earlier proposals that had not been taken up. "In putting forward the silicon section of what became the Alvey Report, in the executive summary, I put the first three pages of the original MoD report, because it seemed to me that set out what we were trying to do better than anything." The MoD plan as such did not form part of the Alvey VLSI proposal, but, since GEC, Plessey, and Ferranti had all been involved in the MoD discussions, the VHPIC thrust was very much incorporated in their Alvey thinking.

In contrast to the VLSI approach of modifying an existing plan, Philip Hughes started almost from scratch in tackling software engineering. (His brief also included communications). He enlisted technical support from Robert Worden and Jeremy Tucker at Logica and from Rob Witty at the Rutherford

Laboratory, commissioned a number of advisory papers, and invited comments from all the major U.K. software companies. Substantial work had already been done within the SERC in organizing, very much along the lines pioneered by the Distributed Computing Systems program, another program known as the Software Technology Initiative (STI), and Rob Witty brought his STI experience to the Alvey task. "We had cooperation from Professor Brian Warboys of Manchester University, who was at that time putting together the ESPRIT strategy in software technology," Witty recalls, "so some of the complementarity between our program and ESPRIT was not an accident."

Charles Read was not an IKBS expert, but he was a man who fully appreciated the significance of the new technologies. In his Alvey task he consulted Professor Needham and engaged Dr. Karen Sparck Jones, a noted researcher in natural language understanding (and Roger Needham's wife), as a full-time consultant for three months to assist in drawing up the IKBS plan. As with VLSI, a model already existed in the shape of the SERC proposal for a specially promoted program in IKBS. "Having at least one specially promoted program in progress was a sort of virility symbol for the SERC committees," notes Needham, "and they had prepared for one in IKBS. They had worked out a program of work which was intended to be the intellectual prospectus for a specially promoted program." Thus the Alvey Committee benefited from the fact that this particular sector of the IT research community had already begun to come together and discuss objectives.

Colin Haley had the toughest job of all in tackling the diverse elements that came together under the banner of MMI. He got the job because he had stressed the need to conduct serious research into how people communicated with IT systems—at all levels, from professionals to casual users. Not only was there no existing plan for this total area, there was no agreed definition of what the area was, nor any existing single MMI community able to discuss it. In assessing this important but difficult new topic, Haley enlisted the technical assistance of a working group chaired by Vic Maller of ICL. Among the members of this group were Chris Barrow of Plessey and Mike Underwood of ICL, both of whom were later to join the Alvey Directorate.

Points of Principle

The committee's critical decision, says Philip Hughes, was the choice of the four areas of technology and the four individuals who would investigate those areas. "That had implications more in what it left out than in what it put in. In particular, there was nothing on architecture, so the work on computer architecture subsequently had to be cobbled together by stealing from other programs."

Ian Barron amplifies the architectures issue:

I wrote papers on architectures in conjunction with Roger Needham. I recommended that we did not have a specific architectures section, because we felt that architectures ran through every other topic, and it would be better to explore the architectures through the topics rather than to create a special free-standing intellectual subject. The consequence of that was that it got left out of everything eventually, and the Alvey Directorate later put it back in attached to IKBS.

Philip Hughes was critical at the time of both the VLSI and the MMI proposals. On VLSI, he recalls, there was no doubt that there would be a program in this area, simply because Derek Roberts of GEC and the Ministry of Defence said there should be one. But he queried the content of the program. "I was absolutely convinced that it would be merely pouring money down a hole which would keep this country two to three years behind what was going on elsewhere—which I'm sure in the event is true. If you were going to do it, the only chance that you had was to concentrate on design methodologies; you had no chance of catching up in terms of process."

Hughes and Roberts were in agreement, however, in opposing the MMI program. "There was more argument about the MMI program than about all the rest put together," says Hughes. "It was a mess. It was really never a program, just a collection of topics. I don't think I was ever in favor of there being an MMI program."

Most members of the Alvey Committee agreed that some kind of national IT program should be mounted. But there were sharp differences of opinion on the style and content of the program. The choice of the technologies to be pursued was one early issue, as noted above; other major points at issue included the degree of direction of the program, the desirability of a central institute, and the level of public funding. And, indeed, there were one or two brave souls who dared to doubt whether any national IT research program was needed.

Derek Roberts and Ian Barron represented opposite extremes of the VLSI spectrum: Roberts a pillar of the U.K. electronics establishment, with a big-company background in Plessey and GEC; Barron the iconoclastic co-founder of an innovative start-up company, Inmos. Not surprisingly, they tended to disagree, but by different routes they had each concluded that a national IT research program might not be such a good idea.

"I was against the Alvey concept," says Barron, for two reasons.

One was that I felt the money would go to companies that had enough money already, and it would not get to the right places. And the second reason was that the U.K. IT problem was not a problem of research. The U.K. has never suffered from a lack of basic ideas. Our problem has been to turn those ideas into commercial success. So I was arguing against the whole concept, saying it was fine for the Japanese to have a fifth-generation computing program, because the problem they had identified was the need to improve their research ability. In the U.K. our problem was not that we weren't good at research, it was that we weren't good at making money.

So I felt that, first, the cash was going in the wrong direction and, secondly, it was misdirecting political attention to be concerned about fifth-generating computing *per se*. Within the committee I expressed these views, formally at the start; thereafter I tried to make sure that what was done was as useful as possible. At the end of the day I had a problem: what do I do about this? I took the view that I should remain quiet, on the basis that £250 million or whatever misspent in computing science was better than nothing spent in computing science.

Derek Roberts's approach was different, though his conclusion was similar. "We might have been better off if we'd never had an Alvey Programme," he says, "if we'd simply put those same resources into strengthening the U.K. participation in ESPRIT. The fact that the two programs, covering broadly the same areas, were being created at the same time, created a lot of problems." One of the problems with ESPRIT, he suggests, was that the DoI was anti-ESPRIT in the beginning, mainly because the department had not been involved in devising the European program—though this attitude changed over the next few years. "If they could have killed ESPRIT at the beginning they would have done. They were going around saying 'It will never fly, it will never happen.' That was their justification for pushing Alvey and ignoring ESPRIT. But it did happen."

Given the choice of the four key technologies, to what extent should the U.K. national program be tightly directed from the center? This proved a controversial issue, linked to the question of the level of support from public funds. Philip Hughes argued for a strongly directed program. "I felt the absolute need to have a directed program in technology," says Hughes, "which, incidentally, I still feel five years later. The Alvey Programme has had its successes and its failures, but I think it was shanghaied from the start, because it never could have been a directed program."

Hughes admires the directed style of both the Japanese collaborative program and the U.S. Defense Advanced Research Projects Agency (DARPA, formerly known as ARPA). "To be fair, I think a directed program would have been difficult, particularly given the breadth of the program; nevertheless I believe that the ARPA mechanism has been an astonishingly interesting way of getting research and development done in the United States." As an example, Hughes quotes packet switching for data communications. "Packet switching was really invented at the National Physical Laboratory in England. But what made it happen, clearly, was Larry Roberts as ARPA director commissioning the Arpanet network."

Highly relevant to the question of a directed program was the envisaged level of support from public funds. Figures of 50 percent, 90 percent, and 100 percent were discussed in the committee. If the figure was to be 100 percent, then clearly the government—or the body set up to run the Alvey Programme—could direct the program completely, specifying exactly what was to be done (and presumably, having paid for the work, owning the resulting intellectual property). If the figure was to be 50 percent, then companies would take a different view, perhaps participating only in research that they would have wanted to pursue in any case. Also, it was argued, a 50 percent figure would act as a barrier to keep small companies out of the program. Certainly the big electronics firms were accustomed to being paid in full for their development work on defense projects.

"I felt very strongly it should be a 100 percent funded program," says Hughes.

Over and over again I quoted the ARPA program in the United States as the kind of model whereby the government places contracts for specific items of work, deciding what the work should be and who should do it, under the direction of a powerful head who is recognized for his grasp of the technology. It has a powerful administrative machine, running a directed program. As far as the big boys on the committee were concerned, this really didn't get much support.

The small-company point has always seemed to me to be a complete irrelevance—a complete and utter red herring. The argument is direction. And the bigger the company, the more you need the power to direct them, ironically. Derek Roberts is a canny old player, and I think he recognized two things: first, as a realist, he judged we'd never get 100 percent through the government; secondly, the big firms didn't want direction.

They certainly did not, the canny old player confirms bluntly. "There was a very strong argument within the Alvey Committee, meeting after meeting," Derek Roberts says,

because there were some people who felt that the right way to do it was to find somebody—God knows who they would have found, some whiz kid, almost inevitably an American—bring him over, give him £350 million or whatever and say "You're the dictator, you spend the money, you tell industry what to do, you tell the universities what to do. It's your program; get on with it." A centrally managed, directed program, run by some brand new organization.

I regarded that as laughable, regardless of whether I thought it was desirable. It seemed to me there was no way the civil servants and the politicians would do it that way. And, apart from anything else, I could not see companies such as GEC and Plessey, who were expected to put up 50 percent of the money for projects, being told by somebody outside what to do. I could never understand why this wasn't obvious to everybody else. The waste of time that took place on that sort of discussion could have been cut short at an earlier stage by one of the civil servants on the committee saying: "Even if you're right, it's a nonstarter, let's not waste time on it."

The Alvey Committee was split very much into two groups, says Iann Barron.

There was the big-company group of GEC, Plessey, Ferranti, and ICL, who wanted one sort of approach; and then there were people like Brian Oakley, Roger Needham, Philip Hughes, and myself who wanted a quite different approach. That split came out in a variety of different ways. The primary one was that GEC, specifically, wanted a program in which all the money was given to one or two major industrial companies, who would then subcontract to the industries and universities to do bits and pieces. Basically they wanted the money to go to big companies, whereas the other people wanted the money to go on a much more disseminated basis to many companies and to a much wider range of research.

Derek Roberts would have preferred a rather different program to the one that emerged:

I always felt it was a mistake for the MoD to hold back from their own program and integrate their requirements into Alvey. I remember at the very first meeting of the Alvey Committee, I arrived about five minutes late, and when I sat down I found myself opposite Hywel Davies, the MoD representative. I'm not very good at being polite to people, and I knew Hywel quite well, and I said "What the hell are you doing here?" I said, "I thought this whole business was really concerned with an industry program; why confuse it with the MoD? It seems to me that you have different objectives. I really think this ought to be DoI and industry."

Personally, I would have kept SERC out of it as well. I was probably wrong, but that was my view. I was in favor of involving the universities in the research, but I wasn't in favor of involving the SERC and hence the Department of Education and Science *and* the DTI *and* the MoD in a three-cornered bureaucracy representing government. In one sense I was right, because there were arguments between the DoI and the SERC, and between the MoD and the DTI, and that three-headed monster contributed to the best part of at least a year's delay in getting the program launched.

Size and Shape of the Program

How did the Alvey Committee reach the figure of £350 million that it recommended should be spent on the national program? John Alvey asked his four authors to "cost up what you need to do"—but bearing in mind such factors as what the government was likely to approve and the feasibility of generating the human resources. "Two hundred and fifty or £350 million over five years is about 1,000 people, with back-up, so that was probably feasible. Obviously 100 people would get you nowhere, and there was no way one could get anywhere near 10,000. This was just another yardstick. And the Westmoreland meeting had been discussing a program of about £250 million."

There was no doubt which technology would take the biggest slice of the cake. "Clearly, from the word go, Derek Roberts's eyes were the biggest," John Alvey says.

And they probably needed to be, because you did need to do a hell of a lot of work in microelectronics to get anywhere. Derek came up with figures of over £100 million for VLSI, while other people at that stage were coming up with much smaller programs. I took the chairman's initiative to an extent and asked the other lads if they'd got their scales of activity right. So they went away and rethought the scale of their exercises. Because IKBS had only a limited population of people who could do it, that part of the program remained a small program, which was why we funded it for the longer period.

The eventual cost breakdown envisaged by the Alvey Committee is shown in table 4.1.

Though the report of the Alvey Committee included this analysis by year and by topic, members now insist that what they were proposing was very much an outline, not a precise plan. "It was not an absolute blueprint," says John Alvey. "We were suggesting a feasible sort of thing which would evolve in the hands of the directorate. All we were saying was 'Look, Government, this is the scale of the thing you ought to be doing, and, at the time of our tabling the report, these are the sensible areas to be working in.'"

Alastair Macdonald adds:

There were many possibilities to choose from. John Alvey stressed that life was too short to seek to cover everything; we had to concentrate on a small number of areas. I recall John Alvey's insistence that these areas were "for instances." John's point was that if the government agreed to a program, then our views should not be taken as the

TABLE 4.1.
Advanced IT Program: Total Cost (£m in 1982)

Activity	\	\	Year	\	\	\	\
	0	1	2	3	4	5	Total
Software engineering	—	8	13	14	18	17	70
VLSI	—	11	18	21	20	20	90
CAD	—	3	4	5	6	7	25
MMI	—	3	8	10	12	11	44
IKBS	—	2	5	5	6	8	26
Communications	1	3	3	3	4	5	19
Demonstrators	—	5	10	13	15	15	58
Education	1	3	3	4	5	4	20*
Total	2	38	64	75	86	87	352

*Software 10, MMI 3, IKBS 7.

last word. They would just show what you *might* do that should help the U.K. industry. We all knew that we were doing this work at fair speed, and we could not be sure that we had chosen to study the "best" areas. So we said to ourselves: "What we are doing is providing some for-instances which others wiser than us will be able to look at critically."

In discussing the style of organization to be adopted for their proposed program, Alvey Committee members considered, and rejected, the concept of a central research institute of the kind set up as the Institute for New Generation Computer Technology (ICOT) under Kazuhiro Fuchi in Japan. "We weren't necessarily against it," says John Alvey, "but ICOT as we saw it was a place where things started and people from the various companies worked together and then took their know-how back into their own organizations. We weren't too sure that that would work terribly well in the U.K." Instead, the view was that the U.K. research groups should be linked by a good network—the communications budget was for this, not for research—to provide a distributed, electronic equivalent to ICOT.

Roger Needham thought the suggestion of a central institute was "a dreadful idea." It is, he says, the sort of thing that is proposed from time to time. "It's something that I oppose whenever I see it, on the grounds that I think such things inevitably become second-rate and also very difficult to stop. And I think you'd have great difficulty in getting good people to go to such a place."

Philip Hughes in principle favored the idea but in practice feared that a certain government establishment would put in a preemptive bid:

I said I am in favor but I'm worried about putting the idea forward because, if it's put forward, someone will accept the idea and use it to dream up yet another way of using Harwell* to do something. I was fearful that, instead of getting fifty top-class people together on a brand-new, ICOT-like site, someone would find that there was a building available at Rutherford or Harwell. I felt it was better to have nothing than to have government-establishment mutton dressed as lamb. My idea was that, as a compromise, you should create a sort of dispersed ICOT based on a high-bandwidth network.

*The Atomic Energy Research Establishment (AERE) has diversified into other areas of technology in recent years.

(There was not universal opposition to a central IT research institute in British academia at the time; Professor Robert Kowalski of Imperial College, for example, had already proposed to Laurence Clarke that such a center should be set up—at Imperial.)

Alvey's People

Many key members of the Alvey Committee contributed their recollections in the research for this book, but Charles Read died in July 1987. Alastair Macdonald describes Read's singular contribution below, but first Macdonald makes a general point on the membership of the committee:

> In our choice of members for the Alvey Committee, which John Alvey discussed with us at the DTI, we could be—and were—criticized for an apparent imbalance, in that too great an attention was paid to the hardware side and large firms and insufficient attention was given to software and small firms. We all should have identified the way technology was going. Several of us, in making speeches during IT82 year and so on, were referring to a great shift in the balance of companies' activity, from 80 percent hardware and 20 percent software in 1975 to forecasts of 10 percent hardware and 90 percent software by 1990. Yet the composition of the committee did not take full account of that change.
>
> Charles Read's contribution was twofold. First, he harnessed very effectively the creativity of people like Karen Sparck Jones and others in the community to get a clear long-term vision of the importance of knowledge-based systems in a way that persuaded the rest of the committee, perhaps rather unwillingly, to accept that in KBS you had to look ten years rather than five years ahead. Several of us were looking for neatness and were saying that the committee ought to be presenting to government an integrated five-year program. At first there was resentment at Charles's saying "Five years is not long enough," and I think his major contribution in terms of the IKBS program was to convince his colleagues that knowledge-based systems would be an integral part of IT for the 1990s and would need a ten-year program. He also did much to show that such systems had a credibility that put at rest the internecine warfare about artificial intelligence of the 1970s.
>
> His second contribution reflected his personal iconoclasm. He sought to reduce all technical discussions to the closest you could get to calling a spade a bloody shovel. And he was prepared to question whether in certain areas the U.K. industrial emperors had any clothes. He had a very good way of puncturing inflated ideas. He was the most individual of all the members of the committee.

The most dominant in terms of personality was Derek Roberts. I believe that intellectually the best piece of work done for the Alvey Committee was that done by Philip Hughes's team on software. There must be a danger that, if that team had not done so well, the software side in Alvey would have suffered.

The Alvey Report

The Alvey Committee made its report[10] to Kenneth Baker in September 1982 (see appendix 1). Collaborative research was essential if Britain was to preserve and strengthen her capability and competitiveness in IT, the committee had concluded. A national program, costing £350 million over five years, should be mounted, with two-thirds of the direct cost of the program coming from public funds. The committee's answer to the funding-level arguments was a compromise: academic research and training would come totally from public funds, as would be expected; while the industrial work should be publicly funded at 90 percent "where very wide dissemination of the results is required," otherwise at 50 percent. The chosen technologies were essential to progress:

• Software engineering, the efficient specification and generation of the instructions for the machines, was crucial to success.

• The interface between man and machine also was crucial. Commercial success would come to those who made their products truly acceptable to their users.

• A prime aspect of the extension of this interface into the machine was the study of intelligent knowledge-based systems. More powerful information-processing systems, with better transfer of human intelligence and knowledge to the computer, were required.

• The hardware to make these systems would be heavily dependent on advances in the very large-scale integration of circuits on silicon.

In software engineering the strategic objective was that the U.K. should become a world leader in this technology by the end of the 1980s. The focus was to develop Information Systems Factories (ISFs)—systems that provide integrated sets of tools for producing IT systems using software engineering techniques. Strategies for innovation, integration, and exploitation were proposed. In MMI a program addressing both man-related and machine-related problems was recommended. The broad area was divided into human factors, input/output devices, and speech and image processing.

In IKBS a ten-year R & D program was needed because the research was difficult and because technological innovation and transfer was inevitably time consuming. The program should expand the infrastructure and the research community, support research programs, and construct a number of demonstrator systems. In VLSI the goal was "to ensure that by the later 1980s the U.K. has secure access to internationally competitive VLSI." This implied one-centimeter-square silicon chips containing about one million logic gates, but this goal would not be achieved in a single step. Advanced facilities for computer-aided design and for various process technologies were needed.

Good communications would be vital to the success of the program, the report noted. Indeed, the need for the program in the first place derived in large measure from the fragmented state of the U.K. IT research community, the components of which needed to be brought out of isolation to work together effectively. The objective therefore was to link participants by means of a network and to support collaborative work by scattered groups.

Discussing the Japanese challenge, the report noted the various joint government/industry programs in that country, of which the fifth-generation program was merely the latest. Others had covered VLSI, pattern information processing systems, high-speed computers, operating systems, and optoelectronics. The option of collaborating with Japan on selected projects might well make sense, and the proposed U.K. national program would "put us in a far stronger position to exercise this option."

As for the ESPRIT proposals from the European Commission, the committee argued that the U.K. program "would assist in feeding in the U.K. input to any EEC program, not least by widening the range of potential U.K. participants to include the small and medium-sized businesses which would otherwise tend to be excluded." ESPRIT was not a substitute for a U.K. program; a U.K. program would help Britain to participate more effectively in any European one.

The committee rejected the central-institute suggestion "because the program must be carried out as far as possible by organizations capable of using and exploiting the results, to ensure maximum industrial relevance." A new directorate should be set up within the Department of Industry to expedite and manage the program. This unit should be "slim and compact," and its director should be "an experienced technical manager with a proven program management track record in this field."

The director should report to a board, which would serve as a steering committee and supervise the overall strategy and management of the program. The Electronics and Avionics Requirements Board (EARB) of the DoI provided the basis for the proposed new board and should be given the task of steering the new program. The director would consult with the board on his overall strategy and present annual plans and programs for approval.

"The main task of the directorate will be to ensure that the technical program is effectively implemented and its targets met," the report stated.

To achieve this, the program must be driven firmly from the center. The director will work with industry and with other technical experts, but he must have sole responsibility for project specifications and for the award of contracts. We are convinced that tight direction of the program is the only way of ensuring effective implementation and of achieving the swift action which is necessary. A responsive approach of waiting for outside organizations to submit proposals would fail to provide sufficient momentum.

As a measure to retain top researchers and make maximum use of their skills, the committee proposed that a national IT Fellowship should be set up. A group of about 30 full-time IT fellows would be based at recognized centers in academia and industry to support the program. They would in effect form a dispersed national IT institute and collectively could be an important source of technical advice to the new directorate.

From the start of its work the Alvey Committee had invited comments and commissioned papers from relevant outside organizations. No fewer than 115 bodies responded, including hardware and software companies; IT-using organizations; universities, polytechnics, and colleges; consultancies; and public and private research centers. Respondents ranged from the Cabinet Office to the National Hospital of Nervous Diseases, and from SESA in France to SRI International in California.

AI Revisited

Parallel with the work of the Alvey Committee, yet another study[11] of the state of artificial intelligence in the United Kingdom was conducted in 1982 within the academic establishment. At the request of the SERC two Cambridge University scientists, professors Sir Peter Swinnerton-Dyer* (Mathematics) and Roger Needham (Computing), reported on the subject. Neither was an AI specialist, and their report made an illuminating contrast with that of Lighthill ten years before.

"The most striking and depressing feature of AI work in the United Kingdom is how little there is of it," the authors noted—particularly when contrasted with the high level of activity in the United States. In Britain, AI had remained in the shadow of the Lighthill Report for the past ten years. In 1973 that report had represented a justifiable view of the state and prospects of the subject, the two authors opined. "The publicists for the subject saw its future in terms which can only be described as millenial: the software packages that were needed to underpin any major work were not available, and there was little realization of how much tedious work would be needed to produce them; worst of all, the hardware which was available or could reasonably be foreseen was quite inadequate to the demands that the practitioners of the AI were likely to make on it."

By 1982, in contrast, things were different:

All this has changed. The intermediate targets of AI are more reasonable than they were ten years ago, much effort (mostly in the United States) has gone into providing the basic software that is needed, and hardware developments have made available amounts of computing power and of memory that could not have been foreseen ten years ago. It must be recognized that the Lighthill Report was right for its day, but that its day is past. AI is a different subject from what it was ten years ago, and it is set in a different context. Then it was the wild blue yonder. Now it is the open frontier of IT—and the frontier on which in the medium term some of the most promising advances are likely to be made. But, as with most frontiers, the maps are inadequate; it is worth paying for explorers, but we cannot yet say exactly where to dig for gold.

*In 1983 Swinnerton-Dyer became chairman of the University Grants Committee (UGC), which oversees public funding (excluding research funding) for universities.

The continuing effect of the Lighthill Report, the authors went on, was that the U.K. now had few AI research workers and teams. AI teaching was extremely limited, and the whole community was demoralized: leading researchers were emigrating to top positions in the U.S., and there was no significant influx of new, high-quality entrants. Interest in the subject was growing among students, but the opportunities to pursue this interest were very restricted. Though university cuts were much to blame for the current position, the community had earlier suffered more severely than was intended from the fallout from Lighthill. "Thus the difficulty of even maintaining AI activity in the mid-1970s, after Lighthill, has left a small, scattered and somewhat defensive community, and has made it difficult for it now to withstand the pressures on the university system as a whole. We believe that this situation must not be allowed to continue."

Swinnerton-Dyer and Needham agreed with the Alvey (and the Japanese) arguments for accelerated R & D into artificial intelligence. In summary, these arguments were:

1. Building intelligent systems was the next task of IT.

2. Easy access to advanced IT was essential to the national economy.

3. Government support was mandatory for R & D effort in this very challenging area.

4. Government support was needed to meet the consequent need for increased teaching and training.

While fully supporting the Alvey IKBS proposals, the authors urged that broader and longer-term AI work also should be pursued. Specifically, they added two further points:

5. Government support was required for very long-range and interdisciplinary AI and AI-related research.

6. Government support was needed for graduate teaching relevant to this wider area.

"The reasons for supporting AI are thus practical, political, and intellectual," Swinnerton-Dyer and Needham concluded. "In the last case we think it particularly important to recognize that computational modeling of complex systems has a contribution to make to other areas, like neurophysiology, complementing that which they may make to AI itself. We also wish to emphasize the timeliness, for its own sake, of fundamental research into cognitive processes."

In the event, the two professors' recommendations were overtaken both by the SERC moves toward a special IKBS program and by the Alvey initiative itself. But their analysis of the scene confirmed the generally depressed state of AI research in Britain in the early 1980s—though their unashamed agreement with Lighthill in 1973 set them apart from key researchers in the AI field, whose bitter hostility to the Lighthill Report continues to this day.

Consultation

John Alvey submitted his committee's report, together with the four main technology working papers, to Kenneth Baker on 3 September 1982. He acknowledged that there were some inconsistencies between the working papers and the main report and also some signs of haste in the report itself, but he judged it to be more important to meet the committee's deadlines than to reconcile the paperwork. Baker was abroad on government business but wrote to thank Alvey on 16 September. In a second letter on 4 October he thanked the committee for producing such a comprehensive report to a very tight timetable, and invited them to make a presentation on the report.

The Alvey Report was officially published on 6 October 1982. The DoI press announcement quoted Kenneth Baker as saying: "The Alvey Committee's report is being reviewed urgently. I am most grateful to the committee and its chairman for the speed and thoroughness with which they completed their report. The DoI would welcome as soon as possible the views of other organizations not represented on the committee before the government comes to a decision on the report's recommendations."

In soliciting the views of industry and other groups on the Alvey recommendations, the Department of Industry went on to pose a wide range of key issues. Was the Alvey technical balance right? Was a U.K. IT capability necessary? How realistic were the Alvey costs? How willing was industry to collaborate? How relevant was the proposed program to industry's own intentions? How could the ideal management needs be met—strong direction, rapid action, full accountability, a top-class yet affordable director? What policy should be adopted toward foreign-owned multinationals? How much could the DoI, MoD, and DES afford?

The Alvey report stimulated wide debate on the proposed program. At the final major event of the IT82 year, a large conference held in December in the Barbican Centre, London at which the prime minister spoke, Kenneth Baker said that the government would be announcing its decisions on the Alvey proposals in the new year. He stressed the importance of bringing industrial and university work closer together. Vicomte Etienne Davignon, Vice-President of the European Commission, told the conference:

> We have read with interest the recommendations of the Alvey Committee and note that these are in tune with the Commission's view on the need for a long-term collaborative research and development program backed up by a coherent industrial strategy. We fully support the perception of Alvey that national efforts should concentrate on national strengths, and national efforts should also be linked to a wider collaborative effort—in this case a program the Commission is calling ESPRIT (European Strategic Programme of Research and Development in Information Technology).

Mrs. Thatcher did not mention Alvey in her speech to the conference.

The Confederation of British Industry (CBI) canvassed its member firms widely and submitted its comments formally to the DoI in January 1983. The confederation welcomed the report and supported the proposed program but warned that much remained to be done to ensure that the research and technology achievement was indeed followed by successful exploitation of the results by a strong U.K. IT industry: "Britain must not once again fail in the marketplace after achieving outstanding success in research." On two aspects of the Alvey Report the CBI was critical. First, it doubted the wisdom of the Alvey approach based on collaborative R & D followed by competitive exploitation. More permanent collaborative groupings were considered essential. Second, the report's treatment of industrial property rights and the dissemination of information was inadequate.

Baker's "urgent review" of the Alvey Committee's proposals involved not only his own Department of Industry. The review was conducted in the context of an IT policy mechanism devised in the Cabinet Office in 1980 to 1981 by Professor John

Ashworth,* Chief Scientist of the Central Policy Review Staff (CPRS), the government's so-called think tank. Working with Ashworth was Adrian Norman, an IT adviser seconded to the CPRS from Arthur D. Little. There were four legs to this mechanism, says Norman:

1. An Information Technology Advisory Panel (ITAP) of outside experts to advise the prime minister and the Cabinet.

2. An interdepartmental committee on IT to coordinate policy across the various government departments.

3. A Minister for Information Technology.

4. A small IT Unit in the Cabinet Office (which Norman joined in 1981 and which was disbanded in 1983).

Whitehall discussion of the Alvey Report was focused on those four elements. The DoI was well placed to know what was going on: Kenneth Baker was the initial chairman of ITAP, and Roy Croft, a DoI Deputy Secretary, chaired the interdepartmental committee. Charles Read was a member (and later chairman) of ITAP, and in October 1982 he agreed to coordinate the panel's reactions to the report. He drafted a letter to the prime minister which was signed by Ivor Cohen of Mullard on behalf of all six ITAP members and sent to Mrs. Thatcher on 13 January 1983. A national IT strategy was urgently needed, the panel told the prime minister, including a national strategy for IT R & D:

> Any successful R & D plan for the late 1980s and for the 1990s must involve selective government investment coupled with industrial investment and commitment, aimed at clear, tangible objectives and managed so as to achieve maximum benefit from coordination and efficient resource utilization. We are firmly convinced that unless the government assumes a strategic planning and intervention role, high-risk projects and long-term-return projects in information technology will not be undertaken, and our national resources will be dissipated on fragmented activities.

ITAP strongly endorsed the Alvey Committee's recommendations, the panel said (Charles Read's interest as a member of the Alvey Committee was properly acknowledged in a postscript). It was vital to achieve close gearing of R & D to the

---

*Ashworth later became vice chancellor of the University of Salford and chairman of the National Computing Centre.

production of wealth-creating products and services aimed at international markets and not merely to indulge in scientific research. "In particular, it is vital to devise technology transfer mechanisms and projects which take account of IT users' needs and reactions."

There was much to be done. "But clearly the first steps are for your government to approve the policy, sanction the expenditure, and set up the directorate." The technology was fast moving and no time should be lost in decision taking if the national interest was to be secured. The French and Japanese governments clearly recognized this and were acting accordingly. The panel concluded: "John Alvey reported in the summer, and it is a matter of some concern to us that we are now entering the new year with no signs of action or reaction. Is there anything which we can do to assist in expediting this matter?"

Replying on 31 January, Mrs. Thatcher thanked the panel for their offer and gave a "Don't phone us, we'll phone you" sort of response. The Department of Industry's consultations on Alvey were now complete, she said, and the government was aiming to announce a decision on Alvey soon.

Action

Mrs. Thatcher's "soon" took another three months. On 28 April 1983 Patrick Jenkin, Secretary of State for Industry (and Kenneth Baker's boss), announced in the House of Commons that the Alvey Committee's recommendation for a national program of collaborative IT research had been accepted and would be implemented (see appendix 2). The government was ready to support a £350 million program—subject to industry's contribution and technical progress—but the publicly funded contribution to industrial projects would be a flat 50 percent. "This is the first time in our history that we shall be embarking on a collaborative research project on anything like this scale," he said. "No one can guarantee success, but the government is convinced that this program will ensure for British industry secure access to the new technology and to the products and processes on which our future prosperity depends." A new, small directorate would be established in the Department of Industry to coordinate the program, Mr Jenkin said; it would be headed by Mr Brian Oakley, currently Secretary of the Science and Engineering Research Council.

II
Directing the Programme

5
Birth of the Programme

Brian Oakley takes up the story of his involvement in the Alvey Programme. In this chapter he describes the birth of the Programme; the attendant political, financial, and staffing problems; and the background to his appointment.

The Part Played by Kenneth Baker

Though I had been involved in the early planning of the Programme, and was a member of the Alvey Committee, I had had little to do with the Alvey movement from the time of the completion of the report in September 1982 until the government made the announcement to proceed in April 1983. During this period Kenneth Baker, as Minister for Information Technology in DTI, had circulated the report to industry and asked for their comments. Some 300 firms and other bodies were asked to comment, and most did so. The Science and Engineering Research Council, of which I was Secretary, was one of the bodies asked to comment. Like most of the respondents, the Council supported the main proposals enthusiastically while disagreeing with certain details. When I formed the Directorate I was too busy to read most of these replies, but I had already seen many of them when they were copied to the SERC. I confess I don't remember taking much notice of the detailed criticism, though it may have made some subliminal impact. Nor was it obvious that it made much impact on Kenneth Baker or on government policy. But his good sense in seeking views from a wide community on the Programme became clear when the proposals were put to the Cabinet for approval in early 1983.

By this date in Mrs Thatcher's first administration the enthusiasm for the support of information technology had begun to wane. Kenneth Baker had been allowed to perform in a way that was really quite countercultural in his enthusiastic encouragement of IT. And though IT82 was a year of systematic publicity for the new technology of computing and microelectronics, Baker's policies in support of IT did require an investment in R & D that at the time and relative to what was to come after seemed quite generous. I can't pretend that my colleagues and I were enthusiastic about the propaganda approach exemplified by IT82, but not for the first time politicians had something to teach civil servants, for it proved a great success. Public awareness of the implications of IT rose enormously. At the same time Baker's enthusiastic support for taking IT into every classroom had resulted in a truly remarkable sale of cheap microcomputers from firms such as Sinclair and Acorn. For a time the U.K. led the world in the micro revolution, with more micros in schools and more per head than any other nation. To a considerable extent this campaign demonstrated the power of government "priming the pump," for a few micros in schools led little Johnny to demand a micro in his Christmas stocking and parents scrambled to buy them in order to be one up on the Joneses next door.

Sir Keith Joseph Plays his Part

In order to conduct this micro-in-schools campaign, Baker, with the largely unseen support of his Secretary of State, Patrick Jenkin, had to persuade the Secretary of State at the Department of Education, Sir Keith Joseph, to invest Education funds in training teachers, etc. Sir Keith was, of course, a much drier character than Baker, but he had been at DTI, and he understood what Baker was about. Much more important from the viewpoint of the Alvey Programme was that Baker persuaded Sir Keith that something had to be done about IT in the higher education sector. In the autumn of 1982 Sir Keith did produce a quite significant sum, approaching £100 million over five years, for the SERC to support conversion courses, fellowships, and R & D in IT. The DES was seen to be doing its bit in the IT revolution that the DTI was pioneering. Indeed, the fact that the DES was actually leading with these funds enabled the SERC, and so the DES, to support the Alvey Programme when it came to Cabinet. Of course, in terms of the Education Bill as a whole such sums were trivial, but in terms of the money that the DES had to dispense directly, rather than through the local authorities, through the so-called "science" vote for the Research Councils that funded research and postgraduate studentships, it was a significant sum. I don't think that the DES obtained new funds from the Treasury.

Incidentally, as well as being vital for the academic part of the Alvey Programme, this money led to the establishment of the one-year postgraduate IT conversion course. This was seen as a way of increasing the IT graduate population rapidly by giving those who had chosen the "wrong" degree course a chance to convert. At a time of high graduate unemployment this proved very attractive. For at this time the monetarist economic policies combined with a laissez-faire attitude to the pound, which was rising sky high, was leading to very considerable unemployment of graduates, part of the tragic unemployment sweeping the country as the old smokestack industries were forced out of business as their exports became uncompetitive. The conversion courses have proved a great success, for they continue to be well supported by excellent applicants, many of whom do not come from any numerate first-degree course. The output of an extra 1,000 IT graduates a year was seen as a way of rapidly stepping up the supply, but in practice the combination of some other first-degree graduates with a one-year IT immersion has proved ideal for many of the IT user companies who wish to add IT skills to their normal graduate recruitment.

Because this DES IT program was arranged at remarkable speed at the time of the autumn estimates, the DES had to turn to the SERC for advice. And for a few weeks it was not clear who was going to administer the conversion-course grants. The SERC stepped into that breach, and I was personally much involved in this work, so I became well known to the DES officials in the University and Science Branch, notably Richard Bird and David Tanner. It was always a pleasure to deal with them. David, in particular, reminded me of all that was best in the old traditions of the civil service. I never saw David out of temper, he was courteous to all and was a good friend to the SERC, to the Alvey Programme, and to me—as I believe he would have been to any individuals trying to forward the causes that his department served.

No doubt the fact that I was working so closely with these officials did me no harm in the Whitehall infighting over the appointment of a Director for the Alvey Programme. And this close involvement continued throughout the winter of 1982–1983, for another of Sir Keith Joseph's sensible actions had been to support a program of so-called "new blood" appointments to ease the age structure in the scientific and engineering departments of the universities. It was somewhat ironic that the cutbacks in the universities were resulting in reductions of staff even in the engineering and computer science departments, despite the government's desire to increase the numbers in these fields, for the democracy of many universities was resulting in misery all round. Indeed in some universities the voluntary early retirements fell disproportionally heavily on these departments because they were the people who could most easily obtain posts outside the academic field. The new-blood appointments served to replace the vacancies left by the cuts. This was a mixed blessing, for though it gave a welcome opportunity to many excellent young people who otherwise could never have got a foothold on the university career ladder, in some places it resulted in some pretty poor appointments. The new-blood scheme had various parents, but the crucial paper was written by Sir Peter Swinnerton-Dyer, at that time a don at Cambridge and a key member of the Advisory Board for Research Councils. He turned to me for help in drafting that paper and in a sense I made the bullets that he fired. Again it can have done no harm to have friends in high places when the choice of director came to be made. As Sir Peter subsequently became chairman of the University Grants Committee throughout much of the Alvey era, he provided another useful ally for the Programme, though the difficult days the UGC were living through meant that the UGC could do little to help those universities who most needed infrastructure support to match the Alvey grant income.

The Alvey Decision in Whitehall

Returning to Kenneth Baker's battle to get the Alvey Programme approved in Whitehall, it was finally approved in the run-up to the 1983 general election. It was not surprising that the Alvey Committee's recommendation for 90 percent support for certain parts of the Programme did not survive. And I have to say that, even though I supported this in the committee as a way of getting a program of R & D started in firms, such as the software houses, who were not used to forward investment in research, I was pleased not to have to administer a program with so much government support. It would have resulted in large numbers of applications from firms who would have been very upset not to have obtained support but who were not really likely to be able to exploit the work. Experience demonstrated that cooperation was not hard to obtain at the 50 percent funding level that was approved. And though 90 percent funding might have resulted in a much more directed program—on the principle that he who pays the piper calls the tunes—I'm not convinced that it would have helped the U.K. industry in the long run. It would certainly have been much harder to administer!

In the end the Programme was approved, but with two emasculating conditions attached—it should not cost the Treasury any "new" money, and there should be no extra complement of civil servants to run it. The DTI agreed that it could fund its share of the Alvey Programme without new funds.

The situation for the MoD was in some ways similar. Defense had been living through a period of a 3 percent per annum increase in real expenditure over a period of several years, for defense and the police were about the only parts of the overall government expenditure scene for which Mrs Thatcher approved an increase in her first administration. So the MoD could afford the £40 million it promised for the Alvey Programme. In practice most if not all the money came from the CVD budget that supported work for research and development of electronic components.

Changes from the Alvey Committee's Recommendations

Before leaving the matter of funds, it seems right to point out that the government reduced its expenditure from 90 percent to 50 percent for parts of the Programme without reducing the total funds asked for by the Alvey Committee. So the community got as much as they had proposed, but distributed over more work. With the benefit of hindsight this seems to me to have been highly satisfactory. It is inconceivable that the officials in the DTI could not have recognized that an opportunity for reducing the total expenditure was being passed over. Whether Kenneth Baker and the Cabinet recognized it, I cannot say. My guess is that the change came in the middle of a hard-fought Cabinet Committee meeting, when the point would have been overlooked. But maybe our friends in the Cabinet did us one more service. In the years to come several ministers who were not directly involved told me that they had fought for the Programme, most noticeably Norman Tebbit, at that time at the Department of Employment. He subsequently became Secretary of State at the DTI and was easily the outstanding holder of that hot seat during the Alvey years. Geoffrey Pattie, at the time Minister of State in the MoD, was a strong supporter of the Programme and also subsequently moved to the DTI. He was always a good friend to the Programme, and if he failed to get approved the follow-on to the Alvey Programme, the program recommended in the Bide Committee report, it was not for want of enthusiasm on his part. A rather more surprising supporter of the Programme was the Secretary of State at the Welsh Department. It was rather a shame that the geography of the IT industry and universities meant that Wales got very little out of the Programme, certainly when compared with Scotland and England. But no doubt he had not had the interests of the principality primarily in mind when the Programme was discussed in Cabinet.

There was one other departure from the Alvey Committee's recommendations and that was over the support for education and training. In fact, though the Alvey Committee had always argued strongly for support for what they rightly saw as these critical activities, they did not come up with any specific recommendations. Even at the time of the writing of the report it was recognized that the DES, UGC, SERC, Manpower Services Commission, and all other bodies with an interest in training would have fought hard to prevent yet another new body, the Alvey Directorate, from trampling on their ground. Discretion was seen as the better part of valor, and there was no strong pressure from any quarter for the Alvey Directorate to have a significant say in these matters. The Alvey Directorate had quite enough to do without this extra burden, but, looking back, I do wish we had had the right to be consulted and to intervene with advice. If I had my time again, I would have appointed someone from the higher education sector to take a special interest in the related education and training activities. As it happens, I believe the Alvey Directorate did have quite an influence in stepping up the supply of high-quality people for the more advanced aspects of IT, such as the AI and integrated circuit CAD fields. But we could, and should, have done more.

The Choice of Director

In searching for a Director for the Alvey Programme the DTI would have been in the lead but would have consulted the SERC and MoD. There would probably have been discreet consultations with various senior industrialists. In the main paper circulating in Whitehall setting out the case for the Alvey Programme was a section describing the duties and desirable characteristics for the Director. I saw a copy of this paper, though I remember thinking at the time that those who had passed it to me probably did not notice that my name was among a group of perhaps five or six names given as examples of possible candidates. The Alvey Committee had seen the post of the Director going to a technologist from industry, with some members of the Committee feeling strongly that the post should be filled by someone who could give a strong technical lead. The example was held up of Larry Roberts, the person who had given a firm lead to the DARPA network project in the United States. I don't remember taking much part in these discussions. At the time I had become very wary of directors who had excellent technical qualifications but little managerial experience. In my experience, all Chairmen of the Science Research Council had felt that the leaders of the SERC laboratories must be outstanding scientists, on the model of the Max Planck Institutes in Germany. From some experience of such people I have become aware that an academic scientist, however eminent, was unlikely to become a great director of a large laboratory unless he had already had considerable experience leading something larger than your average university research team. So I would have been wary about appointing an academic, however eminent, to lead the Alvey Programme, even though at the time I might have been expected to speak up for such an appointment in view of my role as Secretary of the SERC. But the appointment of an industrialist with experience of leading a large industrial research laboratory was quite another matter. Had I been asked, I, like the other members of the Alvey Committee, would have come down in favor of an industrialist, probably one of the names on the list.

Whether they were approached and turned the offer down or their firms refused to release them I can't say. All I do know is that I was approached, in the first place through the Chairman of the SERC, John Kingman. It all happened very fast. The government wanted to make an announcement about its decision on the Alvey Committee's report to Parliament before it was dissolved for the forthcoming election, and it was felt desirable to couple the name of the Director with that announcement. Is it conceivable that I owed my appointment to being the only person around who would say yes at short notice? Perish the thought!

Qualifications for the Director Post?

I could hardly have been appointed on my nonexistent record as an advanced IT worker. It is true that I had been working with computers on and off since 1956, when I was at what is now the Royal Signals and Radar Establishment (RSRE). I was leading a team working on data handling for air-traffic and defense-interceptor control. At that time I was involved in the early days of realtime computing and in the specification of the first realtime defense language, Coral. When I came to Headquarters in 1969 I had worked in the Computer Division of the Ministry of Technology, being responsible for the software industry—insofar as civil servants can be said to have any responsibility for an industry. But after 1972 my responsibilities had widened to general research matters, establishing the requirement boards that brought industrialists into the decision making on government support of R & D. In 1978 I became Secretary of the Science Research Council (SRC) as it then was. So for some years past I had had no direct involvement with computing matters, though I had kept up my interests through the various IT boards and committees over which I had some indirect responsibility.

Perhaps my sole qualification for the post was that I had served in all three sponsoring bodies—the MoD, DTI, and SERC—and was probably the only person around with that distinction, if distinction it be. I had been vaguely noticed by Kenneth Baker at the time when I played a minor part in the Westmoreland Hotel meeting that led to the setting up of the Alvey Committee. And then again he did jokingly refer to me as a possible candidate for the Director post when I spoke up in the discussion of the Alvey Committee's report at one of the consultation meetings with industry held in the late autumn of 1982, after the report was published. I suspect it was Alastair Macdonald who canvassed my name, and for this and his unfailing support throughout the era of the Alvey Directorate I owe him my thanks. The name cannot have had much appeal to industry or even to ministers, who almost certainly wanted someone with a proven entrepreneurial reputation from industry. But it probably won the support of the MoD and SERC—"Better the dog you know!"

To Accept or Not to Accept?

I was given about twelve hours to decide if I would take the job. I had been confident that the Department would appoint an industrialist, so I had not seriously considered the post. But I knew at once that I wanted to take the job. I had been Secretary of the SERC for five years, so it was time for a change. The Alvey Directorate offered a unique opportunity and one I had wanted to have for many years. Way back in my research establishment days I had been concerned at the lack of cooperation between the various firms in the computing industry, each of which could not afford to invest enough to make a major impact on the world scene. If only they would cooperate, especially for common software development, we stood a much better chance of becoming the power in the computing world that our undoubted technical excellence entitled us to believe we could be. So this was an opportunity to help to bring this about. I told the Department that I would take the job on only if industry wanted me and would back me. I think there must have been some consultation with industry, for the key individuals in all the major firms phoned me to offer their support, and what at that moment was even more important, promised to put in good people on secondment to help staff the directorate. It is true that the directorate was seriously understaffed for the first couple of years, but Ron Cooper, the establishment officer of DTI, and the Department's Permanent Secretary, Sir Brian Hayes, took a very supportive attitude to finding the staff.

As far as my rank was concerned, I was offered promotion to deputy secretary to run the Programme. At the time that I had become Secretary of the SERC I had been promoted from under secretary to a point between that and full deputy secretary, a rare post that existed because the Chairman of a Research Council, an appointment always held by an eminent academic on secondment from his university, was that of a full deputy secretary. It was somewhat anomalous to create a post at the deputy secretary level to run the Alvey Directorate, but I think it came about because it was realized in Whitehall that it would require a deputy secretary status and salary to attract a good man from industry. When they switched to offer the post to a civil servant they retained the rank. Shortly after I had accepted the post the part of the Treasury responsible for controlling senior grades in the civil service objected to the rank, but the department claimed it was too late by then, and I was allowed to keep the rank. What would have happened if I had not been offered the promotion I cannot say, though I suspect I would have taken the job as an under secretary. Yet it was, on occasions, important to have the status that the rank confers. It meant that I could report directly to the Permanent Secretary rather than through the Deputy Secretary responsible for Information Technology or through the Chief Scientist. As it happens, the Deputy Secretary for IT through most of the Alvey era was Alastair Macdonald. I could not imagine a finer colleague to work with, and I would have been quite happy to report through him.

The Chairman of the SERC, John Kingman, was very good about my taking on the Alvey job. It must have been a confounded nuisance to him to have to find a new Secretary for the Council, though it is always possible he was only too pleased to see me go! He left the decision entirely to me, though I think that in the background he was very supportive in getting me the post and rank. Throughout my career I have always been very lucky in the men for whom I have worked. Geoffrey Allen, the man who attracted me to become the Secretary of the SERC, was a great chairman from whom I learnt many things, not least about working with people. When in doubt in my Alvey Directorate days I often asked myself how he would have handled the problem. I personally owe a great deal to John Kingman, for he could easily have blocked my appointment to the Directorate.

Before finally telling Ron Cooper that I would take the post I set two conditions. As I have already mentioned, one was that I had the full support and confidence of the main IT firms.

The other was that Ron would give me a first-rate man to stand at my shoulder as administrative director. I had always recognized that it needed someone with very special skills to work successfully with the administrators of Whitehall. Though there have been exceptions, the average outsider needs a first-rate man to help him with the details of Whitehall administration and procedure. Ron agreed to find such a man, and as I shall relate in the next chapter he was as good as his word. So with the auspices for the Programme not set entirely fair, I agreed to do the job, and the announcement was made the next morning.

6
The Directorate Moves into Action

As the Alvey Directorate settled into Millbank Tower, London (former home of the Ministry of Technology set up by Harold Wilson's Labour Government in the late 1960s), there were key posts to fill, technology strategies to be drafted. Brian Oakley traces the course of events as his directorate moved into action.

The Deputy Director

The date announced for the start of the Alvey Programme was 1 May 1983. In fact, because of commitments to the SERC, I was not able to join the office until 2 May, so Laurence Clarke, my deputy, was actually the first person in the Directorate's offices in Millbank Tower. Virtually everything had to be built from scratch, so he had a very bleak introduction to life in the government machine. When I joined the next day I found a rather dispirited Laurence and a secretary, Gwen Lord. It was very satisfactory for me to have Laurence with me from the beginning. GEC had offered to put a good man in the Directorate. I had had my eye on Laurence ever since my name had come up as Director, since I had known him for many years as the GEC research man with most involvement with government. Recently he had chaired the SERC Information Engineering Committee and was being talked about as next Chairman of the Engineering Board. As he had been very influential in the early planning that led up to the Alvey Committee, he was well informed about the objectives of the Programme. Though he had been in the senior ranks of the GEC management for some years it was believed that he had fallen out with a key man in the GEC hierarchy, so his undoubted qualities were not getting proper recognition by a suitable senior appointment in the firm. So it was by mutual agreement with Derek Roberts that I was very happy to have him as my deputy in the Alvey Directorate.

As it turned out, Laurence was first in and virtually last out, for he took over as caretaker when I retired in October 1987. (Timothy Walker was appointed as director for the Information Engineering Directorate that succeeded the Alvey Directorate in December 1987.) I could not have wished for a better deputy. We certainly didn't always agree on the details but were as one over the objectives. He was invaluable as my spur to action in the early days, and throughout the five years he was there pressing for action. It cannot have been easy working with me, but he was loyal to a fault and, even when the temporization of our political masters in the last year drove him to the limits of frustration, he retained his good temper and unflagging spirit. It was essential for me as a lifelong civil servant to have a deputy from industry, and it was highly convenient to have that man from the largest U.K. firm in the IT industry and, as experience was to show, the largest participant in the Programme and the largest contributor to the Directorate. He took the lead in handling the biggest and most difficult projects, the large demonstrators, and he helped me on all aspects of the Directorate's work.

The Key Administrator

Very special skills are required for a scientist to make a success of working closely with the administrators of Whitehall. Many a distinguished scientist appointed to be a chief scientist in a Whitehall department has proved a disappointment because of his inability to learn how to get the best out of the rather special environment. It requires an understanding not just of how to work under ministers but how to work with the mandarins. It requires an intimate knowledge of where the levers of power actually reside. I knew I did not really possess these skills and recognized that I needed someone in the directorate team who really could both work with scientists and administrators and operate effectively as part of the Whitehall machine. It required a person with very special skills.

Ron Cooper and Sir Brian Hayes understood the need for an exceptional civil servant to support me and were prepared to provide one. For that I am eternally grateful. Cooper looked around and came up with Timothy Walker. It cannot have been easy for the Department to make the decision to put one of their valued rising stars into the Directorate. For it was obvious even then that, though in 1983 Timothy was a relatively junior official, he would rise fast—as indeed he has, for in 1988 he became an under secretary and my successor as Director of the Information Engineering Directorate.

In May 1983 Tim Walker was just finishing a year's sabbatical at the London Business School. He could not join the Directorate immediately, which created a problem for us. But it was worth waiting a few months to get such a good man, and Tim helped by time sharing in the last weeks of his course. He had read chemistry at university and had a doctorate, though I had some difficulty in persuading him to use the title Dr. T. Walker in Whitehall. Tim rapidly made some sense of our chaotic administration and acted as the main interface with Whitehall on all matters except those concerned with technical policy and projects. He also provided the lead for us on ESPRIT within Whitehall, which took a great deal of time and effort. There is no doubt that we were short of at least one extra administrator to directly support Tim during the early months. But he worked wonders with what few human resources he had. When, two years later, Cooper asked me to let Tim move on to run the Department's think tank, I knew I was losing a key member of the team. But one has to employ exceptional measures with exceptional people, and by then the pattern of Alvey administration was largely established. I did not feel I could stand in Tim's way, for the think tank job was one that would make him very visible and could well lead to preferment—as indeed time demonstrated. Maybe it needed a different type of man to look after the detailed grind of running the Programme in 1985 from the man required to pioneer the machinery. I think we all felt the loss, but maybe it was for the best in the long run. I enjoyed working with Tim, as I did with his successor Roger Hird in his very different way. I cannot pretend that was true for me with all Whitehall administrators. Administration, as distinct from management, is a rare skill and much underestimated, not least by those who know all about management in industry.

Secondments from Industry

The top priority was to build the directorate team, to establish the strategies and the procedures for applying for grants. I spoke to the technical directors of all the obvious large firms, and they all readily volunteered to put someone in. Usually I was asked who I would like to have, but I found this a difficult way to work. I would suggest the field for which I thought a particular firm might provide a director. For example, I asked ICL for a director for software engineering. All the firms were very good about making it clear that I did not have to accept the first person they offered. In quite a number of cases I did turn down offers, sometimes because I felt the man was not quite right for the job, sometimes because he did not have the specialist skills I wanted. I made at least one mistake, when I turned down an excellent man who happened to be an expert in image processing, not a priority area for the Programme. In retrospect I would have done better to have accepted the best man on offer, even if his technical specialty was not quite right. It would have been possible to find a less senior man to work with him who had the right technical expertise.

Directors from the MoD and SERC

It was obvious that special attention had to be paid to the part that the MoD and SERC would play in the Directorate. The DTI had played the central role in setting up the Programme, the Director was appointed as a deputy secretary in the department, the director of administration and the majority of the administrative staff came from the DTI, and the Directorate was established in Millbank Tower, a building belonging to the DTI. So it was important to show that the MoD and SERC were to be treated as equal partners. As it happened this worked out very readily, with the active encouragement of the key staff in the MoD and SERC. Colin Fielding, the Controller (Establishments Research and Nuclear), had spent much of his early career at the RSRE, an establishment that had long played a vital role in the country's VLSI research. So it seemed to me that an appropriate member of the staff of the RSRE was the obvious man to lead that part of the Programme. Colin Fielding readily agreed and already had his eyes on Bill Fawcett, who was an expert on the technology. It was not easy for him to work in

London, for his home remained in Malvern throughout his three years with the Directorate. In my opinion Bill proved to be a first-rate director. He learned fast and rapidly gained a true grasp of the industrial scene. While he kept me in touch, he got on with the job without bothering me with the details. Perhaps he did have too great an addiction to the RSRE way of doing things, but the relatively few firms in the VLSI field were happy to work with him, since they knew the MoD routines well. We worked very happily together, and I developed growing affection and admiration for him. Whether it was right to put the proportion of the Alvey funds that we did into VLSI technology is a highly contentious issue to which I will return in later chapters. But within the framework of that decision the work went well.

The SERC situation was more complex, but there we had a keen volunteer in David Thomas, who was already the director for all aspects of IT in the SERC. With some hesitation, I agreed that it would be sensible for him to combine that SERC responsibility with that for some aspect of the work of the Directorate. The IKBS field was seen as the most technically advanced, the one where industry had least to contribute, so it was not unreasonable to ask him to take responsibility for this field. The problem was that he knew very little about the field. He was a physicist by background and though he was running the IT field in the SERC he was not very experienced in any aspect of it. Obviously it would be essential to provide him with a deputy who was an expert in IKBS, and, in order to keep the balance in the Directorate, it was highly desirable that that deputy should come from industry. But not one of the volunteers or people proposed by industry had any experience in the field. This was not really very surprising, for there were very few people in industry with any experience of IKBS, let alone at a senior level in the firms at the start of the Alvey Programme. It was one of our objectives to change all that.

I knew David Thomas rather better than I knew the other senior staff of the Directorate. He was a man with considerable leadership qualities and "bottom" but was not a lover of routine administration. He had a rare determined quality, being something of a buccaneer. These qualities tended to make him unpopular with his senior colleagues in the SERC administration. But some of them were the very qualities that appealed to me, and I rather liked having a rebel in the senior ranks of the directorate. It added to the fun and helped to get things done. I'm not sure all my colleagues shared my enthusiasm. It must be admitted that it was a severe disadvantage that neither David nor his senior colleagues helping to run the IKBS part of the Programme had much direct experience or understanding of industry, even though David himself was very sympathetic to the industrial objectives of the Programme.

In retrospect it is quite clear that it was vitally important to have a balance of senior staff in the Directorate drawn from industry, the MoD, and the SERC. In particular, we suffered considerably after Bill Fawcett left us to join industry from the lack of a senior contact with the MoD. And although we retained a senior link with the SERC after David Thomas moved to help Eric Ash, the Rector of Imperial College, there proved to be no substitute for having a senior person from these bodies who also has a practical responsibility for running some part of the Programme.

Directors from Industry

As I have mentioned, ICL was the obvious firm to provide the director for software engineering. After some false starts they proposed David Talbot. We met and discussed the proposition. He had a rather different background than the others, being more of a marketing man than a technical expert. But he knew a great deal about the computer industry and would bring to the team an understanding of the market that the rest of us lacked. In the Rutherford Appleton Laboratory the SERC had a young tiger, Rob Witty, who lacked David's wordly wisdom but had an expert knowledge of the software engineering scene. They made an unlikely couple. Rob had the reputation of being contemptuous of those without his detailed technical knowledge, and so I did not look forward to the first meeting between the two of them. But I need not have worried, for they both recognized that each had properties that the other lacked. They became firm friends and strong partners. As time went by I came to respect David Talbot more and more. He ran his part of the Directorate better than anyone overseeing the other parts, and I came to rely on his judgment. In a strange way he seemed to be older than the rest of us, though this was far from the fact. He became the adviser not only to me but also to the others. It was excellent to have as a member of the Directorate a man wise beyond his years.

With industrial staff from GEC and ICL, and discussions going on for somebody from Plessey, it was important to have somebody from a smaller firm. But the problem for a small firm is that it costs a great deal to second a good man for a couple of years, in terms of salary and even more in the loss of his services. The DTI agreed to help out with some assistance for the salary if we could find a smaller firm that would second a good man. Philip Hughes, Chairman of Logica, came to our help. Logica is a software house that in 1983 had been in existence only some fifteen years. It had grown very fast and in 1983 had a turnover of about £50 million. It continued to grow throughout Alvey's five years and is a small firm no longer, but, compared with GEC, ICL, and Plessey, it then represented a smaller and newer sector of industry. Philip had been a member of the Alvey Committee and had taken the responsibility for the software-engineering working party. He now suggested that we might like to have Derek Barber. I had known Derek slightly for many years. He had been a member of the NPL communications team before joining Logica, where he had been acting as a sort of technical adviser to Philip. Derek is one of that rare breed who always manage to exude enthusiasm. He had a wide knowledge of the data communications scene, so he was the obvious person to take on responsibility for the infrastructure part of the Programme, especially the data network. The Alvey Committee had spent quite a long time discussing whether the projects could be run in a decentralized way, without bringing a team together, as the Japanese had done at the Institute for New Generation Computer Technology (ICOT) or as the Microelectronics and Computer Technology Corporation (MCC) had done at Austin in Texas. Without a center the need for a good infrastructure of communications was obvious to all. I also asked him to handle the communications research part of the Programme. There is, of course, a certain relationship between the provision of a data network and research into data networks, though it is always dangerous to mix a service with research. In fact we did not intend to carry out much communications research under the Alvey Programme. I don't remember the Alvey Committee making any firm decision about this; it probably went by default. But if one reads the report carefully, one can find at least one paragraph of enthusiastic support for broadband communications research. Anyway, we felt it was right to carry out some research on data communications related to the provision, in due course, of a much improved data service. I interpreted this as the creation of a broadband service. Of course, Derek always wanted a larger research program, but he loyally accepted that this was not going to happen, though he never ceased to remind me of the possibilities at all reasonable opportunities.

Interpreting communications to include not just the electronic communications but also the provision of information flow to the IT community by any means enabled me to ask Derek to take on matters such as *Alvey News*. In many ways this was his great achievement: with his boundless enthusiasm and energy he threw himself into creating the journal. He rapidly came up with the idea for the Alvey pentagon symbol, and after some permutations we settled on the one that was used through the Programme. From the second issue of *Alvey News* we adopted a newsletter style that stayed with us throughout.

That left one place to fill on the board. I had decided that the six leaders of the Alvey sectors, together with my deputy, Laurence, and I, should form the Alvey Board. It took some time for the directors, as we agreed to call ourselves, to come together, largely because the others could not just drop their ongoing commitments to their employers. But by September we were together—except for the director for the man/machine interface part of the program. Attempts to find a suitable person from industry had not proved very successful, but Plessey now came up with Chris Barrow. He was not ideal, for he lacked direct experience of the field, but I was very thankful to get the post filled. His background had been with Philips in Eindhoven before joining Plessey in the office automation field. As a member of the ESPRIT planning committee he had learned quite a bit about the human-interface research scene, so he at least came to the post with some views on the priorities in a field about which few people had thought systematically. Unfortunately, soon after taking up the post (some weeks after the other directors) he fell ill, and though his deputy ably held the ship on course, by the time he was back at work the MMI part of the Programme had slipped some six months behind.

Delegation

In retrospect I feel that I made the mistake of leaving too much to the individual directors, especially in administrative matters. It was right to give the directors full responsibility for their own areas, but I would have done better to insist on more standard practices, for example in the way projects were called for. Because the MMI part of the Programme had fallen behind and Barrow had not been present at the Board meetings when the procedures were worked out, he adopted a method closer to the ESPRIT and SERC grant application round than the "anytime" open approach that we adopted across the rest of the Directorate. With such a heterogeneous bunch of directors, all of very different backgrounds and experience, it was essential to spend time to weld us together. That could only be done by fully discussing most of the issues that underlay our running of the Programme. To a very large extent this succeeded, and the directors could be relied upon to see and handle most issues according to a single approach most of the time. It is possible to lay down rules of administration but not really to create rules for the judgment of complex projects, though one can define a checklist of criteria to be taken into account. I will return to this shortly; it is a crucial issue but one not easy to grapple with.

Preparation of the Strategies

Having got the team together the next priority was the preparation of the strategies. The directorate process is a delicate balance of the democracy of widespread consultation and the dictatorship of central interpretation of that advice. I wanted the consultation process to be as widespread as possible but also to avoid the "lowest common denominator" approach that leads to including everything. From long experience of advisory committees in the DTI Requirement Boards and the many SERC committees I know that it is very difficult for a body of part-timers to be selective. If well constituted they are excellent at thinking about all that should be included but very bad at making firm decisions about what should be excluded. This might not matter if the funding and human resources really do allow the whole field to be covered. But this is very rarely the situation, even less so these days. So I was determined that the

Directorate (myself if necessary) would provide the selectivity that the situation demanded. Without a degree of concentration the work would be spread so thinly that critical mass would not be achieved in any area except by chance. At the same time the process had to ensure that truly exceptional proposals that did not meet the selective strategic criterion were still accepted. Of course, the problem was how to recognize those exceptional proposals! In my opinion the ESPRIT task force in the early days in the first part of its program fell into the dual error of having a strategy—the so called "workplan" that was simply a collection of everything the advisory committees could think of—and a lack of flexibility in the project selection procedures that made it impossible to get even the most exceptional proposal accepted if the proposers had failed to line it up with the appropriate words in the workplan. In general I feel that the Alvey Directorate avoided these pitfalls.

One of the early tasks was to establish advisory committees and to put them to work on the strategies. Laurence and I agreed that there were far too many advisory committees already in existence. The SERC, DTI, and MoD all had their committees, often with a degree of overlapping membership. We felt it would be in everybody's interest to thin out this jungle to some extent. While there is some virtue in diversity, especially as far as research-grant administration is concerned, we felt it would be unfortunate if we received too much conflicting advice on key issues. The handling of advisory issues is always a tricky matter. One has to be careful that one gets the best of the advisers' wisdom without falling into the trap of always accepting their advice on matters where the full-time professional may have a wider or more balanced perspective. And then there is the problem of ignoring their advice without destroying their enthusiasm for continuing to proffer further advice. We decided to use existing committees wherever possible, taking care to strengthen them with representatives of the other Alvey communities as appropriate. Tim Walker has now succeeded, where we failed, in thinning out the advisory committee jungle.

The IKBS field was easy, because this was a relatively new field where only the SERC had an appropriate body—the IKBS architecture working party. Typical of the strength and catholic approach of the SERC at this period, the Information Engineering Committee had set up this working party with a representation that went beyond the purely academic. It was chaired by John Taylor of the MoD, who had worked at the RSRE but at the time was at the Admiralty Surface Weapons Establishment (ASWE). Subsequently he joined Hewlett-Packard as director of their Bristol research laboratories. He did a first-rate job as chairman of this working party, and its report was virtually ready-made as the strategy for the IKBS part of the Programme. It is interesting to note that the apparent bias toward inference architectures implied in the title of the working party lies at the heart of the Japanese ICOT program, which has been very much focused on machine building, at least in the early phases of the program. In practice Taylor's report did not place too much emphasis on the architectural aspects, and we were able to use the detailed report as both the published strategy and the basis for much of the program we actually followed.

The VLSI Strategy

The VLSI strategy was largely prepared under the influence of the RSRE team that normally worked to the CVD. I made many attempts to widen the membership of the advisory committees in this field. There was no real difficulty about industrial representation since the number of firms in the field was small and the main firms were well represented. But there was a difficulty about Inmos, not so much because of the RSRE people but because the large U.K. firms were far from happy treating the upstart Inmos as a member of the family. There was some justification for this, because the Inmos VLSI process technology came from Colorado, with no real R & D in this field in their U.K. plant. On the other hand, Iann Barron had had a major influence on the U.K. machine architecture scene; the firm was carrying out excellent CAD development work in the U.K.; and their experts provided a useful independent view of the strategy. Inmos was gradually accepted in the Alvey family, but it was an uphill fight except in the architecture scene, where they rightly played a major role because of the success of the transputer. There was also some problem over the relatively small instrument firms in the VLSI field. But here the problem was the usual one of how to obtain advice from a bunch of small and medium-sized, very independent firms. The RSRE was well acquainted with these firms, many of whom owed their success to RSRE patronage for prototype equipment. In the event, as discussed in later chapters, that part of the Programme proved a considerable success, though it is possible to argue that we should have put more resources into it.

In my view, and that of many others, we put far too small a percentage of our resources into CAD for VLSI. I could have insisted in pressing the point, but it would have been against the advice of the process technologists who dominated the advisory committees. It is possible to argue that, without the strong support of the large process firms, GEC and Plessey, it would not have been possible to obtain the people to operate a larger CAD program. One difficulty that dogged us throughout the Programme in this field was that with the exception of ICL there was no major firm working in the CAD area who did not treat their CAD work as an adjunct of their process technology. Over the course of the Programme I think the realization gradually penetrated that for the U.K. as a whole it was more important to strengthen our CAD capability than our process technology. But in retrospect I do wish that I had fought the point harder at the strategy-writing stage.

The problem of persuading Bill Fawcett and the RSRE gang to accept a proper balance of academic experts was not an easy fight. To some extent this was due to the Alvey Committee, which made the mistake of believing that the academics had little to contribute to the VLSI field. This was an understandable mistake, for it is true that the high cost of a process line meant that only two universities, Edinburgh and Southampton, had the ability to contribute to whole-process technology, and then with a capability well behind the dominant firms. But in practice we found out that universities had a great deal to contribute, largely due to the excellent advanced instrument community that had worked on parts of the frequency spectrum important for fundamental science but only recently important for VLSI technology as the reduction in the feature size forced the frequencies used up out of the optical range. In my opinion, this is the secret of the success of our advanced instruments industry. So the Alvey principle of having a balance of academic, industrial, and government experts on the advisory committees was well demonstrated in the VLSI field, despite our initial doubts. Rather strangely, the academics never made a proper contribution to the CAD field.

The VLSI strategy that emerged from the advisory committee process well demonstrates the challenge of selectivity. We chose to concentrate on silicon technology entirely, leaving out gallium arsenide. This was, of course, a controversial decision, but it was justified both by the need to concentrate our limited resources and because the market for gallium arsenide seemed to be primarily for optical communications applications, at least in the short term. Experience has justified this decision. But far more controversial was the number of different silicon whole processes that we tackled. There were those who felt we should just concentrate on the universal CMOS. Conversely, there were those who felt we should concentrate on the niche areas, such as bipolar and silicon on insulator. My view remains that we were right to plan for a number of processes in the first wave and follow in the second part of the five years by concentrating on just a few whole processes chosen in the light of progress and the market development as it emerged over the first few years. This was just what we tried to do, and though I now wish we had put far fewer resources into VLSI technology, within the framework of that controversial decision I believe the strategy was on the right lines.

Software Engineering Strategy

The software engineering strategy had been pretty fully developed in the working party for the Alvey Committee. So David Talbot concentrated on developing more detailed strategies for each of the major priorities within the overall strategy, such as integrated project support environments, formal methods, and reliability measurement. Though the approach was pretty catholic within each subprogram, it was highly selective in the choice of these. For example the strategy did not make provision for any work on languages, even so-called fourth-generation code generators. But it should be noted that there was considerable work on logic languages and object-oriented languages in the IKBS program. One of the most controversial exclusions was any work on databases. The importance of relational databases can hardly be overstressed, but one felt that with only two British manufacturers of database programs, one of whom dropped out of the market within a couple of years, there was little scope for a cooperative program in the field. However, it is interesting to note that the architecture part of the Programme, when it was introduced after the first couple of years, did contain considerable work on architectures for storage. Though parallel architectures for inference and computation receive all the glamorous attention, the use of parallel architectures to retrieve information from storage may well prove to be the most important application in the short term.

Two other fields that the Programme ignored were operating systems and applications software. The second was not controversial with the Alvey community, but it certainly was with the many small software houses who live by writing custom-applications software. I have absolutely no doubt that it was right to eschew applications software in the software engineering part of the Programme. But in the large demonstrators and in the IKBS part of the Programme there was some applications software, especially for expert systems. The Bide Committee recommended an applications program as a key part of the proposed program to follow Alvey, and I personally wish this recommendation had been accepted. Of course, only a very few applications could be tackled, but it would have been valuable to see whether the Alvey achievement of bringing the research community together could have been repeated by catalyzing some collaboration between users and generators of IT systems. We will return in a later chapter to consider how the Programme developed, but I will simply say at this point that the software engineering part of the Programme proved, at the same time, to have set very ambitious targets that were not all achieved, but was a great success.

IKBS Strategy

The IKBS strategy was rather different from other parts of the Programme since it covered some very short-term aims, such as demonstrating and evaluating working expert systems, as well as tackling some difficult long-term research objectives. We put considerable effort into "awareness" of expert systems, and the community clubs we built up to do this proved a great success. But no one can really argue that this part of the Programme was particularly advanced research. In the event we constructed a considerable number of expert systems in the Alvey Programme, and I think this was right. But it did mean that there was relatively little effort left for long-term research, and a great deal remains to be done in the IKBS field. It should be noted that this part of the Programme was always seen as a ten-year program, as opposed to the five-year duration of the Alvey Programme. The Japanese fifth-generation program was planned as a ten-year program. The IKBS research strategy tended to be a ragbag, for it addressed some eight topics, rather a lowest-common-denominator list. It included image processing, and I did not insist on the rationalizing of the interface with image processing in the MMI program. In practice there were only two projects in this area, and both turned out to be rather good.

The IKBS element was different from other parts of the Programme because we developed two particular aspects after the main strategy, the logic programming initiative and the architecture program. Both were part of the original strategy but were developed in detail only after the first two years. The logic programming initiative was, perhaps, the best organized part of the IKBS program and included much of the natural-language work of the Alvey Programme. The rest of it was in the speech part of the MMI program. When we introduced the architecture subprogram I decided not to appoint a full director because I wished to avoid disrupting the programs where architecture work was in progress, namely VLSI architecture and IKBS architecture. But we did appoint a double-headed pair of program coordinators and publish a systems-architecture strategy for the field. Though they were in theory subordinate to the relevant directors in both financial and program terms, in practice they ran an independent part of the Programme. I was lucky to recruit a first-rate pair of coordinators in Professor Ronan Sleep of the University of East Anglia and Alan Bagshaw, ex-Technical Director of ICL. I got on very well with Ronan, who was a most interesting character; it was some time before I discovered that Ronan was responsible for his own architecture development at UEA, so little did he impose his own interests on the Programme. The architecture coordinators provided another case of a pair of very different people working well together in a manner that complemented each other's skills. Ronan was the expert with a rather academic approach to exploitation and practical matters, whereas Alan Bagshaw brought a practiced industrial outlook to the exploitation of the work. To some extent the architecture strategy was a rationalization of the projects we had or that we knew were being worked up. But we recognized early on that we could only afford to support two or three full project constructions and so put some emphasis on the parallel simulation facility, which perhaps inevitably came to be known as PARSIFAL. In retrospect I feel we should have put more emphasis on the software aspect of parallel architectures, but we did make one major attempt to develop a standard software interface for our parallel architectures, so as to free both the hardware architects and the language and operating systems program writers from the need to know what was happening on the other side of the interface. We did not envisage this interface as being optimal for the final system developments that emerged out of the research work of the Programme because of its routine inefficiencies, though we suspected that for many architectures this would be unimportant.

An Operating System Standard for Alvey

Perhaps this is the point to record that early on in the Programme we made one decision that we have had absolutely no reason to regret. We decided to make Unix the standard operating system environment for all appropriate projects—in practice this meant for an overwhelming number of our projects. By that decision we forwarded the use of Unix in the U.K. to a large extent. I am confident that we made a real contribution to U.K. users and manufacturers alike in helping to advance Unix. This system has, of course, increased in strength, and no one could now seriously challenge the choice, except for the Open Systems purists.

MMI Strategy

I have left to last the consideration of the man/machine interface (MMI) part of the Programme. This is appropriate in the sense that it got off the ground after the rest of the Programme for the staff reasons I have set out above. It was inevitably somewhat of a ragbag, consisting of pattern processing (that is, speech and image processing), display developments, and the human interface. It is interesting that image processing is not strictly an MMI consideration at all; though it may be developed by reference to the way the human being achieves the recognition of images, no human need be involved in a computerized image-processing procedure. In that sense it is more strictly data input. Nevertheless many people insist on lumping speech and image processing together. Though there must be loose parallels, I do not consider the relationship more than skin deep. So we did not run the two subprograms tightly together. We asked John Holmes to help us with the speech program. He had recently retired after many years as director of the Joint Speech Research Unit, a team originally drawn from British Telecom and elsewhere but now merged with the RSRE speech team. We decided to concentrate on speech input and virtually ignore speech synthesis, since the work there was much further developed and seemed all too likely to be dominated by imported chips. Though we did not have the resources to run a large program, when one takes into consideration the speech-input word-processor demonstrator project, the speech program was quite strong and an excellent example of all the teams in the U.K. involved in the subject working together in a coordinated program. We did not do much on image processing but did run a special interest group, pulling together the two AI projects on image processing in the IKBS program with a few projects in the MMI part of the Programme.

The one key strategic decision for the display program was to concentrate on flat-screen, A4-sized displays. We had decided in the Alvey Committee that the only peripheral with sufficient universal applicability to warrant inclusion in the Programme was the display. This was a contentious decision, particularly as it meant the omission of optical disc memory technology. However, it did serve to concentrate our efforts. Though the U.K. has some good research work, especially in rewritable optical memory technology, this is not an area where the U.K. has much share of the market. This is unfortunate, as it forms a very significant part of the whole cost of computing systems. It was my own view that, though we could do some excellent work in developing the technology of flat-screen displays, our firms would not make the investment to exploit the work, though we might make a return through licensing the technology. As I describe in more detail in chapter 7, I was persuaded by the large firms that we should have a display program, but I remain convinced that, good though the research work was, it was a mistake for the U.K. to carry out such a program when the probability of exploitation was so low.

I find it difficult to comment on the strategy of the human-factors part of the Programme. It was drawn up by a large working party chaired by the doyen of the ergonomics community in the U.K., Professor Brian Shackel of Loughborough University. They agreed to concentrate on the "intellectual" rather than the ergonomic interface, on the grounds that much was known about the ergonomic interface. The propagation of this and other knowledge about the desirable properties of a good human/machine interface was seen as a priority, and we eventually established three centers for this that have gone on to do good work. I am not sure that I can say in what way the strategy was deficient, but the human-factors part of the Programme has always seemed to me to be rather formless, without clear and attainable objectives. Maybe this is more a criticism of that community, which of course is newly come together and bringing a wide array—or, more strictly, disarray—of different disciplines together. I have a high regard for centers such as the MRC Applied Psychology Unit at Cambridge, but I do not feel that we have yet achieved a mature community. In retrospect—and how easy it is to be wise after the event—I believe that we would have done better to have had only a small human-factors research program in its own right, concentrating on technology transfer; and to have insisted on the human-factors part of any and all projects through the Alvey Programme being taken seriously. This would have required a strong man to lead the program, probably the overall Programme deputy director. As it happens, I feel the MMI program did achieve a recognition of the importance of human factors in IT that has been a major contribution. In all parts of the U.K. IT community it is now accepted that human factors have to be given due weight wherever they arise in IT projects.

7
The Directorate Process in Action

Distilling a team approach within the Alvey Directorate was an essential early task. How were research proposals to be assessed? What was the role of the Alvey Programme Steering Committee? Would collaboration prove difficult? How could long-term research be accommodated? In this chapter Brian Oakley answers these and other questions.

Board Meetings

It was apparent at the start that we had to take steps to create a common Alvey culture and outlook. With directors who had never before worked closely together, this called for more discussion in common than would be necessary in a body where the staff had worked together perhaps for years. We rapidly established the pattern of holding a board meeting on Monday afternoons. Quite frequently we had presentations, largely from project applicants, at the end of Monday mornings, with lunch around the board table. The board meetings started at 2 p.m. and rarely finished before 5 p.m., often lasting until 6 or even 7 p.m. I allowed the discussions to ramble on, gradually allowing a consensus to emerge. Though it took some months for a true common outlook to develop, and it never really did over a few issues, after this initial period I could rely on directors to express the same approach and attitude to most issues that arose. It was perhaps significant that Chris Barrow, the last director to join and who was absent for several of the early months due to illness, was the one who had most difficulty in working to a common approach. In general, I tried to get a common approach to major issues but left the less important matters to the individual approach of each director. It is easy to see in retrospect that we should have had a common framework for administrative details. Leaving these to individual directors was a mistake, for though a common approach gradually emerged, it would have been much more efficient in the long run to have laid down protocols for administration. It was David Talbot who saw this most clearly and who commissioned a study that led to procedures that were largely adopted throughout the Directorate in due course. I should have insisted on these being applied throughout as soon as they were seen to be sensible. The long board meetings were not universally popular, and I believe several of the directors did not really understand why I felt this approach was desirable, though they all joined in the discussions with a will. In the fourth year we reduced the frequency of the board meetings to every other week.

The Large Demonstrator Projects

One of the first decisions the board made was to introduce a limited number of large demonstrators into the Programme. The idea had stemmed from ICL, which had suggested that the technology projects that would form the major part of the Programme would need some mechanism for integrating and demonstrating the ensuing developments. We decided that it would be appropriate to put some 10 percent of the project funds into these demonstrators. Each would involve as many of the technologies in the Programme as possible. They would be closer to the marketplace than were the normal technology projects. Because of the size of the individual projects it was inevitable that they would be led by the large electronic firms. Laurence Clarke rapidly got down to setting up these projects. Because this could be done through the large firms we were able to get studies started within a couple of months. We received some twenty outline proposals, and the board agreed to support studies of three to six months' duration for the eight most promising proposals. Finally we selected the four best to go forward as full projects. The selection process was far from easy, but it did enable us to hone the choice and application of criteria for project selection.

Evaluation of Project Proposals

We hesitated over whether to have a fixed date for submission of all technical proposals, say two or three times a year as the SERC does, or even once a year as in ESPRIT. This would have the advantage that we could directly compare projects in the same field; it would also simplify the administration and allow more precise control of the budget. It might also be of benefit to the large firms, as it would enable them to plan their total R & D programs. On the other hand it would delay the start of the Programme by many months and would prevent a project being put forward as soon as a consortium was ready to submit it. But what decided us that it would not be an appropriate approach for the Alvey Programme was that we wished to be able to work up the projects interactively with the consortia. This would not be a practical approach if project applications had to be made at a set date, if only because of the peak in the workload. So we encouraged all consortia to come to discuss their proposals with the relevant director at every state of development. This enabled us to steer the Programme, without wasting too much effort in the consortia working up nugatory proposals that we would never approve.

In judging proposals we did, of course, use all the usual criteria of quality of the team, relevance of the proposal to the Directorate's strategies, and whether it seemed likely that the objectives could be achieved in a reasonable timescale. We added criteria of quality of cooperation and other considerations that stemmed from the nature of the cooperative process: were these the most suitable partners, was some team excluded that could significantly contribute, were the geographical constraints acceptable?

The most contentious criteria were those related to the eventual exploitation of the work. We wanted to know who was going to exploit the results of the work, how the results would reach the exploiters, and how the intellectual property was owned and controlled. In placing emphasis on exploitation we became susceptible to pressure from two sides. When Gladstone watched an early demonstration of the dynamo at the Royal Institution he asked what possible use electricity could have, to which Faraday is said to have replied "Prime Minister, before long you will be putting a tax on it." But of course Faraday was a Victorian entrepreneur, perhaps Mrs Thatcher's archetypical image of what a modern scientist should be. In the recent past there has been a generation of academic scientists who, while they recognized that their work might one day bring economic rewards ("What use is a new born baby?" Rutherford is said to have replied to a very similar question), much preferred not to be bothered by the practical problems of exploitation. Over the years I have come to suspect the scientist who agrees his work will bring rich rewards, but not just yet. So it was no surprise that some academics were not very eager to face up to the often rather sordid challenges of the exploitation of their work. But, overwhelmingly, that turned out to be no problem, with the academics at least as keen as the industrialists to see their work exploited.

More of a problem, and with far less excuse, were the industrial scientists who knew that their work should be exploited but who had no clear path to exploitation lined up. The problem is endemic in the central research laboratories of the large electronic firms. Understandably, they wished to see their work supported so that it could continue, but did not, or could not, obtain any firm commitment from their firms to exploit their work if it proved to be as successful as they were sure it would be. I will return to this issue later. But here I will quote the display field as an example of the problem. The Alvey Committee had considered supporting various types of peripherals but had come down firmly on the opinion that only displays were of such a generic nature that they deserved support from the limited Alvey funds. So we had a section of the MMI program dedicated to flat-panel display development. In keeping with the Alvey concept of trying to support the enabling technologies with the widest impact on IT as a whole, I directed this program toward the A4 display target—that is, a display large enough to simulate an A4 piece of paper at normal printed-page resolutions. We received quite a number of proposals, most of them of high quality. But the exploitation probabilities seemed to me low in a market where high capital investment would be required. If competition from Japan (and Korea) was to be fought off, then the U.K. would have to make similar large investment in strongly automated plants, with the financial return coming over a five-year or even a ten-year period, rather than the U.K. norm of eighteen months or at most three years. The large firms, GEC in particular, assured me that they would do this, and finally they overcame my skepticism. It remains to be seen who was right. Of course, failure to exploit through U.K. investment does not mean that an excellent return could not be obtained by licensing the technology to someone (i.e., the Japanese) prepared to make the investment. But I suspect we would have done better to have put those Alvey display funds into other areas where the return comes from a wide take-up of the technology in less capital-intensive areas. The same argument applies to a few other areas of the Programme, essentially any of the mass-production hardware fields and even perhaps the product markets for software of the IPSE type. Time—and our evaluators—will tell. But I do regret that I did not have the courage of my convictions on this matter. I believe most members of the board agreed with me in their heart of hearts, though it would have been asking too much for directors from the electronic "dinosaurs" to have openly agreed with this position—at least in the early years of the Directorate's life.

There was one other criterion for project selection to which increasing attention was given as the Programme continued, namely project management. In academic research this is not usually a matter for consideration, though it certainly is in the "big science" areas of high-energy physics, large-accelerator construction, and space missions. In industrial research it may not attract the attention it deserves, at the research end of the spectrum. It is probably true, as we are always being told, that we are not very good at technology management as a nation. (For some peculiar reason our civil engineering and construction industry management is respected in large international projects. Maybe it is a case of the prophet not being without honor save in his own land.) In collaborative research experience suggests that it is crucial.

It did not prove easy to judge the management potential in project teams. Of course, there were certain obvious clues. For example, project proposals expressed with objectives that could be readily progressed, break points and "deliverables" (ugly words much used in the Alvey Directorate, I regret to say) set out on a timetable, suggested that the project writers knew the importance of project management. No doubt the best evidence was the naming of the single project manager. It was normal to arrange presentations from the project team to the board for large projects before we made a decision. And it was our practice to ask about the project management, if the consortium did not have the good sense to make it a key part of the presentation. But it was not unusual for the project manager not to be chosen at the proposal stage. And the manager was frequently too junior to take a leading part in the presentation. I have to admit that I made matters worse in the early stages by not wishing to insist on a lead contractor. This was because I was so keen to ensure good cooperation that I did not wish to insist on any one body being in the lead. In retrospect it is easy to see that a project without strong management would tend to have weak collaboration. But at the time it was not obvious that it would prove as easy to achieve collaboration as experience taught us that it was. I am still not convinced that it is essential to have a lead contractor, but there is clear evidence that a single project manager is required. He (or she) may be the technical leader, if that is required. In certain projects the manager came from one of the smaller partners, and that seemed quite successful. We were usually quite prepared to see the cost of a specially employed manager as an "allowable" cost, for grant purposes, in the larger projects. It is surely no coincidence that there is a strong correlation between project success and high-quality management in the analysis of the monitoring officer's project reports.

Advisory Committees

In the selection of projects in the Alvey Programme most projects were seen by one or other of the advisory committees. In my opinion the peer-review mechanism works best when at least some of the peers are known by members of the project teams. There is a tendency for academic peers to judge projects by the quality and reputation of the participants, and for research at the basic end of the spectrum this is highly desirable. But for projects at the applied or development end of the spectrum considerations relating to the actual project and its exploitation must be given due weight. Nevertheless, it is a weakness if at least some of the peers do not know the key members of the project teams. On the whole, I think our advisory committees did have this advantage, so I suspect that their advice was as good as one could expect from the peer-review process. And, of course, everybody knows that it is very difficult to propose a better process! However, there were a number of occasions on which the directors, or more often the board, did overturn the advice of the advisory committees. This is always a tricky thing to do, but we felt it necessary to give more attention to our strategic priorities and to exploitation potential. For example, one area of difficulty was over IKBS projects where the rather academic advisory committee tended to turn down projects led by firms on the grounds of their lack of experienced IKBS workers. But to the Directorate it was important to build up that expertise, and projects involving the right academics with the firms would help to build up the industrial expertise, even if they did not roll back the frontiers of knowledge very much. My impression is that the human-factors advisory committee did tend to get too much influence, but in other fields I don't believe we had any significant problems. They were understanding in accepting our overruling of their judgment, provided we were careful to explain why we felt it necessary. Probably David Thomas had the most difficult task in this respect, and he learned to manage it well, despite the fact that it is virtually unheard of for the permanent staff to overrule the various committees in the SERC way of working.

The Alvey Programme Steering Committee

My one real battle with the Alvey Programme Steering Committee was over whether they should have a say in individual project decision-making. From the start of the Directorate I recognized that we would have this problem. It was necessary that the Programme should have some form of advisory committee. I would have liked to have seen it as the representative committee for the funding agencies, the DTI, the SERC, the MoD, and industry. When it was set up it was ruled that it should be small in number and composed primarily of industrialists. Normally, I would have approved of giving industry a key hand in the steering of the Programme, but I did feel it was important in this case to give due weight to the prominence of the partnership between industry and the government bodies. The composition of the Steering Committee was made worse by the insistence by the DTI that the members should be different from those on the Department's own advisory committees. This meant that the liaison between the Steering Committee and the other advisory committees was difficult. The MoD was represented by Colin Fielding, Controller of the MoD Research Establishments, and that was fine. For the DTI, the chief scientist, Oscar Roith, and the head of the IT industry divisions, Roy Croft and, later, Alastair Macdonald were the representatives. As time went by there was a tendency for the IT and LA division heads to attend as well, or instead, which rather overweighted the DTI representation. This was made worse by the underrepresentation of the SERC. The DTI invited an academic, Eric Ash, to represent the SERC. At that time he was an eminent academic at University College, London, well known in the integrated circuit field, and a Fellow of the Royal Society. He was the chairman of the SERC Engineering Board, so it was quite appropriate that he should be on the Steering Committee, on which he played an important part. But it was difficult for him to represent the SERC in the more detailed questions of finance and administration that arose. In addition to the academic representative, I should have liked an SERC official, preferably Tony Egginton, the director responsible for engineering and the directorates. But this would have increased the size of the committee, and the DTI officials were very opposed to this. The lack of direct representation from SERC officials responsible for their end of their administration was a considerable weakening of the usefulness of the committee.

Yet in one major respect the committee was ideal from my viewpoint. The Department appointed Sir Robert Telford to chair the committee and to take an active part in controlling the Programme and its Director! I could not have asked for a better qualified or more helpful appointment. Sir Robert was no newcomer to the Alvey Programme, for he had played a crucial part in bringing it about. At the time of the early discussions about a cooperative program Bob Telford was the chairman of the Marconi Company, the defense arm of GEC. He was a very respected member of the electronics industry "establishment," perhaps its most respected member. This was more because of his personal qualities than because of the preeminence, in terms of turnover, of GEC in the electronics and electrical industries. In the discussion following the presentations at the meeting in the Westmoreland Hotel, when plans for mounting a cooperative research program were first presented to industry, it was Sir Robert who first spoke out, unambiguously, throwing the weight of GEC behind the concept. It was easy for the other firms to follow where GEC led.

In some ways it seemed strange for GEC to back a cooperative program. Superficially, as the largest firm in the industry, it would appear that they had least to gain. And the general attitude created by Sir Arnold Weinstock, Managing Director of GEC, was hardly supportive of cooperation. If a cooperative program backed by public funds was a *fait accompli* then Arnold would demand that GEC got its lion's share. But while the issue was in the balance, he might be expected, on past record, to argue against such a program, especially if it involved taxpayers' money. For more normal single-company support schemes other, less cash-rich companies stood to gain more from public subsidies than did GEC. I have often wondered whether Sir Robert had Sir Arnold's backing for his public support of the cooperative program. Yet a closer examination of the pros and cons of cooperation suggests that it is the large firms who stand most to gain, because they will be the ones that can most readily afford the subsequent exploitation. They have the marketing muscle in place to seize the markets, especially overseas, if they can acquire the basic ideas, the enabling technology on which to build exploitation. In fairness to Sir Arnold, now Lord Weinstock, he did support the Alvey Programme at a crucial later date. From the time of the Westmoreland Hotel meeting Sir Robert was a key element informing and orchestrating the industrial backing for the Programme, so he was the obvious choice to chair the Steering Committee.

Perhaps inevitably, I wanted the Steering Committee to stick to the major issues and to keep out of the details. In my experience it is always difficult for a committee, who inevitably do not have the time to study the details, to make a useful contribution except on broad policy issues. This is made worse if the committee is small in number and so not broadly representative. It is further complicated if members are, wearing other hats, deeply involved in the decisions. The British tradition for such bodies is that, when such issues come up, committee members should "declare an interest" at the start of the discussion. It is normal for the chairman to invite them to stay for the discussion so that advantage can be taken of their intimate knowledge of that subject matter, but to see they retire from the table before the decision is taken. In my experience this works very well, and I have rarely seen it abused. So it seems to me that it is much better to have people on such committees who are actively engaged in the issues than to have eunuchs who are observers but not participators. To have some dispassionate observers on a committee strengthens it enormously, but to have a committee composed of people who aren't really deeply involved in the issues is fatal. However, if the committee is small, it can be disastrous if one or more of the members are absent, for reasons of involvement in an issue or just the inevitable pressure of other engagements. The balance of the committee, which builds up and evolves over many meetings, is destroyed, and unstable policymaking can easily arise. In the limit, I saw the committee's role as being to help the Director, to steer him as far as that was possible, and then to sack him if his policies diverged too far from those of the committee or if he was falling down on the job in other respects. Hardly surprisingly, the committee saw its role in a somewhat different light—as I suppose I would have, had I been an independent member of it!

Sir Robert had the very difficult task of mediating between the extremes of the committee, who felt that they should be involved in all significant decisions, and the Director of the Programme who wanted to minimize their interference in minor decision making. In part this was to help my directors to establish their direct authority and that of the board. It helps a great deal when one is trying to persuade someone to take a given action if he feels that the ultimate decision rests with the persuader. And no doubt my attitude arose in part from the natural desire to be my own boss, to have ultimate control of the Programme. Bob attended many of the board meetings, and I think we all came to like having him there. He never interfered, he brought to bear the wisdom gained in long experience of decision-making at the top of industry, and he provided a link to his Steering Committee that was invaluable. When the committee questioned whether the board was making the right decisions, he was able to give a direct report on the process of board thinking that could never have had the same authority if it had come from me. I have nothing but admiration for the way he handled his role. But then, since in the end he always backed the Director, I suppose I would approve, wouldn't I? Anyway, the Steering Committee did not have much direct influence over the Programme, though I did put major issues, such as the introduction of a parallel architectural theme, to them for decision.

On one major issue it might have been very valuable for the board to have taken a common viewpoint, and that was the support for VLSI. I suppose inevitably the board was split, along the lines of members' firms' direct involvement in integrated circuit manufacture, about the amount of other resources that should go into VLSI R & D. They were all agreed that we were supporting too many different whole processes but were not much help in deciding which to drop, as there was always someone with a vested interest in one or other process. In retrospect I should have taken more notice of their concern that we were supporting too many different processes and made the decision myself on which lines to drop—despite the opposition such a solution would have met. When in the third year we finally came to implement the decisions to drop certain processes, there was opposition from the committee. It was true that this narrowing of our objectives had been foreshadowed in our original strategy, so the board was entirely consistent. But I now believe I should have followed its advice to reduce the number of process projects from the beginning. For those who now, like me, believe we should have put less into VLSI overall, I can only say that the Steering Committee would certainly not have reached an agreed decision to do so at any time.

There was one other field in which I tried to involve the Steering Committee but met with, at best, mixed success. I will describe in chapter 8 the reasons that led me to select academic evaluators from the SPRU and PREST. I wanted to get true independence and felt this was the traditional role of academics. Unfortunately it also brings, or at any rate at that time brought, a degree of naiveté about industry and its motivations that was far from helpful in the evaluators' relations with the Steering Committee. I should have liked to see the Steering Committee taking a leading role in steering the work of the evaluators. But the Steering Committee was far from impartial and found that it had to accept criticism from these academics—who did not always help by conveying their half-formed and sometimes rather naive views in the academic manner that can appear brash to those not accustomed to it. I suspect the Steering Committee would have been much happier if we had employed consultants of the PA or Economist Intelligence Unit type to carry out the work, though I don't think they would have been any happier if the consultants had adopted the standpoint of economists or, worse, social scientists. It is also true that the Steering Committee was never very happy dealing with the "soft science" part of the MMI program, but in that they shared the prejudices of this Director. One thing is absolutely clear. If the Steering Committee had little influence over the Programme and its execution, it certainly cannot be held responsible for the mistakes that were made.

One important role the committee did assume, rather because there was a vacuum to be filled than because it wanted to do it. When it came to establishing a body analogous to the Alvey Committee, it was clear that our ministers at that time were not prepared to repeat the process of acting as the sponsors. So the Alvey community needed to find a body to represent it. The Steering Committee filled this role, and Sir Robert Telford took the lead in asking individuals to join what became known as the Bide Committee. Of course, he took good care to consult ministers and civil servants as well as his Steering Committee. And, inevitably, the secretarial work and much of the advice on members and balance came from the Alvey Directorate. But more of that later. It does suggest that the Steering Committee did have an importance that perhaps most people, including the Director, could not always see.

Cooperation

By the time all the funds were committed the Alvey Programme consisted of some 210 cooperative projects, each lasting an average of three years. The average number of partners was four—typically 2 or 3 firms with 1 or 2 universities. There were 115 firms taking part in the projects, many in more than one project, a few in many. Virtually every university and university college in the country, 19 polytechnics, and some 20 research establishments and research associations took part in the Programme. At the peak we calculated that there were some 2,500 people working in the Programme, rather more from industry than from the academic world.

When we started we were very cautious about the ease with which cooperation would be achieved. It is difficult now to remember how little experience there was then of cooperative research on anything other than a single-firm/single-university team basis. Almost everybody in the Programme was learning about cooperation. But in practice it proved much easier than expected, especially the initial getting together. The very existence of the Alvey Programme, with all the talk about cooperation, and the widespread circulation of *Alvey News*, which went into virtually every research laboratory in the land, helped to create an atmosphere in which it was quite respectable to ask a lifelong competitor if his firm would cooperate. The Directorate did play its part in marriage broking, but was asked to help in this respect less than we had expected. Our services were largely needed by small and especially new firms looking for partners among the larger firms.

One can basically distinguish two types of cooperation: that between a supply-industry firm and another that would be its rival in the market place; and that between a supply-industry firm and one that would not be a direct competitor because it operated in a different part of the market. There is, of course, a third category in which a supply-industry firm cooperates with a potential customer. Though we liked to have a potential user firm in a consortium, there was very little one-to-one supply industry with customer in the Alvey Programme, because the Programme was aimed at cooperation in the precompetitive stage of research in which few user firms participate. In running the Programme I was not very conscious of a distinction between the first and second categories described above. Inevitably in the VLSI part of the Programme the majority of the cooperation was between similar firms, though the instrumentation projects did lead to cooperation between process manufacturing companies and instrument firms. Because a set of clubs, largely run by BT and the RSRE, had existed in the VLSI field for a couple of years, it proved relatively easy to initiate cooperative projects quickly in that field. This pioneering work in developing cooperation was a great help to us, and has been largely ignored. But of course without government catalytic funding it was almost impossible to extend the cooperation beyond talking toward actual project work. So the Alvey Programme fell on very fertile ground as far as the firms that had been talking together in the VLSI clubs were concerned.

In other parts of the Programme it was somewhat more difficult to get cooperation going. I was particularly proud of the large-software-houses club that we formed. The going was pretty tough until Logica took the initiative to discuss all its cooperative projects with its rivals. But though there were projects in which two or more of the larger software houses cooperated, most of the cooperation in the software section was between large and small software houses, and between large software houses and software teams in the large electronic firms. Cooperation in this part of the Programme was relatively difficult to achieve and also proved relatively difficult to sustain. It is interesting to speculate why this should have been so. My own guess is that, because there had been relatively little tradition of research in the large software houses, they had the added difficulty of learning how to conduct research as well as learning how to cooperate. On the whole cooperation in the true research parts of the IKBS program consisted of much smaller consortia, often consisting of just two partners. Part of the difficulty in this field arose because there were so few firms with significant KBS people when the program started. On the other hand the technology-transfer parts of the IKBS program went very well, with typically ten to thirty firms cooperating in the expert-system community clubs.

Cooperation with Universities

Cooperation with the universities grew rapidly in the early days of the Programme. It is a gross calumny to consider the universities, pre-Alvey, as ivory towers. Certainly this was not true of the computing science departments. After all, the British computer industry had stemmed from the cooperation of Ferranti with Manchester University in the early 1950s. But perhaps it was true that cooperation was not as widespread as one might expect for such an applied subject. The Alvey Programme changed all that: virtually every project had academic participation except in the VLSI field, and even there the degree of academic participation was much larger than had been expected. It rapidly became acceptable for a firm to telephone an academic, or perhaps more often the other way round, to ask for cooperation to attack a particular topic. It would be nice to believe that this was entirely due to the culture of collaboration encouraged by the Alvey climate. No doubt this played its part. But it has to be acknowledged that much of the change of heart was due to self-interest. During the Alvey years the universities were feeling the full effect of the stringencies that the government was imposing on them. In order to obtain funds to carry on research the universities had to turn to any possible source—and in the IT field that meant the Alvey Programme. However, I don't wish to suggest that the cooperation was a sham, even if it stemmed from financial motives. I suppose the degree of industrial/academic cooperation that arose could be claimed by the government as a triumph of its approach. Others might feel that there must have been a less destructive way to bring about change. Certainly our overseas competitors, who envied the quality of research ideas that stemmed from the British universities, looked on with amazement as the government seemed to be attempting to kill off the fundamental work that was the envy of less well-endowed lands.

In order to encourage the more basic, longer-term work, we instituted a class of academic-only projects that came to be called "Uncle" projects. The name was suggested by Rob Witty—not the only original contribution he made to the administration of the Programme. It might have been organizationally sound to have left Uncle projects to the SERC to select as well as administer, but I was particularly keen that the same bodies that were making the decisions over the fully cooperative projects should also handle the Uncle projects. This stemmed from my SERC experience, where I had observed the reluctance of certain academic teams to get involved with industry even though their work was ripe for exploitation. I believe they genuinely felt that it was too early to have the complication of industrial involvement, though I am certain it was also partly a defensive measure aimed at not disturbing the even tenor of their ways by the commercialization process. But I had also observed in my career that to delay involvement of the eventual exploiters was a recipe for stimulating the "not invented here" syndrome in the industrial team. In my experience the earlier the industrial team can be involved, the better in the long run, because gradually the project becomes "theirs," and they become the defenders of it within their own companies. Only if the same bodies were making decisions over the two types of projects could one be confident that Uncle status would be bestowed only when it was quite clear that full industrial partners could not be found at this early stage. Each project had to have someone from industry who would take an avuncular interest in the work, steering it toward the exploitable aspects and alerting industry when the possibility of exploitable results emerged.

In the end we had some 113 Uncle projects, representing one-third of all projects. But the teams were relatively small and the capital costs low, so these projects only cost some 6 percent of the total public funds. They are, of course, the most difficult projects to evaluate, being far from the marketplace. I consider it highly desirable to have a stream of more speculative, longer-term work running parallel to the more applied cooperative work, and it will be a very sad day if pressures to obtain funds from industry eliminate this strand of work. It is on the longer-term work that only the universities can do that the future of exploitable work depends. But I strongly suspect that a number of projects sneaked through as Uncle projects that should have been full cooperative prospects. And in certain fields I suspect some of the Uncle projects were not of the quality that deserved support. It is always easy to observe these things after the event, so much more difficult to spot the weak projects at initiation. I do regret that we never took the Uncle side of the projects seriously enough. We did obtain reports from some of the Uncles and know that some of them played their role to the full. But since we never applied real pressure to the others, it is the Directorate that must take the blame if the mechanism did not work as well as it should have. I have been interested to watch the basic-research part of the ESPRIT program evolve, much under the influence of British academics, in particular Brian Randell of Newcastle University. I think that they err in not using the same evaluation teams as are used for the main ESPRIT program. I shall be interested to see if the Uncle monitoring mechanism emerges; it has certainly been proposed by those on the continent who know of our approach. Incidentally, I should add that the best British academics were very happy to work in full collaboration projects as well as keeping some longer-range work going through Uncle projects and other sources. They were not the ones who wished to avoid collaboration.

8
Problems and Other Issues

Directing the Alvey Programme produced its share of problems, some anticipated, some not. Funding the academic part of the Programme; drafting formal agreements between collaborators; satisfying the ambitions of small firms; getting to know ESPRIT, Alvey's European counterpart; and coping with skill shortages are among the thorny topics that kept Brian Oakley busy, as he describes in this chapter.

Where the Responsibility Lay

It tends to be in the the nature of civil servants to be secretive and to hide problems from the public, partly because that leads to a quiet life and partly in order to defend their political masters from attack. After all, under the British constitution it is ministers who take the responsibility for the faults of their servants. Whatever the political constraints within which we worked, we in the Directorate ran the Programme and were responsible for all the decisions. If we can take pride and credit for our successes, so we must take the blame for what went wrong. And to the extent that I ran the Programme in a very personal way, so I must take the lion's share of the blame for the problems that we failed to solve. If I played a much more public role than was usual for a civil servant, it was partly because I was propelled in that direction by the IT community and the press, who seemed to need a focal point. It suited me to have that publicity for the Programme, and I certainly do not complain about the way the press treated me. But if I allowed, indeed encouraged, the public discussion of our problems, I do hope these will be seen in their true perspective. There does seem to be a danger that the unusual openness with which we ran the Programme might have made the problems appear greater than they actually were.

It is a truism that the press likes disasters; they sell copies. I remember listening to an unusually honest analysis of the strengths and weaknesses of the Alvey VLSI program at one of our Alvey conferences, given by a man from Racal, a firm on the periphery of the VLSI industry but in a position to see the picture clearly. It was a truthful and open picture, warts and all. As I listened with pleasure to such an analysis I knew in my heart what would happen and told my companion my fears. Inevitably the press, or parts of it, picked up and published the problems without giving equal weight to the achievements. Often it seems to be the headline writers who create the most distortion. It is not in the nature of headlines to provide a balance.

Funding Problems

It is generally accepted that our biggest problem concerned financing the academic part of the Programme. Unfortunately in a cooperative program such problems directly affecting one set of workers have an impact on their collaborators. Once the funds were allocated it was very rare for the academic partners to fall out or hesitate, though their delays in recruiting staff caused problems, a situation not restricted to the academic partners. On the other hand it was rare in the Alvey years for one or other of the Alvey industrial firms not to be reassessing its research priorities. If this led to their calling a temporary halt to their work, this inevitably rubbed off on their academic partners. We never really did solve the problem of what to do with the academic component of a cooperative project when the main industrial partner dropped out. Inevitably there was a tendency for the academic part to be turned into an Uncle project, though in some cases we were able to find new partners. We almost never shut down such projects completely, if only because the universities were under a contractual obligation to their temporary workers, the research assistants, and it would have been wrong to break those contracts through no fault of the universities. Of course, one can argue that had they been employed by the firms to do precisely the same work they would have been laid off within a short period when the firms' priorities changed. It is an unsolved problem of cooperative work between universities and industry, but not really a major problem, affecting as it does only about 5 percent of the projects.

The funding for academic work proved much more of a problem. When the Alvey Committee made the decisions relating to the funds required it is fair to say that very few of us actually participated in the process. It was all rather hit and miss, with more help from studying the ceiling than from detailed calculation. I remember the panic a few days before the report went to Kenneth Baker, when it was realized that the figures did not add up. Some judicious adjustments were hurriedly made. To add to the confusion, when the government decided to fund 50 percent of all work, not 90 percent of parts as the report asked for, they wisely (accidentally, some would say) kept the total intact. Yet of course that changed significantly the amount of work that could be commissioned.

I don't want to suggest that there was no basis to the figures. We did try to assess how much of the country's IT research effort should go into cooperative work, how much academic effort could be made available. One must remember that for the parts where industry paid half, the firms had to find a considerable sum from their research budgets. This was probably achieved to some extent by redistribution for large firms with central research funds. But for the medium and smaller firms it was money that could be found only by a reduction of distributed profits, with all the dangers that that created for their share price with a City that has difficulty in valuing investment in R & D. We did try to assess the likely academic involvement in the Programme, and got it wrong in the VLSI field, where the appropriate industrialist argued that the academics had little to contribute because of the capital-intensive nature of the work; industry was well ahead of the academics. In one sense this was quite right, if one concentrates on the performance capability of the few centers of VLSI whole-process work in places like Southampton and Edinburgh universities. But experience demonstrated very clearly that academics involved in advanced physics and instrumentation at wavelengths shorter than light had a great deal to contribute, as VLSI resolutions demanded the use of wavelengths shorter than those in which the industrial world had experience.

Though it is not strictly relevant to the problem under discussion, this may be the point to mention another financial problem relating to the VLSI area. The industry had obtained most of its funding for VLSI research work from the MoD through the CVD mechanism. This was a highly respected machine, which formed the model for some of the Alvey Committee's discussion of the Directorate, the other model being the U.S. Department of Defense's DARPA (Defense Advanced Research Projects Agency). But industry was used to receiving 100 percent or rather 90 percent of its costs from the CVD so that the firms could retain the rights. The Alvey process paid only 50 percent of industrial costs, which became a cause of contention with certain firms. In fact, the move to 50 percent funding was already being planned by the MoD before cooperation in the Alvey Programme was proposed, so it was really coincidental that the change occurred with the move to cooperative research.

Thus the Alvey Committee's conclusion that, of the £200 million of public funds, £50 million should come from the SERC for the academic community in the Programme was more than a little arbitrary. I suppose we could have introduced artificial measures to have limited the amount of academic involvement. Certainly we recognized quite early on, after the first year I believe, that the academic proportion was going to exceed the £50 million share. I chose not to do anything to constrain this, leaving it to the individual consortia to find the right balance between academic and industrial work. I argued that any decision by the Directorate to restrain the academic proportion could only be on arbitrary grounds and that, if it meant that less funds would be available to support industrial work in other projects, so be it—the industrialists could see this as well as the Directorate. In retrospect I have a suspicion that we made it just too easy for the academics to take on excessive numbers of research assistants. Unlike their counterparts in the industrial world, the academic supervisors knew that they could always easily dispense with their RAs when the grant was complete, for they were only on temporary employment terms, as RAs always are. Yet it can be argued that these RAs received a first-rate training, and if they then went on to work in industry they were an invaluable source of experienced and highly qualified manpower for industry. I know that to be industry's experience, and there is no better method of technology transfer than on the hoof. My one reservation on this count is that many of the RAs were not British nationals, and so some of them must have returned to their own countries when the grants expired. Though I consider the funds were well spent if they were partly employed in training a pool of high quality people in the frontiers-of-knowledge subjects for British industry, it is somewhat more difficult to justify their training as an aid to the developing countries to which they returned. I should like to see some work done on the country of origin and final destination of RAs working in British universities. As far as I know this has not been done. My rather superficial impression is that foreign workers dominate in some of the less well-known academic laboratories, but for the main centers of excellence they were able to attract workers from U.K. sources or who would largely remain in the U.K. to work at the end of their grants. The point deserves study.

In the event, the academic funds became over allocated, and a cash flow problem developed. I consider that the situation was seriously exacerbated by the general financial difficulties that the SERC was going through at the time. The pound had fallen, making the SERC's overseas commitments including the CERN high-energy physics establishment in Geneva much more expensive. So the SERC had no easy way of balancing the books. And if a moratorium on all grants was called, as it was in more than one year by the SERC as the need to balance the books as the year's end loomed, it was difficult to argue that Alvey cooperative grants should have special priority. We were able to transfer funds between the DTI and the MoD to balance the books on the industrial expenditure, but it was not so easy to transfer funds from the DTI to the SERC, since the remit of the DTI was to fund industrial work, not academic work. In the event, everyone was as helpful as they could have been. The SERC, with backing and financial help from the Advisory Board for Research Councils (ABRC), which advises the Department of Education and Science on the allocation of funds between the Research Councils, came to our aid more than once. The MoD also helped by agreeing to make a small proportion of its total contribution available for the support of universities through the SERC. And finally, just before I left the Directorate, the DTI agreed to transfer some of its funds to the SERC to square off the account. I would claim that in the end the Alvey process of collaboration between the three public funding bodies was vindicated. But the National Audit Office continued to trumpet that industry had been deprived of funds that Parliament had voted for the industrial part of the Programme. I have not found the world so simple, so black and white.

However, I do not deny that the delays caused by the academic funding problem led to very real problems. There were long delays in recruitment, and experienced firms knew that they would eventually receive their money from the public purse if they proceeded on the basis of an "instruction to proceed" rather than if they waited for the grant contract to be released. But the delays were a serious problem. To argue that, without the Alvey Programme, the funds for the additional academic work would not have appeared is probably true, but does not justify the frustration and personal problems caused.

On the subject of funding and delays, I adopted the general policy of proceeding with the allocation of all of the funds as and when good projects became available. I was criticized for not holding funds to release grants in the final years of the Programme, but I thought it was better to get on with the work earlier if the resources were available. As it was there were cash-flow problems in reverse, because the projects were so slow in building up that the expenditure in the first two or three years of the Programme fell well below that planned, compensated of course by overspending in the final years. We were able to find funds for a final round of grant allocation in the autumn and early winter of 1986. I don't feel I have anything to apologize for in the timing of fund commitment.

Support of the U.K. Industry through Capital Purchases

In some ways one of the most expensive errors that we made was for the best of reasons. It was within the first few months of the Directorate's life that we had to make a decision about the bulk purchase of computing equipment to support the Programme. From experience in the SERC we knew that there are very real advantages to be had in using the same infrastructure equipment in geographically separated research centers working in the same field. Though the spread of standard open-systems interfaces is now making it easier to communicate between different equipment, it still is much easier to use the same equipment if computer programs are to be readily exchanged. In 1983 we had no doubt that to use the same infrastructure equipment for teams who were likely to work together would ease cooperation. Moreover, it held out the prospect of creating a standard kit of software tools for a community in a much more economic way than would be possible if they were using a variety of equipment.

There was no doubt that the IKBS academic community would need more computing equipment. It seemed more important to have the same equipment in many of the centers than to worry about what the particular make of that equipment would be. The obvious choice would have been VAX equipment, since it was widely available in the academic community. The problem for the Directorate was that GEC was about to put on the market a VAX-compatible system to be known as the Series 63. All previous experience told us to stick with the well-known and widely available Digital VAX. I knew that we were virtually sure to have delays and software shortages, and soon, if we were to purchase the GEC equipment. But to purchase the British equipment would be an excellent boost for the company at that stage in its life. It is in just that situation that public purchasing can do most good for the U.K. industry. In the long run that might help to cut down imports and even boost exports. At the time of one of the U.K.'s recurring balance of payment crises it was an unattractive prospect to be accused in the press of using our first large expenditure to boost imports. For the public servant it is very difficult to explain a decision not to purchase British equipment by explaining the true reason, if that might damage the potential sales of that manufacturer. So despite our disquiet we announced we were going to make a bulk purchase of Type 63 equipment. Though this might have proved a very excellent decision, saving money and boosting the sales of British equipment, in the event it proved an expensive mistake.

This was not the only occasion on which the Directorate was faced with the choice of supporting new British equipment or making the obvious choice of fashionable imported equipment. I do not regret that we frequently tried to help the British firms, but I do regret that our decisions were so rarely justified in the event. Naturally our ministers were happy to announce our decisions that backed British firms, especially small British firms. But I believe they would not have intervened had we decided to make the foreign purchases.

Where the British purchase has no long-term consequences, the choice is not easy when the risks of backing new equipment are so obvious. But where the IT community is going to have to make an investment in software development with long-term implications, the damage that can be done if the wrong choice of equipment is made can be very considerable. I reluctantly conclude that in such situations it would be prudent to think very carefully about the overall implications before reaching decisions. But it would be a sad day if considerations of the interest of British or European firms were entirely set aside when public funds are involved. The problem is to judge what is in the overall national interest in such cases. Let no one believe that these are easy decisions to take.

In the first years of the Programme we had much trouble with the collaboration agreements between the partners. I had laid it down that every project should have a collaboration agreement relating to matters such as property rights, exploitation, management, and publication. I wanted these to be drawn up at the start of the projects, in order to avoid delays and misunderstandings at the point of exploitation. It was my belief that clarity on these matters would considerably aid the process of achieving exploitation. We had assumed that the firms had had ample experience in drawing up collaborative agreements and so would be able to tackle the task, even if the universities were largely tyros in the matter. This assumption proved wrong, and it took a great deal of time and effort to get the agreements drawn up. However, in due course they appeared, and the problem faded away, though not before it was claimed to have delayed the start of projects. It is true that we refused to pay out on claims until we had the signed agreements in our hands, but we would normally give instructions to proceed, so I doubt that the delays were really caused by the agreements. However, experience has proved what a valuable service drawing up the agreements provides in clarifying important matters such as management issues. I am unrepentant about requiring these agreements to be signed at the start of the projects. If I had my time again I would require them once again!

There were two ways in which I think the Directorate could have helped in the process of drawing up collaboration agreements. Experience demonstrated that it was wrong for the Directorate to stand back and leave the details to the partners. We could have provided some staff help, probably by appropriate people seconded from industry. The experience that they gradually accumulated would have proved invaluable to those trying to draw up agreements for the first time. And it is clear that someone with experience from a neutral corner can help with the process. In practice a few of the Alvey civil servants did provide invaluable help with certain project teams. I'm not sure that a standard agreement, on the lines of the ESPRIT agreement, would have helped. With the ESPRIT agreement much the same battles go on but are relegated to the annexes. But we should have provided a detailed guide to drawing up collaboration agreements. I did get work started on one, on more than one occasion. But for a variety of reasons nothing very useful emerged. The final version was hijacked by officials more concerned with the details of contractual matters between the partners and the government departments than with the issues of property rights, etc. that are problems between the partners with little involvement of the funding agencies. Still, it is not too late for a guide to collaboration agreements based on Alvey (and ESPRIT?) experience to emerge. I hope it does.

Small Firms

Whether it was a real problem or not, the involvement of small firms loomed large in the political mind and in the press. While I have never shared the unalloyed enthusiasm for small firms as the saviors of the national economy that some people exhibit, I do enjoy dealing with small firms and believe that, in the long run, a few of them, a very few, will hit the big time and become significant factors in the national economy. But any belief that high-technology small firms will make any significant impact on the economy or even on unemployment is moonshine. It happened that at the start of the Alvey Programme there were a number of small firms, largely part of the Cambridge phenomenon, that were exhibiting remarkable growth. Unfortunately, most or all of these proved to be rockets, and the sticks came falling back to the ground without the heads' achieving orbit. This was a terrible disappointment to us all. At least one of them survived to achieve more normal growth. Experience suggests that it takes a very long time for start-ups to grow into significant firms under U.K. conditions. In this respect we resemble Japan and Germany and seem to differ from the U.S. It seems easier for firms that depend primarily on people rather than on capital. One has only to consider the steady growth of our independent software houses, such as Logica, which has grown over twenty years into a firm employing several thousand people around the world, with a turnover in the hundreds of millions of pounds.

Despite the picture often conveyed by the press, there were a considerable number of small firms in the Programme. In all, some 113 firms took part in the Programme. Using the European Commission's definition that a small or medium-sized enterprise (SME) has fewer than 400 employees, at least 50 firms in the Programme were SMEs. Incidentally, we had endless trouble determining the number of firms participating in the Programme. We decided early on to classify all subsidiaries of a parent firm under that one name. GEC consists of over 100 separately registered companies. Had we treated them as separate firms, the participation list would have been much larger, perhaps reaching 200 firms. This decision caused us much trouble. Throughout the Programme firms were constantly merging, and since many of them did not lose their separate public identities we were not consistent in revising the tables. For example, it seemed to reduce intelligibility to reclassify Inmos as Thorn-EMI, or Yard as CAP. Would it have been right to reclassify ICL under STC, or the Ferranti semiconductor business under Plessey?

So small firms did participate in the Programme but, of course, it was very difficult for them to find their share of the costs of the research work. Even more difficult for them was to find the high-quality staff required to undertake the work. There is a considerable overhead in working on a cooperative project. For a small firm the best solution seems to be to form a partnership with a large firm and act essentially as a subcontractor. Some small firms played an invaluable part in some of the projects. It would be nice to believe that they benefited from it. Some of them clearly gained considerably from the exposure, along with the big firms. For others it was the technology that they gained, with a relatively small investment to the work of a large consortium.

Collaboration with ESPRIT

One other problem area for us lay in the ESPRIT program. Should we cooperate with it, or should we stay aloof? Would it ruin some of our consortia or provide an outlet for exploitation on the continent? The ESPRIT program is described in more detail in chapter 13, but for the purposes of the problem for Alvey it is important to understand that the program was much in the air at the time the Alvey Committee was meeting. Several members of the committee were involved in the planning for ESPRIT, but there remained much doubt about whether the program would go ahead. The Alvey Committee took the view that the U.K. needed to learn to cooperate through a national program in order to be able to play its full part in the international ESPRIT program. Once the Alvey Directorate was set up we were fully involved in the problems within Whitehall of obtaining the U.K. government agreement to the program and finding the funds. It was readily agreed in the DTI by Alastair Macdonald that the Alvey Directorate should take the lead for the U.K. in handling ESPRIT. Tim Walker had to put a great deal of effort into setting up the U.K. end of ESPRIT, at a time when we could well have used his full-time effort in support of the Alvey Programme. I agreed to one principal working full-time on ESPRIT, and another support post was provided later. I decided to attend the ESPRIT Management Committee meetings, the meetings of representatives of what became the twelve nations. It rapidly became obvious to me that the Alvey Directorate had an important role to play in orchestrating the U.K. input to ESPRIT. At first the Commission's staff were highly suspicious of the Alvey Directorate, but in time they came to recognize the benefit of having a sympathetic focal point in the U.K. In the early years I tried to keep the involvement of the Alvey Directorate staff in ESPRIT matters to a minimum, in order to concentrate our limited effort on Alvey matters, but this gradually changed as time went by. We used *Alvey News* to carry information on ESPRIT, and always set aside a session at the Alvey Conference for the ESPRIT task force, though their involvement in the conference never really worked satisfactorily. One request from the ESPRIT task force was for us to disclose proposals to the Alvey Directorate to them. This I refused to do, though I was happy to let them have some information on the projects once we had agreed to them. But overall we gradually achieved a close cooperation between the Alvey and ESPRIT administrative staffs that I am pleased to see has continued and been extended since I left the scene.

Communications

I have made little mention of the network and communications part of the Programme. We did not see it as a major part of the Programme, but we did wish to support the infrastructure of the Programme. Unlike the Japanese fifth-generation program, with its ICOT research center, and the U.S. MCC program with its center at Austin, Texas, the Alvey Committee had decided that a distributed approach would suit U.K. conditions better. The distances are relatively small, the problems of moving, schools, the "working wife" needing to find employment at a time of high unemployment in professions such as teaching, and the problems of academics leaving their students—all these factors had persuaded the majority of the committee that the project teams should largely remain at their own research centers. But this was far from a unanimous decision, for it was recognized that to bring a team together on a single site could be far more efficient. Moreover, if a common research center were constructed for several similar projects, there would be benefits of interaction among the different project teams and disciplines. However, the clinching argument against a single site was that it would make much greater the problems of technology transfer back into the firms for exploitation. Since we were much concerned to maximize the chance of exploitation, the much-increased ease of exploitation if work was going on in the firms that would exploit it was a powerful argument. In retrospect I have no doubt it was the right decision, though I do wish that we could have had a less distributed program with more centers of concentration. The ANSA systems architecture project was not the only one in which the team chose to work from a single site, but it was the only one in which this was organized on any significant scale.

If the project teams were to be dispersed, it was vital that there should be good communications between the various members of a team. And preferably this should be extended to good communications between all projects. In 1987 the academics were well served by the academic Janet network looked after by the Joint Network Team based at the Rutherford Appleton Laboratory. But this did not extend to industry, and it was comparatively rare then to find industrial research workers using electronic mail in the easy way that their academic partners did. So we saw as one of our first priorities the establishment of Alvey Net (or Alvey Mail), a network that would link the industrial research workers and the academics. The control station was established in the first place at NPL, and was later moved to RAL to be alongside the Janet data exchange on which it was clearly modeled. In the event the network proved to be useful for some, but only some, of the teams. I am not sure why this was, but I suspect that we gave too little attention to the human factors in the terminals. These, of course, covered a vast range of different equipment. It would have been quite easy to develop conversion routines for certain terminals, so that the user could dial a simple address to obtain the mailbox of a remote colleague. But it would have been a very expensive task to have developed routines that "looked" the same for each of the many different terminals.

The high-speed network was even more of a failure. We had envisaged a limited number of projects dedicated to using this network in the first place, and then more and more users joining in as the network became established as a service. In the event the number of projects dropped to two, both deriving from the very successful SERC Universe project that used satellite communications. Some very good work came out of these two projects, though they did not achieve all their objectives. I suspect the next generation of broadband communications owes more to the experience gained by the work on the Alvey high-speed network than is generally acknowledged, if only in matters like network management and control. Nevertheless, the high-speed network was an expensive way of gaining this experience, as so few of the Alvey projects made any use of it.

Far more successful was *Alvey News*, the newsletter we quickly established and distributed free to whoever asked to be placed on the mailing list. In the early days of the Programme Derek Barber was working day and night to get the networks going, to establish the communications research program, and to launch *Alvey News*. It was he who invented the Alvey pentagon logo, one of the few features of the Alvey Programme that seems to have survived the Alvey years to be adopted by the Information Engineering Directorate. Published every two months on our behalf by the IEE and the BCS (in fact by the IEE, since the BCS was a sleeping partner), it provided a channel to keep the Alvey community informed about the progress of the Programme. We also used it to publicize activities such as the Alvey Conference, the program strategies, and the various clubs that we built up around all the projects in particular parts of the Programme. We came increasingly to use it for publicizing ESPRIT program information. Throughout the Alvey years we were well served by two people who contributed to the running of *Alvey News,* Ken Owen as a regular writer and Linda Prior at the Directorate. Owen had been the technology editor of *The Times* at a time when that was something of which to be proud. Since 1978 he had taken a special interest in artificial intelligence.

Though we did discuss holding a conference in 1984, it was not until 1985 that we had the time to launch the first Alvey Conference. This was held in June in Edinburgh, and then followed annual conferences at the same time of the year in Sussex, UMIST, and Swansea. The first conference was largely put together, in short time, by the superhuman efforts of Bill Fawcett and his assistant Linda Prior. As time went by Linda became the focal point for all the work on the conferences under the leadership of Keith Bartlett. Linda was ideal for the job, being excellent at details and able to work with people at all levels. The format started with much of the time devoted to the Alvey directors setting out their programs; year by year more of the time on the conference program was devoted to technical papers deriving from work on individual projects. Certain fixed features of the conferences were established. Under the benign chairmanship of Sir Robert Telford the conference would be opened by the local university vice-chancellor, and then an appropriate minister would speak. There would be a dinner attended by many of the conference delegates. And there was always an informal evening session given over to presentations by the evaluators that were intended to spark discussion on the Programme. Like *Alvey News,* the conference acted as a mechanism for pulling the Alvey community together. I look back with enormous pleasure to those busy days, when several hundred of the best research workers from the academic and industrial research community of the U.K. met together in easy harmony and companionship.

Skill Shortages and Training

Though the Alvey Committee had given considerable thought to the skilled manpower shortages that were then becoming serious, the Alvey Programme was not given any specific responsibility for training matters. No doubt this was due to the feeling that the Alvey Directorate should stick to research and keep out of the training field, where there were all too many bodies such as the DES, the SERC, and the MSC already at work. In fact, at the frontiers of technology training is closely related to research. And though the skill shortages at the frontiers are not as numerous as in the mainstream of IT application, they can be crucial for the rate of transfer from technology development into application. So the Alvey Directorate found itself filling a vacuum for trained manpower around the subjects at the frontier of the Programme. Indeed, some parts of the Programme, such as IKBS, were very much designed to increase the number of workers skilled in the subject in industry. In some ways the biggest contribution we made was through the increase in research assistants in the universities. These are largely either postgraduates (many of whom are also registered for postgraduate degrees) or postdoctorates, though the age range is surprisingly wide. They are normally employed on three-year contracts for the duration of the project, though in some large departments they may be reemployed over and over again. This is very much against the SERC policy, for it is highly desirable that they should leave their universities after the first three years, taking their technology with them to industry. Of course it is nice for the permanent university research workers to be able to employ experienced research assistants, and maybe it is good for the research. But it is not good for the employment prospects of the RAs for them to become eternal students. It is difficult to find any figures for the number of RAs who actually entered industry after training on Alvey projects. Part of the problem is that some, maybe many, of the RAs are not British. How many of these stay on for employment in the U.K. I do not know, probably relatively few. At its peak the Alvey Programme was employing some 3,000 people of whom perhaps 1,000 were RAs, so the number of skilled people joining industry from this source was probably a significant contribution to reducing the skill shortages.

We helped to organize various distance-learning courses, usually with the cooperation of the Open University. In my view good distance-learning material, despite its high cost, is a crucial contribution to overcoming skill shortages at the frontier of the subject. I now feel we should have done more of this, and should have gone systematically through the Alvey field to do it. We did make one significant attempt to organize a supply of distance-learning material for the IT industries, in particular to tackle the reeducation of graduates who wish to take up careers in computing, having graduated in some other discipline. It seemed to fall through because of a temporary downturn in the demand for new graduates, leading to the industry withdrawing its support from the scheme.

The Journeyman scheme was the brainchild of David Thomas. It was based on the concept of the medieval journeyman, who was a cut above an apprentice but carried out essentially the same learning process of sitting at the feet of the master. We organized IKBS schemes at the Turing Institute and Imperial College to enable suitably qualified graduates to go to work with AI experts for six months or so to learn the art, if art it be. In my opinion there is scope for extending the scheme to other fields, such as software engineering and HCI, though perhaps this would not have worked five years ago.

Though it was not our direct responsibility, a tendency developed for the community to turn to the Alvey Directorate to act as the focal point for issues that concerned the whole community but were nobody's specific responsibility. The shortage of skilled people was just such an issue. I suppose the Directorate was able to gather some of the facts on shortages and to give them some publicity. So perhaps it was not surprising that when the government finally set up the Butcher Committee under John Butcher, the DTI junior minister through so much of the Alvey era, I was asked to join the committee. Though I did little of the work, I was able to feed in some of the ideas, and the activity did have the effect of focusing attention on the issue. It became clear to the committee that what was needed was a body to bring together all the bodies with an interest in the matter and with something constructive to contribute. Unfortunately, the government was going through a period when it felt it was not its responsibility to do anything about the situation, so the hunt was on for a body that would act as the focal point. I came under considerable pressure then and from time to time thereafter to make the Alvey Directorate that focal point. I should very much have liked to take on the task, but I was conscious that we were already overloaded in servicing the Alvey Programme. But it would have been nice to have done the job, and it might have helped to get the Directorate recognized as the focus for matters of concern to the whole IT community. In the end the IT Skills Agency was set up, backed by some of the large IT firms and located within the CBI Education Foundation.

In the Eye of the Press

From the time of my appointment I recognized the importance of publicity. I had been taught by Sir Geoffrey Allen at the SERC that publicity could help to mobilize support for the organization in its time of need. But of course this was counter-cultural to the civil service tradition, where one did not speak to the press and left publicity to ministers. And the then current minister, Kenneth Baker, was a master of publicity and certainly welcomed the high profile we adopted. In fairness to his successors, nobody ever attempted to curb my publicity activities. I was always prepared to speak to the press, and of course this was popular with the journalists. I tended to be consulted on a wide range of IT issues. This led to headlines and quotes, particularly in the IT "give aways." For some reason the press seemed to enjoy taking photographs of me, so my picture was frequently appearing in the press. I wrote a constant stream of articles for various journals, and this added to the publicity. Then I started to receive invitations to lecture, and since I normally accepted these they tended to grow in numbers until it was a rare week in which I was not giving one or more lectures. I tended to be quite good at this and so obtained some satisfaction by drawing attention to the Alvey Programme and the impact that the new technologies would have. It is probable that I took this too far and that the benefit to the Alvey Programme was offset by the loss of valuable time that I could have been putting into other aspects of the Programme. Of course, it became a form of escapism for me from the various conflicts inherent in running a program of this type. On the other hand it could be argued that had I spent more time on the internals of the Programme I would have interfered more with the work of my directors. I do believe that I tended to follow my beliefs and left them to get on with the details of their work, even when this meant that their different approaches led to a variety of differences in detail. If I had had more time I might have ironed out some of these differences, but I might have interfered with decisions best left to the man closest to understanding the details of his subject area.

Whether all this publicity did us much good is a matter of contention. Certainly our formal press conferences tended not to be a great success. The press was generally sympathetic to our objectives but critical of our performance. To some extent the criticism was justified, but we did feel that a great deal of it was unbalanced and sensational. The press likes a good horror story, and bad news tends to make better press than good. When it came time to persuade ministers to accept the Bide Committee proposals the press was generally very supportive of the case. Whether the criticism of the past made it more difficult to obtain support for the new program is not clear. My own guess is that it made little difference.

In retrospect I do not regret our high profile and publicity. It helped to create an image and a focal point for the Programme. That was needed, and I regret its passing. Indeed I believe my failure was in not taking the publicity activity further. I should have ensured that all the directors played their part in the publicity campaign. Some did it very well, but most did not.

Monitoring and Evaluation

Before leaving my personal description of the Alvey Programme I would like to record something about the way we monitored and evaluated the Programme. With several hundred projects in progress it was essential that we should have some mechanism for learning, systematically, what was going on, what needed help, and what needed stopping. Early on, we decided to appoint monitoring officers to every industrial project. It took us some time to achieve this, and I do wish we had been able to appoint monitoring officers when the projects were set up, as the officers could have helped us with the early problems like the completion of the collaboration agreements. It was the intention that one monitoring officer should cover a bunch of related projects, but this did not always work out satisfactorily. We obtained regular reports from the monitoring officers, and once a year Laurence Clarke and I spent a long weekend analyzing these reports. We scored their comments under headings like Progress, Quality of Cooperation, Quality of Management. Though not all the directors were happy with this admittedly somewhat arbitrary process, we felt it did give a fair picture of progress, enabling us to pick out those projects that needed attention, and also gave us a feel for how projects were maturing as a whole. As always, we had a few problems with individual monitoring officers. There were a few who wanted to run their projects and a few who were "captured" by their project teams and were no longer independent witnesses of the scene. But the vast majority did a conscientious job. The mark of a good monitoring officer is when the project team comes to respect and value him. This happened enough to make us feel that our rather informal way of selecting monitoring officers, on the basis of the best man we could think of for a particular group of projects, was working satisfactorily.

We saw the monitoring officers as an extension of the Alvey Directorate team. I think we could have made more of them had we developed this relationship by seeing them as a group more frequently. But there is a danger that monitoring officers come between the Directorate and the project teams as a barrier to direct communication. The trick is to use the mechanism as a key part of the communication process but to ensure that the door is also open for direct communication. In general, monitoring officers really earn their keep when something is going wrong with one of their projects.

If monitoring officers are clearly a part of the Directorate team and are seen in that light, the evaluation teams should be seen to be as independent of all parties as they can possibly be. This is not of course easy to arrange for someone has to commission and steer the evaluation teams. Perhaps because I had had a considerable experience of the evaluation process, both in my previous DTI incarnation and as Secretary of the SERC, when I took up the Director's mantle I was determined that the Alvey Programme should be properly evaluated. This meant getting the evaluation teams set up early and taking steps to ensure their independence. At a time when we were all very busy this took some effort away from what others would see as more pressing problems. But I have absolutely no regrets about spending the time on this task. Luckily for me I was strongly backed by Tim Walker, and we had some good help from other members of the Directorate administration team in this work over the years. I cannot say that the rest of the Directorate welcomed the process so enthusiastically! At best my other fellow directors might be said to have tolerated the evaluators.

Because I knew what I wanted in evaluation I found myself chairing the steering committee for the evaluation projects and ultimately being responsible for paying for the work with public funds. There can be no doubt that it would have been better if others had done this; evaluation has got both to be independent and to be seen as independent! One always fools oneself on such matters, but I do believe that I ran the evaluation work with as little interference and bias as possible. I suspect the evaluators will back me on this. But inevitably some bias entered into the process because of the direct involvement of the Directorate. And even if it didn't, the Director will be perceived as having biased the evaluation. At the time that the Programme was being set up it might have been difficult to find someone in Whitehall with the interest and enthusiasm to drive the evaluation work forward. By the end of the Programme the evaluation team in the Cabinet Office was established, and that would have been an ideal group to have taken it on.

I asked two academic teams, one from the Science Policy Research Unit (SPRU) at Sussex University and one from the Programme of Policy Research in Engineering, Science, and Technology (PREST) at Manchester University to form a club to carry out the evaluation work. For a time a team from the London Business School also took part, but we parted company after the first couple of years after members of that team moved to Oxford. Many people felt these teams were too academic in nature, though I suspect this was partly because the critics did not realize how much work these teams had done in the past, with industry as distinct from science. I think, for example, of the pioneering work that the SPRU had done evaluating what makes a successful innovation in industry. But the objection to these teams might have been on the more sustainable grounds that the individuals in the teams were very naive about industrial affairs. Independence and naiveté often seem to be opposite sides of the same coin. It was a mistake not to have fed into the evaluation club at least one team from one of the commercial consultancies. Such people tend to get a reputation either for saying what they think the client wants to hear or for trying to ensure that one piece of work leads to another—which may come down to the same criticism! But a properly chosen team from a professional consultancy would have added some weight to the evaluation and would have prevented the oft-repeated accusation that the evaluators did not understand the industrial viewpoint and imperatives.

The evaluation teams have now produced numerous reports, which are publicly available, though I fear that they are largely unread outside a narrow circle of those directly interested (see appendix 5). Their work did prove very valuable to the Alvey Director and will contain valuable lessons for all involved. I look forward to reading their final report in a year's time. It will be much more balanced than my chapters of this book!

One thing I did learn about evaluation: I knew before I embarked on the Director's job that academics are very sensitive to criticism from independent academic evaluators who are not experts in their field, though they are usually quite happy for their peers in their own disciplines to make similar criticisms in the relative privacy of the peer-review process. What I had not expected to find was that industrialists are similarly sensitive. One can see that public criticism would have serious economic implications for industrialists—and, for that matter, academics. Yet not to publish is to deny the main benefit that stems from independent evaluation, namely that lessons can be learned to make the next program better.

I suppose I should make some reference to the National Audit Office evaluation, since its report was published and Sir Brian Hayes, the long suffering Permanent Secretary of the DTI to whom I directly reported, had to answer its criticism of the Programme before the Public Accounts Committee. The PAC is the most respected—and feared—select committee of Parliament, the body that concerns itself with seeing that the authority of Parliament in financial affairs is not thwarted. I have a certain respect for the PAC and recognize that it is absolutely right to have a Parliamentary watchdog over the Executive, even if the consequences tend to be much nugatory work for civil servants.

The National Audit Office essentially provides the PAC's ferrets. For many years we have criticized the PAC for concerning itself purely with expenditure aspects and not with the policy that leads to the expenditure. So we can hardly complain if the committee encourages its watchdogs to look beyond the points of last-penny accounting to political and policy framework within which the expenditure is incurred. The problem is that this makes the Audit Office deal with considerations that it is ill equipped to evaluate. It seemed inevitable that the NAO would latch on to the Alvey Programme as a novel and possibly trend-setting mechanism. And so it was. I have a fair amount of sympathy with many of their criticisms. My major quarrel with the NAO report is that many of the benefits of the Alvey Programme did not stem from things to which one can apply quantitative cost/benefit analysis. Climates created, bonds formed, attitudes changed, and people trained are not matters on which one can hang a price tag, even if it is fashionable to say that if one can't put a price on it, it's not worth anything. In an increasingly materialistic world it is important not to forget that life is too complex to be reduced to a financial balance sheet.

III
Views For and Against

9
Alvey Observed

The shape of the Alvey Programme, the degree of control by the Alvey Programme Steering Committee, and the different approaches and problems in the various technology areas are among the issues that provoke strong views among those involved in the Alvey exercise. This chapter by Kenneth Owen is based on interviews with members of the Alvey Committee, Steering Committee, and Directorate.

Shape of the Programme

Members of the Alvey Committee did not expect their recommendations to be followed closely by the Directorate (as noted briefly by John Alvey and Alastair Macdonald in chapter 4), and they express surprise that this appeared to happen. They believed that they were indicating the broad areas that should be tackled, as a basis for a further investigation and double-checking by the Directorate before the Programme was defined. In the event, they accept, such a process may have been ruled out by the government's delay in responding to the Alvey Report. "One of the things that greatly surprised the Alvey Committee about the subsequent events was the seriousness with which its budgets and, indeed, the choice of the four areas, was taken," says Roger Needham:

What we expected to happen was that the government would appoint a directorate, which would then sit down and think rather carefully about what it wanted to do.
We certainly envisaged government coming to a more rapid decision, the apparatus being set up, and the directorate spending more time producing its strategies in detail. But by the time they opened for business so much time had elapsed that they would have made a laughing stock of themselves if they'd gone into a monastery for three months to think. They produced their strategy documents in un-

seemly haste. They worked very hard on them—but what they did not have time to do was to query the substrate, to say "Do we want this particular four-legged stool?" What they found themselves having to do was to take something that was meant as a for-instance and treat it as a plan.

This had some peculiar effects, Needham argues. The Alvey Committee in its report had omitted to mention certain areas of work, not because these areas did not merit support but because they were already being supported. But the SERC then "handed practically all of its money for IT research over to Alvey," and research in these other areas suffered drastically.

Iann Barron also stresses that the Alvey Committee had expected further work to be done before the Programme went ahead. "We thought it was an outline to get the money, and the Programme would then be defined." The delay in the government's response did not please the members of the committee. "Everybody was absolutely furious," says Barron, "because we'd had to compromise a whole lot of the things that were done in order to get the report ready in time. We could have spent twice as long and done a much better job."

As the Alvey Programme got under way Professor Eric Ash, who had taken over from Laurence Clarke as chairman of the SERC Information Engineering Committee and who was also a member of the Alvey Programme Steering Committee, was involved in the SERC input to the formulation of the Alvey strategy documents and to the assessment of the subsequent proposals. There was further delay here, he explains:

The draft Alvey strategy documents for the various technologies went to the IEC for comment, and we tried to make changes in them, with rather mixed success. Having agreed the strategies, when the proposals came from the Alvey Directorate, the intention was that they should basically be rubber-stamped as long as they came within the strategy. That's virtually what happened. Despite that, this dual assessment procedure did cause delays—as it did to an even greater extent in the Joint Opto-Electronics Research Scheme (JOERS).

Not that Ash was particular keen on strategy documents anyway. "I do not believe in strategy documents very much. Other than a few paragraphs setting out some key things, I think strategy documents are for the birds. In my view, the Alvey strategy documents didn't provide enough constraints. They were too wide-ranging in what they said." The formulation of these Alvey strategies is discussed later in this chapter.

Role of the Steering Committee

The Alvey Programme Steering Committee steered with a very light hand on the tiller. As Brian Oakley's account (chapter 7) makes clear, the Alvey Director was given considerable freedom by the committee in running the Programme—quite deliberately so, insists Sir Robert Telford, the committee's chairman. This caused frustration among some members of the committee who sought a stronger role. The Alvey Committee had suggested that the existing Electronics and Avionics Requirements Board should form the basis of the steering committee; formally it did not, but informally it did become involved. This also caused friction. In the event, did the steering committee steer at all? Arguably, it did not.

Before, during, and after the Alvey Programme a succession of ministers occupied the Secretary of State's office in the Department of Industry and (as it became in June 1983) the Department of Trade and Industry. In July 1983 the occupant was Cecil Parkinson, and so he was the man who appointed the initial five members of the Steering Committee under Sir Robert Telford. They were:

- Philip Hughes, Chairman of Logica.
- Dr. Keith Warren, Director of Technology and Strategic Planning, Plessey.
- Colin Southgate, Chief Executive, Thorn-EMI Information Technology.
- John Leighfield, Managing Director, BL Systems.
- Professor Eric Ash, Head of the Department of Electronic and Electrical Engineering at University College, London.

Professor Ash was also to represent the SERC; and deputy secretaries Colin Fielding and Roy Croft were to represent the Ministry of Defence and the DTI.

Sir Robert was already chairman of the EARB when the Alvey Programme Steering Committee was set up. Was the steering committee given any terms of reference? "The answer must be no," says Sir Robert. "I saw its role completely as advisory, as supportive to the director." The terms of reference of the steering committee were in fact initially defined as follows: "To oversee the research program and satisfy itself that it is on course; and ensure that the results of the program are quickly translated into marketable products." (At its first meeting in August 1983 the committee quickly spotted the trap inherent in the second of these functions and agreed that, because the committee could ensure no such thing, its task in this area should be to monitor the Programme to ensure that it matched emerging market needs.)

In the early stages, Sir Robert recalls, the various strategy documents produced by the directorate "all came back to the steering committee," where it became clear that "there were people on the steering committee who clearly felt they ought to be in a more directive role." Also, there was a strong division on the committee, with some members opposing the VLSI program on principle.

Sir Robert says he modeled the relationship between the steering committee and the Alvey Programme Director on the GEC-Marconi pattern, where as group managing director he gave the managing directors of his various operating companies full authority. "My job was to create the environment in which they could operate and, if you like, to fire them if they couldn't do the job. The same with Alvey—it's instinctive with me."

Attendance at steering committee meetings was not confined to those appointed by Parkinson, for a rather peculiar reason. The Alvey Report had said that a restructured EARB should form the basis of the new steering committee, and Sir Robert and John Alvey had had "lots of talks" about this. Indeed, Sir Robert had gone ahead and brought new people on to the EARB, "with the agreement of the DTI," in readiness for their expected Alvey roles.

The prime minister, Sir Robert understands, was insistent that the steering committee should be as small as possible—hence the Parkinson list of only five, plus officials. Sir Robert was embarrassed: "There were these people who had been brought in on this basis, who weren't going to play any role, and this was crazy. The other point was that I knew from experience that if you've got only about five busy people on the committee you're not going to get a quorum there." Sir Robert says he pleaded with Kenneth Baker for more members, but to no avail. "What I did then was to invite these key people from the requirements board to join the committee as ex-officio observers, as we were an informal body. One or two of the original members of the committee didn't really like that. They felt I had made it too big." At some meetings, Sir Robert says, there might be only two of the original members present—plus four or five from the EARB. Eventually, "I had to stop this EARB flooding it," but the DTI "allowed me to increase the committee membership by two*—but unofficially. It really was getting to be a bit of a farce."

One of the steering committee members who "didn't really like that" was Philip Hughes. Or, as Hughes puts it, "That was really scandalous." His view of events is as follows:

After the first two meetings I was virtually in despair. The problem was that Bob Telford was a great consultative man. He wanted everybody in, so there was a steering committee, but you never knew what its membership was. Either a guy is a member or he's not. Sometimes Derek Roberts would turn up, but he wasn't a member of the committee. What was he doing there? There was a thing called the EARB, of which Telford was chairman, so sometimes he would co-opt the two together, so that there was this miasma of things. The meetings were ghastly.

Hughes argues that the steering committee should have operated, but did not operate, as the board of a company, to whom the managing director would report. "I don't think Bob Telford saw it that way. I think he saw it as a kind of chat club where industry at large kept in touch and put in views. And Brian, to be fair, saw it as yet another bloody committee to be avoided. I don't think that Brian ever deliberately misled the committee, but to him it was just another chore." Did the Alvey director, for instance, come to the steering committee and say "I propose to do this?" "No," says Hughes:

He'd say "This is what I've done." In a sense one was caught, because one wanted to be supportive of Brian. Given a different kind of chairman, Brian could have used the steering committee to get backing when needed from ministers. But none of that happened.

The steering committee was neither steering nor was it used to fight

---

*New members David Speake (GEC) and Geoffrey Holmes (Systems Designers) were welcomed by the steering committee in April 1986, when appreciation was recorded of the work of Hughes and Southgate, who had "retired" from the committee.

battles. It could have been used to fight the battles. There were four or five key political battles—such as the directorate, the machine architecture, the infrastructure network. I finally resigned from the steering committee in desperation, because I had no enthusiasm for it.

Eric Ash, also, is critical of the steering committee's role. "I do not believe that the steering committee had a large influence on the Programme. The idea that the Programme was done with a great deal of advice from the top—or that the SERC committees had a very major influence on it—was a misreading of what actually happened." As an example, Ash cites the case of the VLSI strategy document.

The VLSI document was really organized and approved at a level "below" the steering committee. When the committee got this document, several of us criticized it. I would say a clear majority of the steering committee criticized it, and what we criticized was that, for a relatively modest budget of £70 million or thereabouts, they were going to look at two whole wafer processes and a large number of different technologies. My personal view is that we would have done better if we had made a list of all the things that you could work on, stuck a pin in the list, picked that one, and put the £70 million into that. We were not able to prevail on this, and the strategy document was not seriously changed as a result.

Another controversial issue for the steering committee was the question of the Alvey large-scale demonstrators (discussed further in the next chapter). Colin Southgate recalls: "I thought we were there to make sure the money was spent in the right way. The thing that really upset me was the question of the large demonstrators. As soon as you asked any questions you were knocked to the boundary because the information was said to be company confidential. We had no worthwhile in-depth insight into a single one of the demonstrators; we had no power over whether they should go ahead or not. I was fundamentally against some of them because I thought they were rubbish." The Directorate's general approach to the large demonstrators was endorsed by the steering committee in September 1983.

In November 1983 the steering committee was presented by the Directorate with the proposed allocation of public funds across the various technologies (table 9.1). Members suggested that more should be spent on software engineering and less on

TABLE 9.1.
Alvey Programme Provisional Public Funding (£m at 1983 prices)

Software engineering	40.9
VLSI	52.8
CAD	17.5
MMI	30.2
IKBS	22.9
Communications	9.1
Demonstrators	21.2
Administration	5.4
Total	200.0

VLSI. One year later a notional £19 million for systems architecture, out of a £225 million total, was allocated (see chapter 12 for actual figures reported by the National Audit Office in 1988).

On the general role of the steering committee, Alastair Macdonald sums up: "I sensed that Sir Robert Telford saw the steering committee as giving a strategic direction to the Programme, while allowing immense day-to-day flexibility to Brian. Sir Robert was most anxious that the steering committee should not be a spanner in the works."

Assorted Technologies

Within the Alvey Directorate different starting points, different professional communities, and different management styles ensured that there would be no standard approach to putting together and running the four "enabling technology" programs. Not that any such standardization was suggested at the time, though a common management information system would certainly have proved valuable as the Alvey Programme developed. So the five initial technology directors—the topic of infrastructure and communications had been added to the four identified in the Alvey Report—had different issues to address.

Bill Fawcett, VLSI

Bill Fawcett, head of the physics group at the RSRE before moving to Alvey, had two starting points in assembling the VLSI program: the Ministry of Defence's planned Very High-

Performance Integrated Circuit (VHPIC) program and the Alvey Committee's proposals. Fawcett outlines the background:

VHPIC had been under discussion for about two years. It was a vertically integrated program that started with the technology and included a number of demonstrators. That program never got off the ground, and the technology part was subsumed into Alvey. The VHPIC demonstrators, which involved military applications, were the subject of a separate MoD demonstrator program which aimed to draw on Alvey technology.

There were two parts of the VLSI program, concerned respectively with the technology and with computer-aided design (CAD). Also, I was trying to put together the architectures aspects in some form. On the technology side there was significant consultation with both semiconductor companies and user companies, trying to assess whether the Alvey targets were right or not.

Out of Fawcett's consultative process came substantial confirmation of the targets—and a basic argument on whether the program should include the whole-process work:

The point at issue was: if you are putting development of whole processes into a semiconductor company, it is not really collaborative research, it is commercial activity that should be funded by the company. I argued against that, for two reason. First, unless you put in a whole process, the whole program became too much of an academic exercise. The other aspect is that you could make those activities collaborative, and I think we demonstrated that. Some people disagreed strongly on this point, because when you start putting in those whole processes it becomes a very costly exercise.

Fawcett took care to set up a comprehensive advisory structure:

It was a two-stage process. I set up independent technical advisory committees on VLSI, CAD, and architectures; and an industrial advisory board that took the technical committees' recommendations and pulled all that together. What we needed to do was really very well defined. That enabled us to get off the ground much more easily and quickly than other parts of the Programme. Even so, there was a hell of a lot of work involved.

I had the impression that VLSI was one of the best organized areas of Alvey, in that people knew what they had to do and had agreed objectives at the beginning. I believe we were never out of control of what we were doing, in terms of projects or in terms of committed funding. We had our own mechanisms, almost independent of the rest of the directorate, because in those early days there was no financial control at all, as far as I could tell.

There was a general ambiguity about the relationships between the sponsoring departments and the Alvey technology programs that became evident in the VLSI area, and (as noted in Brian Oakley's account) a specific dispute arose concerning the influence of the Ministry of Defence:

There was always an underlying current between DTI and MoD in the Alvey Directorate. Chris Barrow came across it badly later on, and I came across it to a lesser extent in the early days. I suspect I should have been more dictatorial on this. It was the sense that DTI and MoD separately had some authority over the money because it was their money coming into the directorate, rather than a recognition that the directorate itself had the authority. Clearly the department, the ministry, and the directorate had different interpretations of the situation.

There was also suspicion that MoD was dominating the VLSI program. I believe this was the one dispute that Brian and I had. Brian thought that my technical advisory committees were MoD-dominated. I always disputed that, because I wanted the best independent advice. To provide that advice, I assembled government people from SERC, DTI, and MoD to vet proposals technically. Not surprisingly, Malvern tended to dominate, and Brian felt that Malvern was MoD. This was the one occasion when the boss instructed me to do something about it, so we reduced the MoD involvement. I still believe to this day that the VLSI program was not defense biased. The technology is equally applicable to civil or defense applications.

A familiar criticism of Alvey, and of Alvey VLSI in particular, is that the Programme was putting money into large companies such as GEC and Plessey for things that they would do themselves anyway. Fawcett's answer is simple:

Putting that around the other way, if you're putting money into GEC and Plessey for things they would *not* do anyway, then either Alvey has got something wrong or GEC and Plessey have. Also, if we don't want to support firms like Plessey and GEC in the VLSI program, who do we want to support? They're the ones in that business.

We tried to get Inmos in, but their view was that they didn't want to collaborate; they were well ahead of the opposition. We tried, but unsuccessfully, to get GEC and Inmos and others to collaborate. Inmos could have contributed significantly more than they did, and it would have been a stronger program with them. The Inmos U.S. connection was not a factor in the early debate, though it might have proved a factor if we had progressed.

Fawcett is pleased at the contribution to Alvey VLSI made by academia and small firms. "The university involvement was very strong and, surprisingly, I think the small-firms involvement was very good as well. We managed to get small instrument makers involved with the bigger companies, and that seemed to work pretty well."

David Talbot, Software Engineering
In tackling software engineering, David Talbot had the benefit of the Alvey Committee's well-researched proposals on the subject, plus the earlier SERC background that Rob Witty brought with him when he joined the directorate as Talbot's second in command. The software engineering thrust was not a gigantic leap; it was an incremental development of work already begun. Part of the job at the start was to spread the gospel; the evangelizing duo talked to well over 1,000 people in their first year at Alvey. The response of the software houses was patchy, Talbot reports; they were accustomed to being paid 100 percent, and some of them took longer than others to adjust to the new circumstances.

Talbot was convinced that the software tooling parts of the program would be well supported, since they would be seen as highly exploitable. Two interesting Integrated Project Support Environment (IPSE) projects were mounted. In formal methods, he expected Britain's world-class academic teams in this area to contribute significantly, which they did, with the bonus of good linkages with some of the more adventurous industrial groups. In a sense, he says, these were the (relatively) easy bits; the predictably difficult areas were those of management and process:

"Management and process" is the thing that really screws projects up. It's the important stuff. Tools and techniques are trivial. The reality about making projects work is the way you manage the project. There are disciplines and processes that are employed to make a project more manageable, more predictable, more tractable, and likely to deliver a more sure product. With one or two exceptions, this is a game that's not interesting for the academics. Alvey was able to raise the professional interest in this and to mount the IPSE 2.5 project, which is concerned above all with process issues.

In the software engineering strategy document much was made of what was called the information systems factory. Talbot explains:

> The concept of the information systems factory is an abstraction. It is the notion of contrasting ad hoc software development practices with the notion of a factory with its organization, investment, tools, and management; and the idea that factories are concerned with things such as getting things out on time, to budget, to specification, to quality etc. The factory notion undoubtedly was seen as a threat to a number of people who saw programming as fun and did not enjoy the notion of moving out of their cottages into a bigger and more disciplined environment. The ISF continues to be an articulation of the central concept of software engineering. It remains valid, and it's being pursued.

One of the several attempts that were made in Alvey to interlink different technologies concerned the prospect of applying IKBS techniques to software engineering. Tony Dignan joined the Alvey software engineering team to pursue this topic. Talbot says he knew this would be difficult, and so it proved:

> We were very much concerned with process management issues, and we wanted to see how IKBS could make a contribution there. The problem that we knew we would encounter was that, in part, the IKBS people had grown out of their AI background, and most of the players were academic. Also, their ability to grasp what was important from an industrial point of view in terms of process was going to be pretty limited. So the chances were that they would contribute to very specifically defined areas. However, we knew that their view would be: "There are a whole raft of new things which will take over the world." Our view was: "You haven't seen the world, Sunshine."
> We set up joint workshops and other initiatives. On the whole, however, all it did was to confirm our view. There's a good deal of intelligent tools work in the Alvey Programme, and that's very positive. We thought that's what would happen at the very least, and we have got at least the very least. But a completely new way of handling the total software engineering process with revolutionary approaches and tools—absolutely not.

The absence of an overall Alvey project management and financial control system meant that the various technology directors went their own various ways in this, at least at the start of the Programme. Software engineering took this seriously, and Talbot brought in consultants—not to write a report, as consultants tend to do, but to build a system:

Alvey was a major project, and that requires management staffing and support. What we needed was some infrastructure, and one of the first things that I did was to commission PA to build us a system that would help us manage the program. Management processes are not something that researchers think about, or academics think about, or Whitehall thinks about. But, if you get a handle on that, you get a bigger payoff than introducing fancy new design methods. That's why good project managers are hired guns, and they come hired with pretty high price tags.

With hindsight, Talbot believes he tried to do too much, too quickly.

The industrial take-up of software engineering principles, and of innovation generally, can take a long time—one study of the innovation cycle quoted eighteen years from conception to application. Against that background we were being very simplistic in thinking (a) that it could be done quickly, and (b) that if we solved the various individual problems—for example, scale, attitude to investment, showing people that it pays off—then we had solved the whole thing. The reality is that you need to do many more things, and they're much more subtle.

David Thomas, IKBS
David Thomas was unique among Alvey directors in that he wrote no Alvey IKBS strategy document. He was able to adopt an existing three-volume report that filled the bill. In a sense the IKBS community had jumped the gun and had begun to formulate a national program in the subject without waiting for the Alvey go-ahead. This move arose from the SERC IKBS special program proposal (described in chapter 2), from the IKBS recommendations in the Alvey Report, and from a Research Area Review Meeting (a traditional SERC mechanism) in September 1982 at which the IKBS community—academic, industrial, and governmental—had got together for the first time. After publication of the Alvey Report the SERC and the DoI agreed to fund what was known as the IKBS Architecture Study, chaired by John Taylor, to explore issues and devise an outline for a national IKBS program. Whether or not the Alvey

recommendations were adopted, the aim was to go ahead to prepare for such a program. Taylor enlisted the support of Bill Sharpe of the Rutherford Laboratory to provide technical staff work for what became a substantial program of meetings, workshops, and commissioned papers. (During 1982 Taylor was diverted somewhat from his IKBS efforts by the need to turn his attention, as head of the Command, Control, Communications, and Intelligence Department of the Admiralty Surface Weapons Establishment, to the more urgent question of why Royal Navy ships were being sunk off the Falklands. "So the IKBS work was purely spare-time stuff," says Taylor. "It took quite a lot of time. God bless the Admiralty.")

God bless Taylor and his associates, David Thomas might well have echoed, as he took their final report[12] and declared it to be his Alvey IKBS strategy document. "The important thing was, it was available on Day 1," says Thomas. "I couldn't have done the job without it." The program contained three elements—research and development, awareness and marketing, and infrastructure and support. The R & D program embraced five types of activity: "show me" projects based on existing technology; short-term development; IKBS demonstrator projects; directed research in selected themes; and speculative general research.

One major issue that emerged under the IKBS umbrella, though its importance was much wider, was that of systems architecture (reported in chapter 10). Originally the IKBS budget was about £23 million, says Thomas; eventually, with the inclusion of architectures and some creative accounting (urging the spending of Alvey money on IKBS today rather than on VLSI tomorrow) the total came to about £44 million.

A main criticism of the IKBS program by the evaluators was that it was not industry-led, says Thomas. "When we started, there wasn't really any industry. We could have put together a pseudo-industrial strategy, but there were very few active industrial groups. Part of the job was growing the team, and people didn't like the fact that we were supporting unproven people. They were good people, unproven in IKBS. Our view was that the biggest problem was to grow the manpower. There was no way we could have waited until the teams had proven IKBS experience. One had to have faith and get on and support them."

Chris Barrow, MMI

The subject of the man/machine interface, as adopted by the Alvey Directorate, was not one subject but four: human interface, vision, speech, and displays. At the start there were thus four communities to consult and four advisory committees (plus one overall advisory board) to advise in trying to put together a strategy. "Some people said I had drawn the short straw," says Chris Barrow, "and in a way I had." Later the bulk of the displays work was moved into the LA Division of the DTI. Barrow's aides in Alvey MMI were Dick Chorley and Mike Underwood, later to be joined by Nigel Bevan. There was a speech community focus in the Joint Speech Research Unit led by John Holmes and another focus for human factors around the Loughborough University HUSAT team led by Professor Brian Shackel. But Barrow continued to face two tough obstacles: the diverse technologies and communities involved and a widespread suspicion of the "soft" technology of human factors among his non-MMI colleagues in the directorate.

"There were a lot of people who didn't believe in the human interface work," says Barrow. "It is as much applied psychology as it is anything else. Brian had tremendous difficulty with it. It was very difficult for engineering-trained people to take the area seriously." Another disadvantage for the HI proponents was that the subject lacked the sort of strong community connections that IKBS and software engineering had with the SERC or that VLSI had with the Ministry of Defence. In assessing proposals Barrow believed strongly (as did Thomas in IKBS) in backing small, possibly untried groups. His unwritten policy to get the major companies involved clashed with his HI advisory board's strict assessments of technical merit. After "a big set-to with them" Barrow won his point.

When Barrow returned to Plessey after three years in the Alvey directorate, MMI disappeared as a distinct technology area in the Programme and responsibility for its three constituent elements—human factors, speech, and vision—was distributed between two other Alvey directors. Barrow does not argue that this change was wrong; it was probably a realistic acceptance that the various communities had remained separate. "It would have been difficult for anyone outside to identify with the MMI area," he says:

It was always a bit of a Cinderella.

I always thought that was not right, because the human interface is totally ubiquitous. It is very important to get it right. It was probably the single most important area to support, simply because it wasn't being supported. When I came to Alvey I already had an interest in the subject. In the end I became almost a religious maniac, because you had to be a believer. There wasn't much evidence. We were *avant-garde*, trying to say there was a better way of doing things, and a lot of what we were trying to say is now accepted. The human-factors input to the post-Alvey program shows how far the community has come.

The fact that we had no such input at the start of Alvey was part of the pain but also part of the pleasure. In the human-interface area the community was split, and there was very little belief in it, even within the directorate. Some of them were kind, but most were sceptical. Maybe that didn't do us any harm, because maybe we had to work even harder and think more deeply. But there were occasions when I felt we could have had more support.

Apart from the difficulty of producing a good MMI strategy, another difficulty was that we came up with a ratio of academic to industrial expenditure that was about 1:1, not 1:3 as had been originally envisaged. It was always a bone of contention: why was industry not putting its money in? I was the only Alvey director who had been in R & D in industry, and I had the feeling that not too much was understood by the others about the difficulty of moving into a new field within industry. It is so difficult to persuade people to put money into a new area.

ESPRIT does not attach appropriate importance to HCI. Alvey was the one chance we had, and whether we blew it or not I don't know. Five years is not long enough to change people's minds. You've got to do a lot in five years to strengthen the area so that it doesn't need any further support. But we did strengthen the base.

Derek Barber, Infrastructure and Communications

In a sense, Infrastructure and Communications appeared as a minor-league player in the Alvey Directorate, not because the subject was unimportant but because of a who-does-what confusion, an abysmal shortage of resources, and uncertainty over whether it was about research or providing a service. It was in fact about both, but the distinction was far from clear at the start. Derek Barber had the unenviable job of sorting it out:

It wasn't clear whether communications was regarded as research or providing a service. I always felt slightly a second-class citizen in the directorate. I had only a nominal budget of £5m, because there had been no remit for infrastructure or communications in the original

Alvey Report. Philip Hughes told me the Alvey Committee had assumed that the DoI would deal with that.

So there I was with this £5m budget and feeling second-class because I didn't have any terms of reference laid down by the committee. For nine months I had only a secretary and no further assistance whatsoever. I was amazed at how much the other directors were doing; I didn't realize at the time that David Talbot had all the Rutherford work already going, and David Thomas had a lot of SERC IKBS work going. So I formed a tiny group of friends whose opinion I valued, and they became my steering group; and I commissioned a small study to look at a possible program of research in communications.

Then I started to think about infrastructure, and I wrote a fairly long strategy document. Some years earlier, I had had the problems of setting up an infrastructure for the European Informatics Network project. But in Alvey this infrastructure strategy never got carried through because there wasn't the support; the technology directors, to an extent, were creating their own infrastructures. In a sense, there was a lot of competition which was outside my control. There was also the group at Rutherford Appleton Laboratory, who had already set up various elements of SERC infrastructure. So I had the problem of living with a number of de facto situations.

I tried to argue for a high-bandwidth communications network which would link major Alvey projects, but with a budget of only £5m it was very difficult. The other input was the very successful Universe project. I then gradually put together the idea of a high-speed network to support the expanded Universe teams working on what became the Admiral and Unison communications research projects. I hoped and expected that other big projects would come in on that network as users. My intention was that there would be the high-speed network itself, provided by BT; Admiral would be in effect a ring around that, dealing with network services and how they were managed; and Unison would be around that, providing the user interface to other Alvey projects. I never managed to pull it off—partly, I suppose, because I didn't really get support from the other directors. Looking back on it, that really was a failure.

After nine months I was joined by Arthur Griggs, and his support transformed the situation. We implemented the Xionics electronic office system for the directorate, and this was complemented by the Alvey Mail electronic mail service. Since an early date we had been publishing *Alvey News*, our bimonthly newsletter, which was a great success.

One problem was that the high-speed network cost more than expected because instead of British Telecom seeing it as a project, they wanted to recover the cost. My original budget couldn't have coped. I raised my budget to £11m by putting papers to the board for various items, and eventually I believe I spent £13m plus just because the accounting system wasn't all that good.

I would have liked to mount a significant research program, including work on cordless open networks, for example, and on distributed systems more generally. This would have cost about £30m, but this was not forthcoming—it would have had to come out of other people's budgets. So we had the strategy and the R & D in high-speed networks, but we were unable to pursue my proposed further program of communications research because of shortage of money.

Infrastructure work was going on in parallel at Rutherford and other places. The order for the GEC Series 63 computers and the choice of workstations, for example, were infrastructure decisions with which I was not involved. It would have made much more sense to have pooled all the infrastructure money and then decided how to spend it.

Administration

As the technology directors came aboard and the Alvey Programme got under way, Timothy Walker had a threefold initial task as administration director: first, to help get the team together and in particular to explain the DTI way of life to those coming in from outside; second, to handle the many day-to-day problems that inevitably arose; and third, to work out detailed relationships with the SERC, with the MoD, and with the rest of the DTI. "Basically my job was that of a fixer," he says.

Next question: central or distributed administration?

I felt very strongly that we didn't want a central administration which did everything, with the technology directors just doing the technical work. The danger there is that they then become interested only in the research, that they lose interest in how it's to be managed and what the commercial implications are—and that all the problems that then inevitably arise are blamed on the administration. I was very keen that each director should think about the wider implications of what he was doing. That was bound to result in differences of approach. I didn't see that as wrong. We did try—perhaps not hard enough—to have a central management information system. The difficulty was, until we'd actually been running cooperative projects, we didn't know what we needed.

The contracting mechanism was the next issue—again, central or dispersed? "People have argued that it was a mistake to have three separate contracting organizations," says Walker.

The fact is, the three departments were not prepared to give up their independence. It took long enough for them to operate their own systems in a way that was compatible with a collaborative program. If we had tried to get them to change completely, or delegate to one of them, it would have taken forever. It was fairly immediately apparent that central contracting wouldn't happen. As it was, there were a lot of difficulties, particularly for MoD and SERC in preparing new kinds of contracts to reflect the collaborative aspects of the Programme.

The words "collaboration agreements" will forever be etched on the memories of those who took part in the Alvey Programme. Few topics caused more agony in the early days. Walker took a firm stand on this:

Collaboration agreements were a sensitive issue that seemed to generate more heat than light, largely because most of the people who complained didn't know much about collaboration agreements. They simply wanted to get on with the research. Mine was the strongest voice arguing that that was inappropriate. My worry was that Alvey would just become a research program; I wanted people to focus on how they were going to manage the projects and how they were going to exploit the results.

Collaboration agreements weren't just about intellectual property rights; they were about how the project was going to be managed, how changes would be organized, how you cope with a collaborator withdrawing—issues that cannot be left until the problems arise. Often the commercial and managerial people in the companies and universities didn't get involved until the technical people had taken, as they thought, all the decisions. This led to delays, which were in a sense necessary, as people thought through what the project meant for the commercial strategy of the company or what it meant to the university.

At that time few people had experience of collaboration, so they didn't know what the problems were. Again I argued it was not for the directorate to decide all these things; the collaborators had to work them out for themselves (though on the demonstrators and one or two others we did put effort in from the directorate). It was a learning process that people had to go through. If we hadn't done that, Alvey would have become just a research program, with no link to exploitation.

It was a condition of the grant that the Secretary of State could compulsorily license if the work was not exploited within a certain time. As part of their appraisal of projects directors looked at the route to exploitation. The broad Alvey framework, which I negotiated with industry and the universities and the SERC, gave the basic background and rules; people then had to implement that framework in the light of their projects. We required people to sign that they actually had the right to license all the necessary IPR, as background, to their collaborators. Everyone would say "Yes, no problem," but on many occasions at the last moment they would suddenly discover that they did not have that right.

The other big issue that occupied a lot of Walker's time in the first year was ESPRIT. "When Alvey started, ESPRIT was not yet approved. At least half my time over much of that period was spent in dealing with whether ESPRIT was going to be approved at all and, if so, how large it was going to be. Having done that, we then had to build up our relationship with the ESPRIT team. Also, we had to work out what the relationship should be between a national program and a European one. In addition, I had all the governmental aspects of ESPRIT and Alvey to deal with, plus all the usual budgetary arguments."

Within the directorate Walker's role was that of the professional bureaucrat, not always popular with his colleagues.

It was often my job to say why people couldn't do things or why they had to present things in another way. That is not an attractive role to have to play. I had to be able to do that while still being recognized as trying to be helpful. I realized early on that I had to get Brian's respect and that, once I'd got that, he'd listen to me even if he didn't like what I was saying. I think I did achieve that. But he's an impatient man, and because he is prepared to work twenty-four hours a day he expects other people to do the same. One's junior staff don't always want to do that. I don't think he wanted to know about the detailed problems of administration. On collaboration agreements he really didn't agree with me; he wanted the work to go ahead. So those kinds of tensions were always there; on the other hand Brian attached great importance to the fact that I was a scientist who understood the research process.

With hindsight, Walker says, if he had been doing the job again he would have worked harder to strengthen the links with the SERC:

The links into SERC administration were always rather tenuous and just didn't work well enough. This caused some delays, though these were not always the directorate's fault. More important were problems concerned with the flow of information between DTI and SERC; the implications of what everything meant were not as apparent early on as they might have been. Brian and I took the view that we wanted to get on and commit things quickly, and I think we would have done that anyway. But the process of dealing with that could have been managed better.

I'm not sure about staff members. The directors always wanted more staff, and sometimes I thought that was partly because they weren't managing themselves and their existing staff as best they might—although they were all under very heavy pressure. The problem was that when everything started it was the directors who had to do the work. Later, much of their work could be pushed down to a lower level. We didn't manage the resulting increase in junior staff very well, largely because it's very difficult to predict the timing of that sort of change. It's easy to say with hindsight we could have done it better, knowing what we know now. It's less easy to see that we could have predicted the flow of work.

10
Errors and Additions

As the Programme progressed, its technical content was adjusted—in particular, the subject of systems architectures was added as a topic in its own right. Problems emerged and were tackled. Outside critics sniped at aspects of Alvey, and within the Programme there was friction also as perceived national policy clashed with research needs. Kenneth Owen continues the story as told by those involved.

Architectures are Added

The thinking behind the decision to add advanced computing architectures to the Alvey enabling technologies has been outlined earlier by Brian Oakley. Ronan Sleep and Alan Bagshaw were appointed coordinators for this area, formally responsible for academic and industrial coordination respectively but in practice working together as a team. Bagshaw was later appointed Alvey systems architecture director.

A key event in formulating Alvey architectures strategy was a two-day meeting on fifth-generation architectures held at Warwick University in July 1984. Three reports were presented and discussed: an interim guidelines report by the Alvey Architectures Strategy Group, chaired by Dr Sleep; a report of the working party on an Alvey Compiler Target Language, also chaired by Dr Sleep; and the proceedings of a workshop on architectures for large knowledge bases, led by Professor Simon Lavington of Manchester University. Dr Sleep also contributed a personal paper outlining a proposed plan of action for U.K. work on parallel architectures. An informal after-dinner discussion provided a vigorous example of Alvey industry/academic interaction.

The Alvey architectures strategy document was drafted by Sleep and published in April 1985. At that summer's Alvey Conference Bagshaw outlined the program that had been approved: twelve main projects costing over £28 million in total (including almost £18 million from Alvey funds), plus related projects in the IKBS and MMI areas. The main thrust was indicated by five large projects: Advanced Network Systems Architecture (ANSA), Flagship (a £15 million project forming the central focus of the program, drawing on research at Imperial College and Manchester University); Persistent Information Space Architecture (PISA), Conceptual and Relational Database Server (CARDS); and the "Transputer Rack" parallel simulation engine.

"Systems architecture is one of the main interfaces between what the users require and what the combination of hardware and software can provide," says Bagshaw.

It is very much a combination of hardware facilities and the software to exploit those facilities. The amount of money that could be set aside for an architecture program was limited, and so we had to be very selective. The main focus came down heavily on the exploitation of parallelism.

Even within our limited budget we decided there was no point putting all the money into raw processor power. One of the problems had always been to get the availability of data to match the speed at which you could process it. So one significant wing of our program was concerned with intelligent file store concepts, and the exploitation of parallelism within the accessing of data as well as the processing of data. There were other activities, including mapping user requirements in architecture on to silicon efficiently, but generally we looked at the combination of parallelism in the processing of data and parallelism and other forms of intelligence in the management and the accessing of very large databases and knowledge bases.

The systems architecture club and the various special interest groups (SIGs) that were created proved tremendously effective. As we began to work closely with the club members and the SIGs, certain things emerged as having real importance. One of them is the exploitation of the latent power and capability that these new systems offer. Unless we study this exploitation, it is rather like building a five-speed gearbox and bolting it down in bottom gear.

Alvey in general and Alvey architectures in particular brought the U.K. into the whole area of parallel computing, says Bagshaw, so strengthening enormously the U.K.'s negotiating position in ESPRIT.

Everybody emphasizes that the great achievement of the Alvey Programme was to get this enormous degree of collaboration, not only between academics and industry but between industry and industry, and academics and academics. I believe it has prepared the way for us to be more active in Europe. The fact that we've learned how to collaborate with each other in the U.K. has created a mental attitude which is much more amenable to collaborating within Europe.

That was an obvious advantage. Behind it was the fact that ideas that had been almost dormant within academic faculties found a route through into industrial awareness. Also, during the course of the Programme we came to recognize the importance of some of these other things which merited proper study and proper research in order to preserve the U.K. strength.

Previously an architectures community existed, but it was not recognized as a separate entity; it tended to be submerged as a subsection of IKBS. This had disadvantages, because it meant that architecture's liaison with the other technology areas was that much weaker. Within the directorate the VLSI staff in particular were very positive about architectural aspects of their technology. David Thomas in IKBS and Chris Barrow in MMI also developed close links with us on architecture. The ANSA project was classified as a large demonstrator because of its origin as a workstation-orientated proposal, but technically it rapidly evolved into a systems architecture project.

Large-Scale Demonstrators

The concept of large-scale demonstrators, projects that would act as a focus to bring together various technologies into practical pilot systems, was not included in the program recommended by the Alvey Committee. It had formed part of the earlier SERC/DoI proposals for IT87, and it was readopted by the Alvey Directorate under the guidance of Laurence Clarke. "The demonstrators will serve dual purposes," the DTI stated in announcing the first definition studies in November 1983, "both aimed at improving the exploitation of Alvey research. The most immediate is the setting of market-led goals for the research programs in the individual technologies. These goals will be used to influence the work plans at the start of the Programme. The second purpose will be to demonstrate, in real-life applications, the advances made by the Alvey Programme in all the enabling technologies."

In the event, those goals were not achieved, though the demonstrator projects made significant progress in their own right (not without hitting major problems, as reported later). Four such projects were funded:

• A system to apply new computing technologies to assist legislation-based organizations, and in particular the Department of Health and Social Security, in formulating, interpreting, and applying complex policies and rules. This project was led by ICL.

• A range of mobile information systems, including the provision of route guidance, electricity supply fault diagnosis, and a mobile electronic office (led by Racal Research).

• A "design-to-product" system to demonstrate the automation of the total production process from design through manufacture to field maintenance (led by GEC Electrical Projects).

• A speech-input word processor and workstation (led by Plessey).

Professor Roger Needham describes the anomaly of the large-scale demonstrators as he sees it:

> To my mind, demonstrators were things that didn't take very long in elapsed time and were started toward the end of the Programme, when you could see where the rest of the technologies were going. To my very great surprise bids were sought for large demonstrators very soon. There were two strangenesses about this. Strangeness Number 1 was this: how the hell can you have large demonstration projects which claw on the underlying technologies, if the proposers of them are having to think about what to put in at a time when the strategies are hardly there, let alone when there is any knowledge of how successfully those strategies are being implemented? The other thing was the natural reaction of the industrial characters, at any rate as far as I was concerned, to be pretty damn conservative.

The idea of integrating the various technologies also seems a doubtful one to the Cambridge professor. "I suspect not a lot of integration took place. I think it's a consequence of prudence. I remember being told years ago by my father that if you have something made up of several components, prudent advance consists of trying out improved versions of each component in turn, not together. And that if you insist on taking too many jumps at once you'll go broke, and he was probably right. It's a question of risk."

Laurence Clarke defends his approach to the large-scale demonstrators but admits the view with hindsight is different:

When we started, we said these projects had to demonstrate the results of the technology and had to form demands for the research strategies. Those were the twin aims. That's why they had to be five-year projects, and that's why we had to start early, in order that they could influence the research and in order that they could, at the far end, use the research. To some extent they succeeded in this. But I now believe that a much more realistic picture is that an application or demonstrator project takes the majority of its technology from yesterday. That was not our picture at the beginning. We might have thought that 30 to 50 percent would be new technology, whereas in practice I think now the proportion is probably only 5 to 15 percent. But that 5 percent might be pretty damn crucial to that demonstrator.

The intention was that the demonstrators should actually guide the enabling technology research rather than take whatever results came from the community. I believe that this mechanism failed because individual directors and their advisers had fixed ideas on their strategies and were unwilling to be swayed. None of the demonstrator teams was interested in Flagship, for instance. Their main need was an operating environment which could take existing rapid prototyping and turn it into rigorous, large-scale software on cost-effective parallel systems, rather than a system dedicated to a particular declarative language.

With the benefit of hindsight one could say that in principle Alvey 1 technology should be for the most part exploited in Alvey 2 demonstrators, Alvey 2 technology in Alvey 3 demonstrators, and so on. What we were actually doing in our Alvey 1 demonstrators was twofold: we were demonstrating some of the latest pre-Alvey technology but also feeding in some Alvey technology. In the case of the chips used in the Racal demonstrator, for instance, the viability of that is going to be totally dependent upon Alvey VLSI work; IKBS research fed into the ICL and GEC demonstrators; and clearly the speech-input demonstrator depends on Edinburgh's speech research.

All the large demonstrators had their problems. Union opposition to the DHSS project, for example, obstructed the task of obtaining relevant local-office information. The Racal mobile information demonstrator had to be substantially revised. But the trickiest of all proved to be the speech-input workstation project.

Speech Input, Confused Output

The story of the speech-input workstation, arguably the most ambitious of the Alvey large demonstrators, underlines the sort of problems that can arise in academic/industrial collaboration. It is an extreme case but one that merits a fairly full description, not simply to establish the facts but also to illuminate the wider issues of principle. First, Professor John Laver, head of Edinburgh University's Speech Technology Research Centre and the project coordinator at Edinburgh, describes the course of events:

I believe Brian Oakley acted as a marriage broker in bringing us together with Plessey, who envisaged a continuous speech recognition system as a speech-driven word processor. We assembled a consortium, which eventually consisted of not only Plessey and Edinburgh but also HUSAT at Loughborough and Imperial College, with the possibility of Shell as the user participant. We put in our application in about March 1984. After negotiations with the directorate we were given the go-ahead in principle in the early summer, with a start date timed for 1 October. In September we were still negotiating on the collaboration agreement, but we were fully anticipating that we would start on 1 October. At the university we then launched into recruitment—including advertising on Arpanet in the U.S.A.

By 1 October the necessary decision by the Plessey board had not been taken. The university decided to go ahead, in the belief that Plessey would join us soon. In late November the Plessey board decided not to decide, and that left the university in an extremely exposed position. We had no industrial contract. We had employed by that stage some twelve researchers. We had spent a good deal of our initial tranche of capital equipment money from SERC, and the SERC contract had been dependent on the collaboration agreement being signed.

Brian Oakley came to our rescue. He persuaded SERC to carry on with the contract in the hope that Plessey would soon join us. I settled down to develop a management model and a technical plan which would allow us to work more or less autonomously on the speech recognition technology for the project. Fortunately, a management contract had been signed with Plessey under which I had the services of an administrative manager, Harold Blackburn, at Edinburgh. He was a crucial underpinning of the management effort. So we carried on working and carried on negotiating and finally, in December 1985, Plessey joined the consortium.

We were not privy to the rationale behind the long delay, nor to the motivations of the two main proposers within Plessey, nor to the thinking of the Plessey board. There was always a sense of a slightly hidden agenda, and that emerged rather clearly when, in May 1987, Plessey decided to withdraw. I believe the root problem was that the promoters of the project managed to launch the process of getting agreement in principle but never managed to pin down an ongoing corporate commitment from the Plessey board. They were driven from one solution to another, and finally the solution they came to was that the only way the Plessey board was likely to support the work was to find venture capital to support it as a commercial venture.

In the demonstrator philosophy, of course, that was very premature. It was never envisaged that products would flow from the demonstrator program until perhaps two years after the actual demonstration. So in midstream to impose the requirement that one should be able to convince venture capitalists to invest at that time seemed to me unrealistic. We did cooperate with Plessey in giving demonstrations to venture capitalists and others, but the attempt to persuade venture capitalists to invest was a failure. Therefore, at the end of May 1987, the Plessey board decided not to continue to support the demonstrator.

That is not quite the same thing as deciding to withdraw, because they continued to be members of the consortium. This was seen as important to enable the consortium to survive and to give a transition period in which replacement partners could be sought. Work stopped on 30 May 1987. Plessey disbanded their team but continued to hold all the intellectual property rights.

When Plessey withdrew, Brian Oakley wrote a letter to leading IT companies asking if they were interested in joining a revised consortium and suggesting the possibility of a change of direction if necessary. A number of companies expressed initial interest, but it was GEC Marconi that followed it through. In 1988 Plessey agreed to reassign intellectual property to its originators, in order that it could be further assigned to the new partners. Imperial College's contribution had changed since the early negotiations, when we had been strongly linked to the Flagship project. That gradually fell away as Plessey plans for their parallel implementation changed. But HUSAT had continued to participate throughout. Shell fell away as the user group, and alternative arrangements were planned.

We agreed to the change of direction with GEC Marconi in December 1987. This was broadly to bring in domain constraints, to focus the work much more sharply. It is no longer a speech-driven word processor.

Laver identifies the basic problem as follows: "The Plessey involvement was driven by the aspirations of a small group of people within the company who never succeeded in convincing the main board. When Plessey did withdraw, they withdrew on the grounds that it was not, in their commercial judgment, a viable project at that time". He adds: "It was the time when GEC had entered a takeover bid for Plessey, and my personal interpretation, not based on any inside information, is that the effort to resist the takeover bid made it imperative that Plessey withdraw to their main areas of business, and that did not include speculative ventures such as the speech demonstrator." Thus, he argues, a train of events completely external to the Alvey Programme and to the technical merits of the work that had been done brought about Plessey's withdrawal from the project. "It was never a comment on the technical quality of the work done."

The main lesson that Laver draws from the speech demonstrator is that in any collaborative program it is crucial that each party should satisfy itself that all the other parties are fully committed.

If any party has a suspicion that that is not the case, this really should be ironed out before the project gets going. To let one party start a program without the support of its partners is inviting problems. We have been extremely fortunate that the strong moral and active support of the Alvey Directorate allowed us to survive long enough to bring in the industrial partner eventually. There's no doubt that if the program had had the solid backing of Plessey from the very beginning—at a corporate level—the results would have been faster and stronger than has in the event been possible.

The Plessey view of events, not surprisingly, is rather different. Dr. Keith Warren, Managing Director of Plessey Research and Technology (and a member of the Alvey Committee and of the Alvey Programme Steering Committee) says in essence that the project was overambitious; its cost was such that the company's main board had to review it; and, without wider commercial backing for a follow-up development program, withdrawal was the inevitable business decision. Resolving problems was not helped by the fact that, while the company and university project teams worked well together, Warren and Peter Schwarz, project manager at Plessey, personally found it difficult to work with Laver.

"The collaboration agreement was a very difficult agreement to put together," says Warren.

It was a monster. At that stage we had produced the biggest possible demonstrator you could have, and at the end, because of the size of the project, it became a Plessey main board matter. I had to say the chances of success were no better than 50/50. Eventually we got main board approval, and then it took time to assemble the full team and get them rolling.

Our technical view changed when we received the first speech work from Edinburgh. It was in the right direction and we were happy with it, but it showed that the computing power that was going to be needed on the desk was 200 mips or more. This horrified our technical director, William Gosling, who believed this would not happen for at least five years. Also, we were beginning to recognize that the AI languages were much less developed than we thought, so we began to get cold feet. We'd started nicely, but now we began to discover that all the planning we'd done was probably overoptimistic. We were going to produce something that in computing terms was going to be as big as a house, if we weren't careful. That wasn't the objective of the project, so we were very unhappy with this.

Taking the original objectives and assuming we could solve these problems, we then decided to see if we could get an objective view of the marketplace. Supposing we did produce such a machine, would the market accept it? We got a lot of people interested, but when we invited their participation in a consortium to develop it further they did their homework and concluded that it was too expensive and too long-term. I told my chairman the project still appeared a 50/50 risk, except that we now knew we could not do the computing function in the time available, and the time to a marketable product was debatable but was between five and ten years. As we had tried and failed to put a consortium together, the chairman said he was sorry but he was not going to put that sort of money into that project.

We were talking about what would follow the Alvey project. We weren't putting that money in for nothing; the demonstrator was meant to lead to a real product. Our judgment on the prospects had changed, and that was why the board decision was made. Reluctantly, we decided to withdraw from the project. We told Alvey that we were not prepared to continue the project as it was, but that there was a lot of good technology there which GEC could usefully pickup. They had set themselves a nearer target which would fit the technology well.

On the suggestion that Warren and Schwarz did not have the backing of their main board, Warren says:

You could say that, but you have to recognize that it was an unusual research project in that it had a very long lead time—ten-plus years. Virtually no company in the sort of business that Plessey is in is prepared to put large sums of money into something with such a questionable payback. Because the project was large, it came under query. No public company could make that bet, and the consortium candidates confirmed that the program was about five years too early. I don't think you can blame the board or the Plessey company for this; you have to blame if you like the fact that we in charge of the project proposed a demonstrator that was too ambitious for an industrial participation. We had a number of technologies where we were pushing the frontiers back; that's why we were looking at a ten-year horizon. Any one of them was soluble; put them all together, and the probability was dropping rapidly. I think Peter Schwarz and John Laver got it right on the speech techniques to pursue; they were just five years too early.

156   Views For and Against

Warren sums up: "I guess we let a research project get out of hand." Behind the problems of this particular project lurks one of the generic problems of the large demonstrators: an all-too-easy confusion between research, prototype development, and product development.

The Series 63 Mistake

Behind the text of a DTI press notice of 26 January 1984 on the purchase of computers for the Alvey Programme lay a difficult decision by Brian Oakley. Ahead of it, so to speak, lay a sorry story that remains a sore point with many Alvey researchers. First, the 26 January text:

The Alvey Directorate announced today the purchase of ten GEC series 63 computers and five Systime 8750 computers to support its research program in intelligent knowledge based systems (IKBS) and software engineering. This is a first step toward establishing a coherent national approach to the development of a suitable hardware and software infrastructure for these parts of the Alvey Programme. The machines will be located in research centers throughout the country, linked together through Alvey-net, the network which will connect all the main Alvey research centers.

An associated software development program has been agreed which will involve at least 150 man-years of effort over the next five years. This work will be done by industry (principally by GEC Computers Ltd.) and by universities and government laboratories as part of a collaborative project approved by the Alvey Directorate. Unix has been adopted as an operating system common to all machines. Prolog, Poplog, and Lisp will be made available initially on these machines as languages for IKBS. For software engineering Pascal, Ada, and Modula 2 will be among the languages supported.

It has also been agreed that the DEC-10 machine at Edinburgh Regional Computing Centre, which has been the workhorse for much of the artificial intelligence research so far undertaken in the U.K., will continue in operation, with Alvey Programme funding, for a further six months after its scheduled closure date of October 1984. This will ease the transfer of work to the new infrastructure machines. The cost of procurement of the 15 computers is approaching £2 million and at least an equal amount will be spent on software development over the next four years.

This had been one of Brian Oakley's first major decisions as Alvey Programme Director, and one that he had raised at the first meeting of the Alvey Programme Steering Committee the previous August. The steering committee had approved—though some members were concerned about the cost and duration of the software conversion.

John Taylor, from his close connection with the SERC IKBS initiatives, had (and still has) strong views on this issue. He outlines the background to the purchase, and the resulting impact on the IKBS community:

One part of the background was Rob Witty's work within the SERC in promulgating the so-called common-base policy, concerned with a common base of computing systems infrastructure for SERC-supported research. I understood the need for that but I argued that, if our job in the SERC was to promote and enable world-class research to take place in universities, then we ought to be very clear that world-class researchers needed world-class kit. I held and still hold the belief that you have to be rather clear in your thinking: are we trying to do world-class research or trying to support the British industry? You can't necessarily do both.

In our attempts to relaunch AI research in Britain in a sensible, focused way we realized there was a lot of catching up to be done. We needed to expand the community, we needed to give these people some tools, and the only appropriate tool on the scene at that time was the American DEC VAX. The only machine the U.K. community had of any real power was the aging DEC-10 in Edinburgh. So the last thing I did as chairman of the IEC Computing and Communications Subcommittee was to sign the paper that said there should be an order for a big bunch of VAXes.

The first thing that hit Brian Oakley's desk as he came in as Director of the Alvey Programme was this. I had a meeting with him in Millbank Tower and tried to argue the case for ordering these VAXes. Brian said "How can I possibly come into this job and as my first decision go out and buy a whole lot of American machines?" In the end there was this compromise. The great reservation that we all had was that there wasn't any software around for the Series 63. As it transpired, software was indeed the main problem with the GEC machines. First, it meant that you couldn't move into business because it wasn't there, and secondly it meant that quite a number of university people who should have spent their time doing research spent their time instead writing system software for the GEC Series 63.

Aaron Sloman, Professor of Artificial Intelligence and Cognitive Science at the University of Sussex, also felt strongly about the GEC machines. In September 1984 he wrote[13] to the prime minister about it, and in 1986 he returned to the subject in a long letter[14] to Sir Austin Bide during the after-Alvey program debate. The Alvey purchase of the Series 63 computer, he told Mrs. Thatcher, "is widely acknowledged to have been an unmitigated disaster—malfunctioning hardware and software, unavailable software, inability to deliver the promised performance and a consequent enormous waste of very precious and scarce software talent in the universities and other establishments, fighting to produce or use software on a machine with no future and in many cases deprived of much needed research support which could have been provided on other machines."

In his letter to Sir Austin, Sloman cited the Series 63 episode as an example of mistakes made in Alvey that should be avoided in any successor program. This mistake, he indicated, was "forcing people to use totally unsuitable hardware and software just because it is British, thereby holding up significant research and diverting precious highly skilled manpower from advanced research to low-level software development."

Derek Roberts, Deputy Managing Director of GEC, admits that his company got it wrong with the Series 63, which he describes as ill-conceived. According to his account, the trouble began when a U.S. office-equipment subsidiary of GEC thought it could get into the minicomputer business. At the time that the Alvey Programme was being launched the Series 63 also was being launched, Roberts recalls, and on paper it looked like a good match—it was a British product, a Unix engine, and a very powerful machine.

The fact was that we made a mess of it. In one sense we should never have started it. It was ill conceived. It was conceived in outline by Geoffrey Cross,* when he was running A. B. Dick in the United States. The trouble was his ambition to turn A. B. Dick from an office equipment company into a computer company. He launched what became the 63 Series project. Frankly, it made no sense. There we were, struggling to make coffee machines and printers and so on, and all the resources were going into this powerful minicomputer, because that was his personal ambition.

To try to make a bit more sense out of it, people like Laurence Clarke† and I insisted that GEC Computers should share the project with them. When the bubble burst at A. B. Dick and Geoffrey Cross left, the people running it passed the 63 project completely over to

---

*Geoffrey Cross, ex-Univac, was managing director of ICL from 1972 to 1977.
†This was pre-Alvey. At the Alvey Directorate Laurence Clarke was not involved in the GEC Series 63 decision.

GEC Computers. In terms of the financial resources and the people resources, because the bulk of the work had been done in the United States, this created a problem. I was nervous that GEC Computers wouldn't have the resource to finish the job completely. And that's what happened—a lack of resources to write the software that was needed.

So was it true that Alvey scientists had to spend their time writing Series 63 system software instead of doing research?

Absolutely, and it was quite wrong, because they just wanted a machine that they could plug into the mains and use.

It's easy to be clever after the event, and it's not obvious, even if you could do it all again, that you'd do it any differently. I can remember getting involved at the time in discussions with the GEC Computers people about the fact that, in pushing the 63 Series, they knew they were taking a gamble. But they knew also that, if they did not push it, they would never sell it. If they got it into these key university slots and it went well, sales would grow from there and they would have a success on their hands. If they played it safe and said "Sorry, we're not ready to ship for another year," then the Alvey opportunity window would have been closed for ever.

It's easy to say we got it wrong, and in terms of the effect it had on the Alvey Programme we did get it wrong, because we caused a lot of disturbance. But GEC Computers was in a no-win situation. If they'd played it safe, they'd have had to close the project down anyway. They gambled, it still finished up as a failure, and they screwed people up in the Alvey Programme. Eventually the project was closed down. But it was a fair commercial risk to take. It wasn't totally stupid.

(The Alvey researchers were not the only ones to suffer from the deficiencies of the GEC Series 63. Derek Roberts had ordered the first three machines for GEC laboratories in Wembley, Great Baddow, and Whetstone. "I know it's one of the black marks on my record, because the blokes in the labs didn't want them. They were the last things they wanted. I said: 'You're bloody well having them, and furthermore you're going to use them.' They were using DECs.")

Professor Jim Howe of Edinburgh University, Chairman of the Alvey IKBS Advisory Group, adds another strand to the background to the Series 63 decision:

Infrastructure aspects of the Alvey IKBS program were delegated to the Special Interest Group in Artificial Intelligence (SIGAI), a SERC group which became a joint SERC/DTI operation. I was chairman of SIGAI at the start of the Alvey Programme. One of my tasks previously had been to define a hardware/software infrastructure strategy for AI/IKBS. That strategy was adopted by David Thomas for Alvey but when it came to implementation, we ran into trouble. For good technical reasons, I had specified that the machine should run the Berkeley Unix operating system. At that time the DEC VAX was the only machine that met this specification.

Accordingly, we recommended the purchase of VAX machines for the program. Brian rejected our advice in favor of the purchase of GEC machines which did not offer the required functionality in the operating system, nor had any AI languages been implemented on that machine at that time. Fortunately, the Sun 2 workstation arrived on the scene earlier than predicted. A shift away from multi-user minicomputers to single-user workstations got us out of the mess that we were in.

Within the Alvey Programme, the IKBS community suffered more from the Series 63 mistake than did the software engineers. Rob Witty says the software community already had in place an infrastructure policy that had provided them with VAXes, and they took only two of the ten Series 63s and none of the Systime VAXes. Also, he suggests, the IKBS community made a tactical error in demanding computer power on Day 1 of Alvey. So the software engineering community was better placed not to suffer unduly? "They were better placed because they had a more sensible infrastructure policy; they were better served because they had a wiser management. The IKBS community made a major tactical mistake. I have every sympathy with them."

A brief postscript to the Series 63 decision appeared in the 1988 Alvey Programme Annual Report. David Shorter, IKBS Director, reported: "The GEC machines which had ultimately been developed into a useful facility were closed down in March 1988 and have been disposed of." Those involved knew what Shorter meant by "ultimately."

A U.S. Critic

It was hardly surprising that the Alvey Programme had its critics. Millbank Tower was a prominent building and a convenient metaphorical target, and the directorate that worked there had a high profile also. The critics came from both within and outside the Programme—and indeed from both within Britain and abroad.

Professor Edward Feigenbaum of Stanford University is one of the acknowledged pioneers of artificial intelligence in general and of expert systems in particular. He was an invited speaker at the Tokyo fifth-generation conference in 1981 and has close personal links with Japan. He was co-author of a popular book[15] on the fifth-generation program and was in great and increasingly expensive demand for many of the fifth-generation conferences that sprang up in the early 1980s. As the Alvey Programme got under way, Ed Feigenbaum was one of its critics.

At a fifth-generation conference organized in London in September 1983 by the SPL International software house, Feigenbaum (on videotape) explained his pessimism. To be fair, he prefaced his "case for pessimism" with a brief "case for optimism"—little time had been wasted in launching Alvey, and British scientists had a good track record of innovation in AI. But he remained pessimistic—first, because Britain needed but would never get a concentrated focus for its IT research. British scientists and technologists (unlike the Japanese) were "strikingly self-willed, fiercely independent and intellectually competitive, heterogeneous and multifaceted." Logic dictated that, in a small island nation like Britain, a national center for IT should be possible. But the British scientific character defied such logic.

Britain's pool of talent for fifth-generation work was dispersed across a number of small laboratories. The Alvey Report itself was a compromise and in no way an adequate response to the highly focused Japanese program. Feigenbaum noted Britain's "missing generation" of AI scientists, following the impact of the 1973 Lighthill Report. This generation, people who could have been project leaders and technical managers in Alvey, was in the United States—people like Michael Brady of MIT. "Can this generation be recruited back to Britain? I think not."

Projects of great scope and importance demanded great leaders, Feigenbaum continued: people with technical depth, managerial skills, decisiveness, vision, and charisma. It had been said that big projects required both a chief surgeon and a hospital administrator. Alvey had an able administrator—but where was the chief surgeon? Also important was vision. "I have observed a tension in the U.K. between short-term needs for resources and the longer-term goals and visions that are needed for the next generation." This tension needed to be resolved in favor of the ten-year horizon, as had happened in Japan.

Feigenbaum saved for last what he considered his most serious grounds for pessimism. Building intelligent knowledge-based systems was the most difficult endeavor ever undertaken by computer science and engineering. Success would require not just money but a mobilization of the national technical will, based on the accepted credibility of the underlying science of artificial intelligence. In the U.S. this credibility was widely accepted, not so in the U.K. "It appears that the spirit of the Lighthill Report still lives in the land, poisoning the national technical will.... The doubts implanted by the Lighthill Report persist like an enfeebling virus that stubbornly resists treatment." How would the spirit of Lighthill be finally exorcised from the British mind?

Just before the image of the Stanford professor in his campus office faded from the conference screen in London, Feigenbaum said that he hoped the course of events would show that his case for pessimism was misguided. Five years later, at least partial misguidance was evident: Mike Brady and several other expatriates were back home from the United States, alive and well and pursuing advanced IT research in such places as Oxford, Manchester, and Aberdeen. And the "strikingly self-willed, fiercely independent and intellectually competitive, heterogeneous and multi-faceted" British scientists and technologists had somehow managed to work together quite well.

The MMI Scene

Of all the Alvey technologies, as indicated in the previous chapter, the man/machine interface was the trickiest to organize and to run. Professor Brian Shackel of Loughborough University of Technology had helped Vic Maller in providing MMI support for Colin Haley on the Alvey Committee, and had chaired an SERC panel preparing a report on a possible national MMI program (confined to human factors and the interface) in the period between the Alvey Report and the Alvey Programme go-ahead. Unlike the SERC IKBS plan, which was adopted without change as the Alvey IKBS strategy, the SERC MMI report was not similarly adopted, though it formed an important input to Chris Barrow in writing the overall Alvey MMI strategy document. Shackel gives an inside view of Alvey MMI that illuminates some of the general problems posed by the SERC/Alvey mechanisms:

> I was appointed to the SERC Information Engineering Committee as the Alvey representative for MMI, in the same way that Jim Howe was Alvey representative for IKBS. We were meant to be the academic link between the committee and Alvey in those technologies. It had been decided that the IEC would approve the Alvey strategies, the directorate would go ahead and make decisions, and the committee would then monitor and evaluate on behalf of SERC. The SERC IKBS document came before the committee as the Alvey strategy and was approved, followed by the VLSI and software engineering ones. We had produced our MMI report at the end of September, but Chris Barrow's full fifty-five-page MMI document was not completed until December. Chris had formed his own committees and asked me to chair the MMI advisory board.

The MMI document was considered in January 1984 by the IEC, when it was approved in principle but with a request for a shorter, more focused version that would highlight the main themes. Shackel comments:

> My interpretation of the situation was that the committee had got increasingly unhappy with the successive strategies, as it realized more and more what a proportion of the SERC IT budget was now being decided upon by the Alvey Directorate. Behind the committee's straightforward questions on the MMI document and the desire for a focused executive summary, I believe there was also the feeling that the IEC should remind the directorate that the committee was not going to be overridden and did have power to say no to a strategy and to evaluate against the strategy later on. Whatever the true interpretation, there was a further delay of three months in getting started. Not until April 1984 was there an agreed strategy document.

Shackel maintains that the criticisms that have been made that human factors formed the weak link in Alvey were totally unfair. They neglect the fact of the long delay in starting, he argues, and reflect a widespread misunderstanding of the subject. On the content of the MMI program, he says:

> It was as good as it could be in the circumstances, because Chris Barrow had to make a lot of compromises. The more advisers you get the more problems you've got, and he got two almost completely opposing views on image and vision research and to some extent on speech as well, because there were strongly opposed philosophies.

It was difficult to get the various communities together, because they don't recognize each other. And there are a range of human science disciplines that are relevant, from sociology, organizational psychology, and occupational psychology through to ergonomics. Individuals and groups in these disciplines argue among themselves as strongly as do different groups within, say, speech recognition—but the technology world looks to the human factors side and expects to receive one answer and expects to see one discipline. It is not one discipline.

The way in which the Alvey Directorate and the SERC agreed to handle the Programme raises very important issues, Shackel argues:

I believe there was a lot of resistance on the SERC side, because we all thought that the Alvey Report was going to lead to extra money. It only gradually became clear that, at least in part, it was not extra money and that SERC was told to apportion a certain amount of its budget to Alvey. When that became clear, I sense there was an SERC feeling that "We was robbed," despite the fact that the IEC budget was going up. Also, there was this feeling that "It's our money, but we're not able to make the decisions on it."

The system of monitoring that was approved was that, IEC having approved the strategies, there would be an annual monitoring meeting of the committee at which formal reports from review panels would be discussed. The MMI review panel brought together reports from four subpanels—interface, vision, speech, and image. Those reviews served as a good counterbalance process, helped to ensure academic balance, and made Alvey directors realize that they had to report to us.

The Alvey MMI director set up two procedures. One was an appraisal review committee for each of the four subsectors in MMI, and the second was an overriding review committee, which had succeeded his earlier advisory board. On that committee we looked at the program overall every six months, and I insisted that we review things as thoroughly as did SERC, with full peer review. Among the lessons we learned was that most academics were not good at assessing potential. And, however much time you spend, you still will not be right all the time. But, above all, why did SERC and Alvey have this split administration? Also, we learned that you cannot write proposals against the Alvey criteria—sound research work, with good marketing potential—from one base, whether academic or industrial. You have to be collaborating from the start.

An insight into the overall SERC process is given by Dr. David Worsnip, former Secretary to the Information Engineering Committee:

In agreeing that SERC money could be approved for spending on grants by the Alvey Board, as opposed to an SERC committee or board, or council for that matter, we lost sovereignty on that sum of money. The Alvey Board approved where it should be spent, and we merely turned that approval into the issue of grants.

One of the conditions SERC adopted in its agreement to lose sovereignty on that money was that we would carry out a review of the academic element of the Alvey Programme on an annual basis. In the summer and autumn of each year from 1984 to 1987 we conducted those reviews, to see whether in normal circumstances in a peer-review system the projects would have been funded and whether the appropriate standards were being met. We also looked at rejected applications in the early reviews. In each year the SERC was broadly satisfied that peer-review standards were being maintained. The intention was to protect our interests, quite independent of any Alvey evaluation or monitoring.

Individual Views

A wide-ranging critique of the Alvey Programme was included in the fourteen-page letter[14] written in 1986 by Professor Aaron Sloman to Sir Austin Bide, whose IT86 Committee was preparing plans for an after-Alvey program (see chapter 14). Alvey's greatest contribution had probably been the enormously increased industry/university communication, including some fruitful collaboration, Sloman wrote. But multi-site projects could impose an administrative burden that wasted precious research talent and blurred research goals to fit a common denominator. "I've seen appalling multi-site grant applications containing buried single-site jewels that should have been presented alone." Open reporting at early stages would aid technology transfer and allow genuinely complementary potential collaborators to discover one another. "We need more true marriages and fewer consortia whose only real common objective is easy government money."

Sloman went on to complain of administrative delays. "An Alvey infrastructure contract on which many other projects depended took several months (including at least three on a desk at Swindon) after all the details had been tied up and the funds allocated. Why?" (The reference to Swindon was to SERC headquarters.) Perhaps there should be a contracts ombudsman to investigate delays, he suggested. After addressing other aspects of Alvey, Sloman concluded:

166   *Views For and Against*

Despite what its critics may say, the Alvey Programme has had a tremendously important role in attracting more people into the IT area and causing many in academe and industry to expand their horizons. It has helped to change attitudes to collaboration and communication in industry and in academe. These will be lasting benefits. Nevertheless in many areas there are still far too few people whose knowledge and experience in the Alvey fields reach back more than two or three years, and consequently there is still a serious lag in the U.K. What Alvey has done is vastly increase the number of people with even that much (or little) experience. Because of the lag I do not expect spectacular commercial results to follow quickly. . . . We need to think of the Alvey Programme as having taken the nation to a launching pad. A real launch will require more.

Sloman's complaints about delays were echoed in many projects. The DTI told the House of Commons Committee of Public Accounts in May 1988 that the longest delay between the offer of a grant and the conclusion of a collaboration agreement was twenty-eight months, from February 1985 to July 1987. The main reason for the delay on this project* was disagreement between an industrial and an academic partner over royalties for intellectual property rights.

Delays also occurred in the periods before the offers of grants and after the conclusion of collaboration agreements, for various reasons. One academic who feels strongly about delays caused by Alvey procedures is Professor Michael Duff of University College, London, whose CLIP parallel processing systems are used for the processing of images (the systems use one processing element for each picture element in the image). Duff's SERC funding for CLIP development was interrupted by the launch of the Alvey Programme, which meant that his project now had to conform with Alvey MMI rules and procedures. From the Alvey point of view, Chris Barrow indicated in a letter to Duff in February 1984, the project was an uneasy mixture of basic generic research and applications-oriented research, and it needed stronger industrial involvement. Negotiating the collaboration agreement took a long time (Duff is

---

*A £1.8-million MMI project concerned with algorithms for speech analysis, recognition, and synthesis and originally involving GEC; Plessey; University College, London; Imperial College; and Leeds University. Plessey withdrew in early 1987. The disagreement was between Imperial College and GEC, but the prolonged negotiations did not delay the work, which began on 1 April 1985.

critical of the lack of Alvey help in this phase), and there was then a further delay in issuing the contract. Not until July 1986 was an SERC grant, backdated to April 1986, received.

The UCL professor also criticizes one particular event in the formulation of Alvey MMI strategy: a weekend workshop on image processing and analysis in February 1984. Syndicates were expected to recommend the scale of effort needed (in man-years of research) to achieve significant advances in thirty-nine individual research topics. This he regards as "absolutely cloud-cuckoo land" and "the height of naiveté." The workshop then went on to estimate what the U.K. markets for relevant applications would be, leading to estimates of added value and to the rating of the research topics in terms of relative priorities, as an indication of where the research emphasis should be placed. "They did say that these results should be treated with caution," says Duff. "What they didn't say was that these results should be thrown away, which they should have been."

A fourth example of delay is quoted by Dr. Austin Tate, Director of Edinburgh University's Artificial Intelligence Applications Institute (AIAI). "We got final go-ahead on 23 June 1988 for one project that should have started on 1 April 1986," he says. "We started work in advance of that date—though we revised the formal start date to 1 October 1986 eventually." Despite the delays Tate is positive about the overall Alvey achievement. Generally, he says, Alvey forged a real community of IT workers across the industry/academic line; people now know each other much better, and effective teams are much easier to put together. Specifically, Alvey helped in establishing two major AIAI laboratories at Edinburgh that are pulling through individual Alvey technologies and promoting technology transfer in KBS techniques.

Professor Donald Michie, who moved from Edinburgh to Glasgow in 1984 to set up the Turing Institute, disagreed with Alvey policy on two main issues. First, Michie favored "at least one national center." The second issue, he says, was "the risk we perceived that neither IKBS nor software engineering would or could break important new ground with visible payback unless the newly developed technology of machine learning were centrally incorporated." Michie is a leading advocate of machine learning—the automatic induction of expert-system rules from examples—but on this point and on the national center he and Brian Oakley agreed to disagree. The Turing

Institute, however, was chosen as one of two centers of excellence on which the Alvey IKBS Journeyman training scheme was based (the other was Imperial College, London).

Search for Surgeons

Ed Feigenbaum (as quoted earlier in this chapter) believed strongly that Alvey needed a "chief surgeon" as well as the "hospital administrator," as he regarded Brian Oakley. On another occasion[16] he made the same point by saying that the leader should be "a young and charismatic technology hero." Some Alvey participants would agree but point to practical difficulties in finding an appropriately heroic figure. Professor Roger Needham notes that the original intention was to recruit someone from industry:

What is unclear to me is whether you could have had the chief-surgeon approach because of the great spread of the subject matter. It seems to me that the essence of the chief-surgeon approach is that he is somebody whose judgment you are prepared to trust, and I do not know anybody who is in that position across the complete area of the Alvey Programme. It is certainly arguable that things would have gone better if the level in the Alvey hierarchy at which you had people who were technically reputable was higher. But in some ways, for the top post, one is looking for that which is impossible, because of the relative youthfulness of the field.

11
Breaking the Mold

The lessons and achievements of the Alvey Programme are seen differently by different people, though the achievement of collaboration tops most people's lists. This chapter concentrates on some of the positive results of the Alvey Programme, as reported through the Alvey years and as described to Kenneth Owen by participants and others during the research for this book.

Collaboration

Some are born collaborators, some achieve collaboration, and some have collaboration thrust upon them. Certainly the Alvey Programme was in business to do some thrusting of collaboration on people, and in this it achieved considerable success—though not without considerable pain in some cases. The achievement of collaboration between the various groups involved in Alvey has been quoted so many times that it has become a cliché, but it remains a notable achievement. It had not been done on this scale before, and it might not have worked.

Many people interviewed for this book put successful collaboration at the top of their lists of Alvey achievements. A perceptive academic view of the lessons of Alvey in the light of collaboration is given by Professor John Laver, whose experience with the speech-input demonstrator was outlined in the previous chapter:

I believe the most salient outcome of the Alvey 1 phase has been the change of culture, particularly in universities. It has now become not only possible but respectable academically to strive for ambitious applied goals. There was a time when application was thought not to be universities' business; they were about only fundamental research. That is a radically mistaken view. There is as much intellectual challenge in ambitious applied work as there is in ambitious fundamental work. And this applied work implies collaboration with industry.

Despite the history of the speech demonstrator, I am not saying that my experience of industrial collaboration has been bad. I have certainly learned a great deal from it which has stood me in good stead in negotiating other contracts. One of the successes of the Alvey Programme to me, ironically, has been a very rapid education to the point where I can address issues of that sort in a way which has been of great benefit to my university—greater than if I had had a more gentle introduction to some of the warfare that goes on in these circumstances.

As to collaboration between British universities and industry generally, universities are, perforce, having to learn some very hard lessons rapidly about their financial viability. One of the major ways of doing that is to engage in a different culture in their relationship with industry. Two instruments have encouraged universities to do that. One has been withdrawal of funds by central government for university efforts, but the other consists of the pro-active things such as the Alvey initiative. One should try to quantify what the mutual benefit might be. It is clear that universities in general are not going to get rich from the royalty proceeds of the Alvey Programme. But I do believe that universities are getting rich in a whole variety of other ways. certainly rich in experience and rich in the perception of opportunities which allow them to take their place on a world stage.

Also, there is a richness in terms of a perception of the universities' potential contribution to society through providing trained manpower, where the individual might just as easily work in industry as in academia, and there is no difference of valuation of that person in either event. Previously university products, particularly Ph.D.s, very often seemed to conclude that the only natural objective was continued employment within the university. It is still very early to say that there has been a radical shift of attitude, but there has been a shift in that direction. Apart from anything else, that integrates universities a little more closely in society in general.

Professor Laver sums up in words that many British researchers would echo: "They were exciting days. One had the sense in Alvey 1 that, nationally speaking, a particular range of technology was moving fast, we were shoulder to shoulder with our international peers, and in some cases we were considerably out in the lead. That's a very pleasant and energizing feeling. The next wave is transferring those clever technological ideas into real products."

Professor Eric Ash agrees with many others that the achievement of collaboration has been the biggest success of the Alvey initiative:

I don't think we'll go back to the way things were before. Somehow or other there will continue to be more collaboration between universities and industry and between industry and industry—which is perhaps the most important thing that happened. People are used to collaboration now. My other conclusion from the Alvey experience is that the only way to do a program of this kind is to have a take-it-or-leave-it contract for all participants. Keep the lawyers out of it. One of the problems that Alvey encountered and failed to solve was that of the delays between acceptance of an idea and its implementation. My father was a lawyer, and some of my best friends are lawyers, but on this sort of thing they're in the wrong place. Lawyers are trained to look for snags, and of course they find snags.

In a paper[17] presented in October 1987 Ash commented on the overall academic contribution to Alvey, which originally was intended to amount to £50 million of the £350 million total—about 14 percent:

By now almost all of the contracts have been let, and the picture looks rather different. It turns out that the university spend was in fact £70 million, with the government-funded industrial component reduced to £130 million. So the university share of the total rose to 21 percent. That in fact is not the whole story. Those universities that found themselves involved with a lot of Alvey contracts discovered something that should have been obvious to all of us—that the contracts contained no kind of overhead element. Imperial College eventually had more Alvey contracts than any other university—and we discovered, as did several other universities, that it was an exceedingly reliable path to ruin.

Fortunately the UGC did react to this problem and has now introduced a method of providing some partial compensation for the missing overheads in all research council grants. If we now take the overhead contribution into account, the total percentage of the Alvey action associated with the universities is now seen to be 27 percent. In short, when put to the test, universities turned out to be much more useful than had been anticipated at the outset.

Professor Roger Needham identifies different patterns of collaboration, wonders which Alvey projects fitted which patterns, and waxes caustic over what might be called "designer collaboration" in the tendency to attach the collaboration label rather indiscriminately simply because it is regarded as this year's fashion. In one model of collaboration, says Needham, the key parts of the project are handled separately by different individual partners, and the real collaboration process is concerned with fitting these parts together. In another model, which applied in Project Universe, key areas are worked on by more than one partner, who therefore collaborate on a very close basis. A third model is for each partner to try a different approach to the overall problem; if one approach is successful, all partners share in the proceeds.

"There is another type of collaboration which, as far as I know, has never happened. A company working on subject X, and necessarily pursuing a slightly conservative approach to maximize the chances the project will work, would be associated with a university which pursues a much longer-haired approach to the same subject in parallel. The university would not be relied upon for certain results but would be a contributing partner. I would like to see that."

On collaboration in general Needham says that in pre-Alvey days "university collaboration with industry was not at that time regarded as the shibboleth it has since become." By this he means that today it is difficult for universities to mount large projects without industrial collaboration, for reasons of exploitation, management, and the fact that collaboration is fashionable. He strongly resents being told—by civil servants—that academics cannot set objectives.

The AI Scene

Artificial intelligence, to give IKBS its proper name, was a central plank in the Japanese fifth-generation program and was the initial focus also of the proposed U.K. national program that later emerged in wider terms as the Alvey Programme. Professor Jim Howe, Chairman of the Alvey IKBS Advisory Group, assesses the success of Alvey in this field:

> Given the plight that AI was in prior to the Alvey Programme, I believe that the IKBS program has been successful. Now in both academia and industry there is a strong U.K. AI community. And more and more of my colleagues in other disciplines here at Edinburgh want to apply AI technology, particularly expert-systems technology, in both research and teaching. There is also some evidence of the use of AI technology by the larger companies, but we can't expect real evidence of use until the mid-1990s. In the meantime I suspect we are going to see the closure of a number of small AI spin-off companies. I only hope that this downturn won't be associated with the Programme.

There have been some disappointments. Within IKBS little work was commissioned in the area of intelligent training systems because of the difficulty of attracting commercial participants. Also, I was never happy about vision being split between IKBS and MMI. The resulting program of work was much less effective than it might have been, since the AI and non-AI communities were encouraged to remain separate rather than to come together. Natural language and speech also were split in a similar way in the Alvey Programme, again to the detriment of both communities.

Despite cross-membership of committees, the relationship between the MMI and IKBS program was weak. Again, this was unfortunate since in my view many of the problems that we face in constructing computing systems that are properly symbiotic to users require computational solutions, based on existing or yet to be discovered AI techniques. Finally, the links between Software Engineering and IKBS were quite weak. The notion now is that they can be drawn together in the new program by putting both into Systems Engineering. Indeed, some people envisage that both activities will merge. In one sense they are right. Vendors who want to build AI systems using known methods and proven technology should do so in the kind of disciplined way that we associate with software engineering approaches to software production. Here we are talking about delivery systems. But much academic AI is not concerned with delivery; it is concerned with formulating problems and finding and testing solutions, usually incrementally. Software engineering does not provide an appropriate methodology for much of this kind of AI work.

Another Edinburgh AI scientist, Professor Alan Bundy, approves the general principle, and practice, of the Alvey Uncle research projects: "These have been a wonderful way of permitting basic strategic research under this Programme, that is, funding long-term research with an ultimate application potential and with contact with an industrial researcher who can proffer advice. I also found the Alvey workshops very valuable for keeping in touch with other researchers and meeting new ones, especially industrial ones. My contact with the latter increased enormously during the Programme."

Industrial Views

A comprehensive review of the impact of Alvey from industry's viewpoint was given in July 1987 at that year's Alvey Conference by Mike Watson, Director of Marketing and Technical Strategy for ICL. Prior to Alvey, he stressed, there had been no overall government strategy for exploiting or supporting industrial and academic R & D in information technology. There were over fifty DTI and MoD support schemes, but they fitted in to no overall national framework. At the same time the decision-making processes in academia were largely separated from those of industry—to the detriment of both sides and to the competitiveness of the U.K.

Alvey had managed to establish at least an outline of an overall framework aimed at increasing U.K. competitiveness in world markets, and for the first time the academic effort had become integrated into the national industrial R & D framework. It was inconceivable that an effort of this size sustained over five years would not improve the competitiveness of the U.K. Discussing specific Alvey achievements, Watson noted progress in the soft technologies of software engineering, IKBS, and MMI. Although in many cases the results of Alvey projects had not yet emerged into the marketplace, it was already evident in a number of companies that basic research in these areas was being translated into direct commercial benefit. In VLSI, though some excellent progress had been made in certain areas, the coupling between the semiconductor industry and the equipment industry still had a long way to go.

Industry had also learned a number of important management lessons, notably in collaborative ventures. On the national scale a major lesson was that it was both possible and necessary to establish a broad national framework from which industry and academia could work jointly toward common competitive goals. The national IT ambitions of Japan, the U.S., and France had been sustained jointly by industry, academia, and government over a long period. Alvey was the first tentative step along this road for Britain.

Information technology was no respecter of national or regional boundaries, Watson continued, and U.K. companies were playing for high stakes in markets where international competitors were able to deploy resources and move them around the world on unprecedented scales and timescales. Success demanded access to world-class technology across a very wide spectrum—yet clearly the U.K. could afford to own only a very small percentage of this technology. The challenge for industry, hopefully working closely with government, was to focus on that small part of the technology spectrum in which the U.K. would seek to be preeminent and, by a clear process of bartering, ensure access to the whole spectrum.

Thus Alvey had produced excellent technical results, drawn the industry closer together, and provided valuable management input. If all sectors of industry were to benefit from IT, however, a close coupling was required at all stages in the value-added chain between the technology supplier and the technology user. There was no value in having an advanced U.K. microelectronics resource if to the user this represented poor value for money because of the lack of an integrated design automation process or of an established high-performance interconnect and packaging system.

There was no value to the software systems company if it was offered world-class tooling that did not integrate with an effective management control system for the development of large-scale software systems projects. And there was no value to the eventual user of IT-based systems if these systems did not adequately integrate in a recognized framework or architecture together with a spectrum of tools and resources that could be utilized and deployed to reflect his specific needs. Summarizing the industrial benefits achieved, Watson listed four points:

- At an industry-to-industry level Alvey had acted as a major catalyst to build cooperative relations. This had accelerated the cross-transfer of up-to-date technology in engineering processes and practices.
- The links with academia had significantly accelerated both the transfer of new technology into industry and the closer coupling between industry and academia, building up shared views of critical technology issues.
- The provision of financing had allowed earlier starts and take-up of highly innovative projects by industry, helping to offset the inherent risk.
- The Programme had led to a greater consensus between industry, government, and academia on the need for an overall industrial framework to increase our competitiveness.

Nigel Horne of STC adds another industrial view of Alvey:

The Number 1, really powerful good thing was the achievement of the academic/industry links. In many companies, however, that perhaps has not been pulled through adequately. The fact that a certain percentage of Alvey projects may have failed is inevitable. If that were not the case, the Programme wouldn't have been worthwhile. My Number 2 good thing is that we've done some things that we would not otherwise have done. With collaboration you can see the logic for things that individually you wouldn't do.

The main problem in collaboration was of course that of IPR. I think it was very unfortunate that the terms of contract were not universally the same, as they are in ESPRIT, because that makes the playing field uneven and creates suspicion among the partners. That's a lesson learned. I believe that trying to catch up on technology—in the semiconductor area, for example—is a mistake. Trying organically to research it and rush to the finish line, when the other guy is ahead and around the corner already, is very difficult. I criticize ESPRIT for the same reason.

The quality of the collaboration, says Derek Roberts of GEC, was probably better than one expected it to be. "To be honest, there was in many people's minds at the outset a feeling that the collaboration was going to be a sham, that it was collaboration on paper as a justification for getting the money—to get the money and run and then do our own thing. If one could have done a lie-detector job on most people, I think that there was an element of that. In the event, that wasn't the case, at least not in VLSI."

The people involved came to realize that their partners were just as competent and just as honest as themselves, says Roberts:

You give a bit and you get a bit, and you give a bit more and you get a bit more, and before you know where you are, there's no point in not talking totally openly. In one or two of these programs it was necessary for people like myself to sit in at an early stage with our people and really spell it out—read the riot act and say "Never mind what you think it is, company policy is to be collaborative and to be open, and no nonsense." It was necessary to insist, so that people really got the message that we were committed to the open flow of information. And the other companies did the same. It took most people by surprise. In the long term I believe the creation of that atmosphere, not just among companies but among the companies and universities, may prove to be the more longstanding benefit of Alvey, rather than the technology advances. This is much more pervasive.

VLSI collaboration between GEC and Plessey on CMOS and between GEC and RSRE on silicon on sapphire was surprisingly good, says Roberts. Ironically, GEC failed to exploit the Plessey collaboration because of a business decision to withdraw from the field:

You could argue that the present Plessey CMOS capability has been added to by GEC spending its money and putting its people into collaboration. I wouldn't want to make a big issue of it, but I believe the Plessey people, if they were honest—and I've no reason to think that they're not—would admit that there are certain parts of what they see as their technology today which stem from work done at GEC Wembley. In principle it could have worked the other way, with Plessey work flowing into GEC. Had we not changed our commercial policy, had we gone ahead as we'd originally envisaged, then our business would have benefited dramatically from the Plessey input. The fact that Plessey has exploited the joint work and GEC hasn't is our fault. It wasn't the fault of Alvey.

Here Roberts touches on a basic dilemma for many companies participating in Alvey projects—the conflict between a firm's commercial judgment to withdraw and the national interest of continuing projects through to completion. Certainly a number of firms' withdrawals from projects caused headaches for the Alvey Directorate. The problem is one of timing, Roberts says, going back to the delay between the publication of the Alvey Committee's recommendations and the start of the programme, and he is unrepentant about his company's decisions to rock the Alvey boat on a number of occasions:

If two years have elapsed before you begin to implement an agreed program, it's almost a miracle if that same program is still opportune or stands as high in the priority table of where you want to put resources. I would argue that for companies to withdraw from Alvey projects is a healthy feature of the Alvey Programme. There are examples from the past when joint technology support programs have failed because participants were afraid to make needed changes in projects that continued for five years. In company-funded programs you don't just let them continue for five years, you tune them in the light of opportunities and changes in the competition and problems as they arise, and if necessary you cancel them.

When Alvey started, I made it clear within GEC that even though the projects were funded on a 50/50 basis we were going to exercise the same quality of management—good, bad, or indifferent—as if they were 100 percent ours. And that we were not going to continue to do things just because the Programme was still funding them, if they were things we no longer believed in. So I feel more comfortable about the fact that there were a few cancellations, rather than everything that had been planned simply steaming ahead.

Defense Interests

Ministry of Defence interests in the Alvey Programme were spelled out at the 1986 Alvey Conference by Sir Colin Fielding, MoD Controller of Research. Progress in electronics would be the pace-setter for virtually all future defense equipment developments, he said, and information technology would be the major component. The ministry's involvement in Alvey reflected its desire to exploit the fruits of Alvey research in specific defense applications by supporting a common technology base within industry. The greater part of the MoD's financial contribution to Alvey went into the VLSI area; here the ministry's interest was directed at high performance in terms of speed and processing power. There was no prospect for a special silicon technology process simply to meet military needs; the cost would be too high. Despite special needs such as nuclear hardness, the MoD must derive its VLSI circuits from a commercially viable product line meeting civil needs. The Alvey whole-process projects were central to defense needs, and it was recognized that much work would be needed to engineer them for full production.

This was a post-Alvey activity crucial for the exploitation of what had already been achieved. Obviously microcircuit technology did not begin with Alvey, it certainly must not end with Alvey, and a consolidation of options and the manner in which they were brought to full exploitation was desirable. The MoD had its own program of applications demonstrators to exploit the emerging VLSI technologies.

Defense interests were involved not only in VLSI but in all the Alvey technologies, and all of them would continue to be vital. Though much had been achieved, the MoD had to procure its technologies and equipment in a highly competitive marketplace, particularly within Europe. The U.K. must keep pace in these disciplines and capitalize quickly on the work that had already been done. It was important to preserve the momentum that had been established.

New Mechanisms

The idea of a new central institute that, ICOT-like, would mastermind the entire Alvey Programme was one that stood little chance of acceptance in the United Kingdom, for a variety of reasons. It was not surprising that the concept, though discussed at the start, was not pursued. In general, for pragmatic reasons, the Alvey Programme consisted of research projects that were distributed across existing academic and industrial laboratories. But there were exceptions to that general rule, and these included two significant new specialized research centers—both of which happened to be set up in Cambridge. One was Alvey's Advanced Networked Systems Architecture (ANSA) project, and the other was a research-club approach to the natural language area of IKBS. A third key innovation involved a communal approach to expert-systems development.

The £4 million ANSA project was unique in Alvey in that it was conducted by a joint team at a single, dedicated site independent of the collaborators. Their broad aim was to develop an all-encompassing architecture for networked systems. The project, which involved a group of nine collaborating firms, developed as a redefined version of the Advanced Workstation and System Architecture Project (AWSAP), the subject of an initial definition study in 1984. ANSA dropped the workstation emphasis to concentrate on the system architecture. A chief architect and a project director were recruited, and a small team of professionals (some seconded from the participating firms and some directly recruited) started work in Cambridge.

The decision by the Alvey Directorate to run the ANSA project in this way was a courageous one, says Bill Talbot, Project Director since 1986, and this model of collaboration has proved successful. Discussing the project in *Alvey News* in December 1987 Dr. Andrew Herbert, Chief Architect, enthused on the benefits of single-site working. "The most valuable thing is the amount of informal discussion," he said. "The difficulty with a distributed project is that the opportunity for close collaboration is fairly rare." He added: "I don't see how I could have done without the central structure. All good ideas come out of informal conversations. You need to build some sort of community spirit."

Bill Talbot argues that the ANSA model should be used more extensively for collaborative research—with or without government support and not just in IT but also in other areas of technology. Indeed, he has developed the concept further in proposing a new mechanism to bridge the gap (as Alvey and

ESPRIT projects are doing) between research and industrial exploitation. This new mechanism would be based on what Talbot calls "theme institutes," organizations that would provide a critical mass for applied research in areas of technology by linking the work of universities (and of a central ANSA-like research group) to the requirements of industry. The institutes would identify research gaps, act as a clearing house and promote standards, and ideally would be set up on a European basis. "This could be one subject in the lessons to be drawn from the Alvey experience," he says.

The second Cambridge unit embraces a similar club approach, in which a group of companies collaborate to share the cost of a defined research project. In this case the research is aimed at developing a set of natural-language processing tools, and in particular what is known as a core-language engine. The main difference compared with ANSA is that the laboratory is not an Alvey unit but is operated by SRI International (formerly Stanford Research Institute) of Menlo Park, California. The £1.2 million, three-year Alvey project served as the launch project for the new SRI Cambridge laboratory.

The scheme grew out of an earlier link between SRI and the Computer Laboratory of the University of Cambridge and was seen by David Thomas, Alvey IKBS Director, as an effective way to transfer natural-language technology from SRI to U.K. industry. After delays in assembling the industrial consortium the laboratory began work in the summer of 1986. The "U.K." industry represented in the eight founder members of the consortium included British-based elements of Hewlett-Packard (U.S.), Olivetti (Italy), Philips (the Netherlands), and SRI itself (U.S.), plus Shell Research (Anglo-Dutch) and the indigenous British Aerospace, British Telecom, and ICL.

As with ANSA there was a clear benefit to the participating companies in that they were gaining access to research worth £1.2 million for a subscription of only £75,000 each (since Alvey was contributing half of the total). But Robert Worden of Logica, a member of the Alvey IKBS Advisory Committee, criticizes the project for not involving the U.K. IT industry (except for ICL) and for subsidizing a U.S. competitor in setting up in Britain. "This was the one thing we disagreed with Brian about at the time," he says.

Alvey was spending a lot of its money in helping one of our competitors to set up essentially an outpost in the U.K., bidding for business. We felt that if you're bringing SRI over to transfer technology, it should go into the IT industry as well; we wanted to be part of the contractor team and learning, and then the technology would have been in the British IT industry and could then have been spread across various industry sectors. It seems to me that having a direct transfer from SRI into Shell and so on is not actually going to spread it around so much. We felt it wasn't the best use of Alvey money.

One Alvey mechanism that undoubtedly did succeed in transferring new technology widely across various sectors of British industry was the group of expert-system community clubs. These clubs represented the applications end of the Alvey IKBS program; they were short-term projects intended to produce working expert systems for various sectors of industry and commerce. They had nothing to do with research; as part of David Thomas's IKBS awareness campaign (and originally designated "show-me" projects) they aimed to put available technology into practice.

Typically a club would have about twenty member firms, plus one or more academic members. Each industrial member paid a subscription of up to £10,000; the total sum was matched by an equal amount from Alvey, and so the club would be able to commission a contractor to develop an expert system worth up to £400,000. Nine such clubs were formed, covering the areas of insurance, planning, process control, finance, the water industry, quantity surveying, econometric modeling, transport and travel, and data processing. As this list indicates, some of the clubs served individual industry sectors, while others represented a profession or function across different sectors.

The clubs served different communities and chose a variety of objectives and approaches. Members all gained experience, many ended up with working systems that they could use in their businesses, and some clubs produced commercial products that could be marketed. The success of this particular experiment was clear: a number of the Alvey clubs decided to continue with their own follow-up projects, and the Department of Trade and Industry picked up the idea and launched a number of similar clubs aimed more directly at marketable products. The Alvey style of expert-system clubs had taken root, and AI awareness in British industry had grown significantly.

Breaking the Mold

Sir Robert Telford has no doubt that Alvey broke the mold of the reactive-type programs to which the U.K. government was accustomed. The Alvey strategies were not imposed from the top by government but evolved through a process of consultation with the whole community. Then the reactive process got under way with calls for proposals, plus further action by the directorate to fill gaps and divert duplications. That was a new style and itself a great achievement, he says. Against that framework the Alvey achievements—and in particular the achievement of collaboration—outstripped expectations. "You met academics who were bubbling over, working together with industrial people and finding great satisfaction out of it. It gave me a most extraordinary feeling ."

Sir Robert sums up: "The Alvey Programme was the most significant innovation in the management of national, large-scale research that we've had in the United Kingdom since the Second World War. In wartime you had to harness the research. Alvey put three government departments together. It put universities together. It had this top-down plus bottom-up approach. Many of these follow-on developments are stealing Alvey's clothes, so to speak, apparently without realizing it, certainly without giving credit."

As described earlier, a number of pre-Alvey collaborative initiatives had been mounted by the Science and Engineering Research Council. There was thus a double challenge in the Alvey Programme, says Tony Egginton, Engineering Director of SERC during the Alvey years:

The challenge that Alvey represented was that it was a culmination of the process of attempting to take this active role between universities, SERC, and industry to a much larger scale and at the same time to create a collaborative enterprise between three agencies of government. Nothing like this had ever been done before. The chance for both customers (MoD, DTI, and the SERC) and contractors (universities and companies) to come together and agree objectives was a quite remarkable thing.

In its train, of course, it threw up a lot of issues. Financial management was one of them: how to keep ourselves in step—which we didn't. I have to say that sometimes Brian was the cause of our problems. He had the job as director to run the Programme as a whole;

he had imperatives that he perceived as necessary to help to get the Programme going and that involved him, I have to say, in overcommitting SERC money. Overall, he did bloody well to achieve the harmonization of our policies and our monetary interests. Nevertheless, that was one of the problems.

I believe too little regard was taken at times of the Information Engineering Committee view on the strategies that were adopted. It's easy for me to say that; Brian had to square the circle with the demands from n different directions. But the view that came out of IEC at times was critical of the way that the Alvey Programme proceeded, and this view was not totally heeded. Eric Ash was the chairman of IEC, and he was the representative of the SERC on the steering committee. Looking back, it probably would have been sensible if I had been a member of that steering committee too. These are minor flaws by comparison with the overall achievement of Alvey, which was quite remarkable.

The Alvey Programme has been criticized (see chapter 12) for not achieving more of its technical goals and for a lack of exploitation of the Alvey research. Tony Egginton points out the fallacy here:

There is a terrible tendency for a lot of people to have overoptimistic ambitions of the timescale needed to move from what is essentially a basic piece of science through a precompetitive research program into a competitive R & D activity and into exploitation. Even in a fast-moving field like IT it is hard to encompass that timescale in less than eight to ten years, and we are still only halfway along that timescale. For people to think that we would have done it faster is just cloud-cuckoo land. Criticism of a lack of exploitation at this stage is completely wrong. The key achievement was the achievement of collaboration between such an enormous group of academic and industrial people who had never worked in that way before.

On the technical content of the Alvey Programme, the balance between pure and applied research might have swung too far toward the applied end. The trick is somehow to construct a program in which you have routes leading to actual exploitation while not cutting off the supply of new ideas. It may be that we oscillated slightly too far toward the more applied end in creating the Programme, but overall it was such a remarkable achievement that I think we should be prepared to accept that. If we had been working on the originally foreseen ten-year timescale, that might not have been a difficulty. But the government's rigid five-year view caused serious problems as the SERC became so short of money.

Expats Return

In IT in general and in artificial intelligence in particular a number of leading British scientists were working in the United States[18] at the start of the Alvey Programme. During the course of the Programme a number of these expatriates returned to work in Britain. Among these were Michael Brady, Derek Sleeman, David Warren, Alec Broers, and Graham Nudd. Was the existence of the Alvey Programme a factor in their decision to return at that time? "Absolutely," says Brady, formerly Associate Director of the Artificial Intelligence Laboratory at Massachusetts Institute of Technology (MIT), who returned in 1985 to take up the new post of professor of information engineering at the University of Oxford. "The reason I came back was the transformation of the IT scene in the U.K., and Alvey was a major contributor to that change of scene."

"Yes," says Sleeman, who returned in 1986 from Stanford to be professor of computing science at the University of Aberdeen. "The existence of Alvey did influence my decision to return. I saw it as a sign that IT was being viewed by the government as an important component in their strategy for the country's long-term growth." He adds: "Had I waited a year, I may well have made a different decision."

"Yes," says Broers, a VLSI expert who returned in 1984 after twenty years with IBM in the U.S.A. to be professor of electrical engineering at the University of Cambridge (despite an eighty-percent cut in salary). "There was a very positive climate—a sort of renaissance in component development in Britain. That and Alvey made it look very positive." He echoes Sleeman's postscript: "Unfortunately a lot of it has just faded away at this stage."

"Alvey was a contributing factor," says Nudd, another VLSI expert who returned in 1984 from Hughes Aircraft to be Lucas Professor of Electronics at the University of Warwick. "Following my return Alvey projects helped me to get started rapidly, and I was welcomed into the club very positively. I received a number of offers to return to the U.S.; had it not been for Alvey, I would probably have accepted one of them."

"No," says Warren, formerly with SRI International and Quintus Computer Systems and an international authority on logic programming, "though the Alvey Programme helped to stimulate the work I was interested in. I had intended to spend four to five years in the U.S. and then return, for family reasons." Warren returned in 1985 to take up the new post of professor of computational logic at the University of Manchester and has since moved to Bristol.

Baker's Baby

The Alvey Programme was regarded at the time very much as Kenneth Baker's baby. Others in Parliament and in Whitehall suggest that this is an overstatement (though they admit that he might have been the consultant gynecologist at the birth). Baker takes the paternal view—as well he might, for a program that he described in the House of Commons on 4 July 1984 as "by far the most important research and development program undertaken in Britain since the war—probably since the development of the jet engine." In 1988 he says:

I accept paternity for Alvey. I was an enthusiast for IT and for the Alvey Programme. I was keen to get partnerships between industry and universities, but I wouldn't agree to the 90 percent support figure proposed by the Alvey Committee; I wanted much more commitment from industry. In the event we got good support from industry. I decided we should have a small team and appointed Brian Oakley as Director. Industrialists were considered for that post, but all were too engagé with their respective companies. I was very keen to bring the Alvey precompetitive research to the market, and I told Brian Oakley this.
  If we had not carried out the Alvey Programme we would have been in a much worse position that we now are. Certainly the cooperation has been valuable, and I hope that valuable technical results are coming through for the participants. I saw Alvey not as a fifth-generation program in itself but as moving toward a fifth-generation program. Various countries would be tackling this route."

The Second Wave

The original Alvey directors had had the pain and the pleasure of getting the Programme moving, but it was not expected that they would stay with the Programme for its five-year lifetime. Tim Walker moved on in April 1985 to head the DTI's Policy and Planning Unit, to be succeeded as administration director by Roger Hird from the Department's Mechanical and Electrical Engineering Division. Derek Barber returned to Logica in

October 1985 and was succeeded by Keith Bartlett from the IT Standards Unit of the DTI. Bill Fawcett left to move into industry in February 1986, to be succeeded on VLSI by Robert Morland of PA Technology.

At the 1986 Alvey Conference on the Sussex University campus at Falmer, near Brighton, Brian Oakley made a succession of brief farewell/welcome speeches following technology directors' reviews. Farewell David Talbot, returning to ICL; welcome to his deputy, Rob Witty. Farewell Chris Barrow, returning to Plessey. Farewell David Thomas, moving to Imperial College; welcome aboard David Shorter from Systems Designers. No new MMI director followed Barrow, whose technologies were divided between Laurence Clarke (human interface), Keith Bartlett (image and speech), and Robert Morland (MMI displays). In November 1986 David Morgan was seconded to the directorate from Plessey, taking over as software engineering director from Rob Witty the following month.

In consolidating and advancing their predecessors' work the second wave of directors had more of the pain and less of the pleasure. In general their appointments marked a transition in the Programme from a rapid growth phase to a relatively steady state, and from negotiating contracts to monitoring them. Projects continued across the board, but most of the ensuing action was in VLSI and software engineering.

Rob Morland brought energy to his VLSI work and Filofax to Alvey board meetings. He committed the remaining funds to an extension program, including a major new CAD project. Three industrial changes affected his program: the withdrawal from a number of Alvey projects by British Telecom, following that organization's privatization; the withdrawal from a number of projects by GEC, following a reappraisal by the company of its research activities; and the acquisition by Plessey of the semiconductor interests of Ferranti. The British Telecom withdrawal was reasonably well managed (in VLSI if not in other areas), but that of GEC caused difficulties. "I think the decisions that were taken in GEC were taken without really any consideration of such things as collaborative programs," says Morland. "Luckily, a lot of the technology had already been developed and transferred to the partners who were going to exploit." As for the Plessey acquisition of the Ferranti interests, Morland reported in the 1988 Alvey Programme annual report that this was welcomed as a major step toward the strengthening of the U.K. semiconductor industry but had inevitably caused difficulties in a number of projects.

Morland produced a brochure[19] in 1987 that described Alvey VLSI and CAD technologies ripe for exploitation. He comments:

We were accused of not having an ambitious enough VLSI strategy. The result of that is that we've almost entirely achieved our goals. But research is not the problem in the U.K.; the issue is exploitation. In the VLSI area we've got a research program which could support a semiconductor industry five to ten times the present size of the industry. There are two options: either you chop down the research program, which would be a disaster; or you grow the industry. At the moment we have no lever to allow us to grow that industry. The incentive to invest is just not there.

In software engineering David Morgan inherited what he describes as the best organized part of the directorate; he kept this organization running, tightened up on internal reporting, and initiated a thrust toward exploitation. A special study related projects to the overall scene and confirmed that the technology was percolating out quite widely. "The three-year exploitation limit can turn out to be a barrier to exploitation," says Morgan, "because if the industrial partners who hold the IPR do not wish to exploit—for good commercial reasons—then the exploitation process can be held up." He does not agree with suggestions that the period should be reduced to one year, but suggests a sliding system under which IPRs would be renewed on evidence that exploitation was being taken seriously.

Alvey software engineering developed a good relationship with the IT Division of the DTI, which was running a number of software engineering awareness initiatives. From his Alvey experience Morgan notes that the Programme has changed firms' and universities' approaches to collaborative research significantly and, whatever the effect of Alvey on firms' total R & D spending, has had a crucial impact in the choice of R & D areas to pursue. More is being spent on Alvey technology areas and in IT generally. (In 1988 Morgan was given scope to pursue his personal commitment to the closer integration of individual technologies as part of the DTI reorganization described in chapter 15.)

In IKBS David Shorter's initial problem was to catch up on what was happening, not only in the research and awareness projects but also in a number of looser Alvey initiatives involving the community. "One of the frustrations," he says, "was that David (Thomas) had spent nearly all the money." His predecessor had not concentrated overly on the monitoring of projects, Shorter judged, so "we toughened up our monitoring." Progress on the IKBS demonstrators was mixed, and the reasons for success or failure were not always clear. Certainly the Alvey expert-systems community clubs, as reported earlier in this chapter, were recognized as a major success. These clubs were among the responsibilities of Shorter's deputy, Adrian Wheldon, at the directorate. As in VLSI some IKBS projects were hit by policy changes in companies, and some positive lessons were learned about project management.

In administration, Roger Hird suggested in his first contribution to *Alvey News,* in December 1985, that the fact that he had little to say about IPR and collaboration agreements was "perhaps a hopeful sign that past problems are in sight of solution." He went on to brief readers about ESPRIT, Eureka, an Alvey industrial mission to Japan the previous May, and a return visit by an ICOT team in June. In the April 1987 issue of *Alvey News* he commented: "One day someone will write an interesting account of how and why it comes to be that well over halfway into the Programme the Alvey Directorate still does not have a comprehensive central management information system for the Programme." Such a system was forthcoming, Hird stated, but would require that monitoring officers ensure that the specified project spending forecasts were provided. The directorate had been pretty relaxed about this in the past, but, Hird warned, "we are going to get very tough indeed and will heartlessly bounce back any claims that come to us without the necessary information."

One year later, after three years with Alvey, Hird contributed his "Parting thoughts" to *Alvey News.* They had been three fulfilling and exciting years, he said—if sometimes exhausting and frustrating. He had one main regret: the feeling that many people involved in Alvey projects still did not fully realize the importance of collaboration or the significance of the Programme. In bringing together a large proportion of the U.K.'s advanced IT research into a program of collaborative projects, Alvey had attempted to create a community of researchers able to give the U.K. the technological basis it needed to compete in the demanding international market of the 1990s. It was thus worrying, from time to time, to come across industrial research teams or university professors who regarded Alvey simply as a means of funding their own pet projects.

In infrastructure and communications, Keith Bartlett found that the arguments over research versus services that had troubled Derek Barber in the early days of the Programme were no longer a major issue. The two communications research projects, Admiral and Unison, were in business and were using the Alvey high-speed network, but the bulk of the work was to continue the infrastructure support services. "I didn't launch any new research projects at all," says Bartlett, "and I didn't launch any new services either." Indeed, he cut back the research elements that had survived in the high-speed network, so that the network was purely a piece of infrastructure for the two research projects. After inheriting responsibility for the speech and vision parts of the MMI program Bartlett delegated the running of these elements to Nigel Kay of the National Engineering Laboratory (NEL). Bartlett became involved in the Alvey ANSA architecture project and in 1986 began an association with the Eureka COSINE project—to harmonize the data networking environments for research across Europe—that was to occupy him to an even greater extent after the post-Alvey DTI reorganization of 1988.

Bartlett's responsibilities included the organization of the Alvey Conferences, and he rightly points to the Manchester event of 1987 as being particularly significant—not for the conference itself but for the associated exhibition of Alvey projects. There had been small exhibitions associated with the two previous conferences, but 1987 was the year in which it was possible to mount a full-scale, comprehensive presentation of Alvey achievements. This coincided with the publication of an achievements brochure[20] which reviewed progress in the various Alvey technologies and summarized projects that had reached or were nearing fruition. This marked the start of a determined effort to make known the exploitation possibilities of Alvey projects, both throughout the Alvey community and beyond.

12
The Evaluators

The Alvey Programme came under close scrutiny from outside bodies, including a continuing and official scrutiny paid for by the Alvey Directorate. This "realtime evaluation" was intended as an aid to the directorate in its management of the Programme. Another outside body, the National Audit Office, decided to audit the administration of the directorate without waiting for an invitation. Many individuals, both inside and outside the Programme, held strong views on the Programme—and on the evaluators, as reported in this chapter by Kenneth Owen.

Evaluation—Official

The decision to appoint teams at the Science Policy Research Unit (SPRU) at Sussex University; the Programme of Policy Research in Engineering, Science, and Technology (PREST) at Manchester University; and the Centre for Business Strategy (CBS) at London Business School as official Alvey evaluators has been described in earlier chapters by Brian Oakley. In broad terms PREST was assessing the structure and organization of the Programme; SPRU was concerned with the effectiveness of Alvey in the context of the U.K. economy; and CBS was examining the U.K. software industry. The CBS role was later shared with Templeton College, Oxford, until this part of the evaluation was completed in late 1986.

The evaluators produced a stream of reports to the directorate, and reported to the Alvey community at large at the annual conferences of 1985, 1986, 1987, and 1988. At the 1985 event they spoke in one of the formal conference sessions, at which their academic background was evident; at the later conferences they led informal discussions at which their growing familiarity with the subject was welcomed.

One-day seminars on the Alvey evaluation were held by the directorate in September 1986 (chaired by Oscar Roith, Chief Engineer and Scientist at the DTI) and October 1987 (chaired by John Fairclough, the government's Chief Scientific Adviser). At the latter event the draft interim report on the evaluation by SPRU and PREST was circulated and discussed; it attracted criticism from Fairclough (who amplifies his views later in this chapter) and from other speakers. Vivian Brown, head of the Cabinet Office Assessment Office, suggested that the evaluation had been too narrow; it had clearly been useful to the directorate, but he doubted its value to the decision makers who had to assess Alvey in relation to other R & D needs.

Three broad issues were addressed in the interim report:[21] the implementation of the Programme, its progress and impact, and its appropriateness. It appeared that Alvey had doubled the U.K. activity in the IT enabling technologies, the evaluators said, as the Alvey Report had recommended. The most important impact on the research community had been the development of a collaborative culture. The Alvey choice of technologies was in line with world thinking. Discussing the Alvey emphasis on precompetitive research, the evaluators noted that the case for such research rested on the need to strengthen the IT community through academic/industrial links, to facilitate collaboration, to match foreign initiatives, to avoid the higher risk pitfalls of picking winners nearer the exploitation stage, and to resolve the market failure arising from a lack of industrial commitment and finance for long-term work.

But there were also convincing arguments for support of development and market stimulation. Though Alvey had embraced some of these elements, it was expected to concern itself primarily with precompetitive research. In the event, Alvey had tried to fulfill some of the functions of a broader industrial policy by incorporating a number of mechanisms designed to further exploitation, with some limited success. There *was* a need for a program of precompetitive IT research in the early 1980s—but there was also a case for other complementary policy measures.

Discussing the impact of Alvey on academic research, the evaluators said that though most projects appeared to be on schedule over 60 percent of teams had reported obstacles in achieving their research goals. The main problem was that of recruiting staff. On the industrial side there was little evidence to suggest that Alvey funding had simply substituted for previously earmarked in-house funding.

Motivations for collaboration included risk sharing, cost sharing, complementarity between firms, user/supplier collaborations, standards, knowledge transfer, defensive collaboration against competitors, and collaboration as a precursor to other links. The costs of collaboration included communication costs, more-complex decision-making structures, and uneven benefits of knowledge transfer. Collaboration also involved a loss of control through compromises in project definition and implementation, and loss of flexibility through difficulty of withdrawal or vulnerability to withdrawal by a collaborator. Nevertheless, the overwhelming opinion was that, on balance, collaboration was of positive benefit to technical progress.

With the possible exception of SERC funding problems, the report said, collaboration agreements had proved the major source of delay in Alvey. The Alvey technologies had been chosen both to build on existing strengths and to plug gaps in areas of relative weakness, but could the U.K. afford to do both? There were arguments both for selectivity and a broad-based approach. The Alvey strategy of attempting both was sound, though this had led to problems.

Distribution of the limited Alvey resources raised a number of issues. Alvey's "big bang" approach of committing funds as rapidly as possible certainly created a momentum but also led to problems. In a five-year program early decisions could become outdated as new technological opportunities arose; a rolling program would give more flexibility. Also, was the scale of projects correct, or should the total amount of money have been divided among more, or fewer, projects? Alvey had over 300 projects, including almost 200 industrial ones, and they ranged in cost from a few thousand to 16 million pounds. Most project teams considered their funding levels to be about right, the evaluators reported. Additional resources would yield rapidly diminishing returns in achieving faster or greater progress.

The interim report went into considerable detail in its description of the background to Alvey and its assessment of the individual Alvey technologies. The report's conclusions are reproduced in appendix 5.

No Audit Plaudit

Alvey evaluators SPRU and PREST had painted their picture of the Programme, warts and all, as commissioned independent consultants. In March 1988 another picture of Alvey was published,[22] this time by a body which not only is independent but tends to concentrate on the warts, whoever its subject may happen to be. This body is the National Audit Office, headed by the Comptroller and Auditor General. "He, and the NAO, are totally independent of Government," a note prefacing NAO publications states. "He certifies the accounts of all government departments and a wide range of other public sector bodies; and he has statutory authority to report to Parliament on the economy, efficiency, and effectiveness with which departments and other bodies use their resources."

The scope of the NAO investigation was wide. The office examined the administration and financial control of the Programme, collaboration, the exploitation of Alvey research, the effect of skills shortages on the Programme, the relationship of Alvey research to other publicly funded schemes, and the proposals for an after-Alvey program. On Alvey administration and financial control the NAO found "material weaknesses." The involvement of three government departments led to problems in contracting, financial control, and project funding; the directorate did not initially establish central management and financial information systems; the influence of the external evaluators on the direction of the Programme was limited; project appraisals were thorough but the appraisal process caused delays; and departmental monitoring varied in standard and approach. In spite of these weaknesses, possibly caused in part by a lack of resources, Alvey succeeded in drawing up detailed strategies within fourteen months and in getting 300 projects under way by March 1987.

The NAO found that the Programme had generated a substantial amount of cooperation. But difficulties in establishing collaboration agreements had caused significant delays and withdrawals; participation in projects was dominated by large firms; and more was spent on academic research and on administration and infrastructure than was originally intended, resulting in £35 million less being spent by government and also by industry on industrial collaborative projects (see tables 12.1 and 12.2).

TABLE 12.1.
Alvey Programme Expenditure (£m)

	83	84	85	Financial Years 86	87	88	89	90	91	Total
Project spend:										
VLSI	—	3.0	14.3	16.0	19.6	13.5	5.7	1.6	—	73.8
SE	—	1.7	4.0	8.6	8.8	4.9	1.1	0.2	—	29.3
IKBS	—	1.7	6.4	7.7	7.4	5.1	1.8	0.1	*	30.2
MMI	—	0.2	2.3	4.7	9.2	5.4	1.8	0.2	*	23.8
Large demonstrators	—	1.0	3.0	3.4	4.8	4.8	3.0	0.3	*	20.5
Total (project)	—	7.7	29.9	40.4	49.8	33.8	13.5	2.4	*	177.6
Non-project spend:										
DTI I&C	2.0	1.2	1.9	3.1	2.3	0.8	0.3	—	—	11.6
DTI consultancy	—	1.0	1.2	1.6	2.0	1.1	0.6	—	—	7.5
DTI awareness**	—	—	*	0.1	0.2	0.1	*	—	—	0.6
SERC support***	—	1.0	2.6	3.2	3.4	1.7	—	—	—	11.8
SERC administration	—	0.4	0.4	0.4	0.4	0.4	—	—	—	2.0
Total (non-project)	2.0	3.5	6.2	8.4	8.3	4.1	1.0	—	—	33.4
Total	2.0	11.2	36.1	48.8	58.0	37.9	14.5	2.4	*	211.0

Notes: Amounts are rounded to the nearest £100,000.
Amounts for years 1987–91 are estimates.
Amounts marked * are less than £100,000.
**Includes publicity.
***Includes infrastructure and coordination.
Source: Alvey Directorate/National Audit Office report.

TABLE 12.2.
Sources of Alvey Funding (£m)

	Original Allocation	Commitment by 1987	NAO Final Estimate (Research)
Public funds at 100%:			
SERC academic research	50.0	61.4	60.0
SERC infrastructure	—	11.8	
SERC administration	—	2.0	
DTI large demo. management	—	3.8	
DTI infrastructure	—	7.4	
DTI consultancies, etc.	—	8.1	
Public funds at 50%:			
DTI industrial research	110.0	72.9)	115.0
MoD industrial research	40.0	43.6)	
Industry funds at 50%	150.0	116.5	115.0
Total	350.0	233.0	290.0

Note: Columns 1 and 2 are taken from a table in the National Audit Office report (reference 22). The third column gives approximate estimates of total Alvey spending on research (i.e. excluding infrastructure, etc.) taken from the text of the NAO report and leading to the NAO view that final Alvey spending on research is likely to be £60 million less than was intended.

On exploitation of Alvey research the NAO noted that the Programme was not yet complete, but reported that in 1987 a directorate publication showed that 10 out of approximately 200 industrial projects had put products on the market or had improved existing production processes, and a further 77 projects had products at the prototype stage. Most of these were in the VLSI/CAD area. In software engineering no products were yet being marketed although 16 were at the prototype stage. The directorate considered that evidence of exploitable results from nearly half the 200 industrial projects at that stage of the Programme was highly encouraging.

The NAO found considerable evidence of continuing IT skills shortages. Staffing difficulties had been reported in over 50 percent of the 42 projects examined, which had contributed to delays, extensions and withdrawals and to the need to employ foreign experts. The directorate had contributed significantly to the formulation and execution of central government initiatives for skilled IT manpower. The NAO considered whether duplication of work or multiple funding could occur between Alvey and other schemes but concluded that this was unlikely. The office noted that most future U.K. IT research funds would be channeled toward Europe, with a more limited national program.

Overall, the NAO concluded, it would probably be some years before it was possible to make a measured judgment of the impact of the Alvey Programme on the U.K.'s competitiveness in IT. It was clear that a substantial amount had been achieved in terms of new research commissioned and projects supported and of closer cooperation within and between industry and academic institutions.

Then came the sting in the tail:

> However, in the NAO's view, the rate of exploitation of Alvey-funded research appears lower than the Alvey Committee expected. And there have been other indications that the Programme might have been more effective given more staff and better management information systems at the outset and if the balance of program expenditure between work in industry and SERC-funded work in universities and higher education institutions had been closer to that originally envisaged by the Alvey Committee. The Alvey Directorate could also have taken a more positive role in securing more prompt and effective collaboration; and the framework which governed exploitation of IPR by participants could have recognized the special nature of IT development and required results to be made available under licence earlier than for other DTI programs.

The National Audit Office report, in essence, was a combination of familiar criticism drawing heavily on the SPRU/PREST work and new criticism based on a singular interpretation of the weight attached by the Alvey Committee to the words of its report six years earlier. In particular the NAO's search for products and exploitation represented a worthy example of the goalpost-moving syndrome, a phenomenon noted by Alvey participants elsewhere in this book.

Most Monitored Program

"This was, I suppose, the most examined, dissected, vivisected, monitored, audited program that my department has ever had any connection with." The speaker was Sir Brian Hayes, Permanent Secretary at the Department of Trade and Industry, giving evidence[23] on 4 May 1988 to the Committee of Public Accounts of the House of Commons. The committee was looking into the National Audit Office report on Alvey, and Sir Brian, the DTI's top official, was critical of some of the NAO conclusions.

There was a twofold explanation of why the initial Alvey staff resources were so small, Sir Brian said. First, "We were intent that this should be a very streamlined operation, that we should not have a great bureaucratic army in charge of the Programme.... It was a conscious decision of government to try to run this in the most economical way." Secondly, "No one really understood at the outset of what was a very novel program exactly what demands it would make on the staff who were attempting to run and supervise it.... We did not at the outset appreciate just how heavy the demands on them would be."

As for the suggestion that the Programme suffered because more was spent on academic research, and so industry's research and financial contribution was reduced, Sir Brian declared "This is a quite misguided criticism." He went on:

What happened was that as the Programme went forward it became clear that the best value for money would come by using rather more research capability from the universities and rather less from industry. That came about not by *diktat* from above but by the decisions of the actual project managers....

One must not assume that because more work was done in the universities and less in industry than the Alvey Committee had foreseen either that meant the work was on average less good or less relevant to industry or indeed that there was in toto less high-quality effort being put into the Programme. I emphasize that point on quality because there is a danger of looking at all of this in terms of quantity, of the amount of research. That is an input. The output is exploitable results, and that depends on the quality of the research and its relevance to industrial need.

Did the permanent secretary still maintain that a largely hands-off approach to collaboration agreements was the right approach?

Yes.... My own feeling is that Mr. Oakley, who disagreed with my view and who said that he believed more effort should have been put in from the center, is letting his self-criticism get the better of him, because it does seem to me that it is essentially for the partners to negotiate the terms on which they are to collaborate, and that an attempt to dictate to them from the outside world would have led to more delay and to a less willing collaboration. Alvey is all about free collaboration; that is what it is intended to achieve. I think that it is best left to the partners to do that themselves.

The Alvey evaluators' interim report had borne out very strongly the view that the Alvey Programme had been successful insofar as one could measure success at this still early stage, Sir Brian said. He did not believe that the rate of exploitation of Alvey-funded research was lower than expected. "That is the view of the National Audit Office. It is based on a misunderstanding of what is meant by exploitation—or, at least, what the Alvey Committee themselves meant by exploitation:

What Alvey meant was two things. First of all, this research should provide a basis, a precompetitive research basis, on which companies could later themselves mount competitive research and development leading to products and processes. Secondly, it should bring about improved tools and methods which could be applied at once in the industries concerned but which do not take the form of products. It is quite clear if one reads the report that the NAO think solely in terms of marketable products, and that is not the correct way to evaluate the Programme, nor indeed does it conform to what the Alvey Committee themselves expected.

Sir Brian was asked what injury had been done to the Alvey Programme by the haphazard filing of documents, as reported by the NAO. He replied: "I doubt very much whether this did any damage to the Programme, and it is interesting that the NAO in highlighting all these failures of administration do not adduce any evidence to support the theory that damage was done to the Programme." Industrial secondees were not familiar with government practice. "Companies do not go in for great filing systems as government departments do. . . . I do not wish to criticize the practice of using secondees; they greatly increase the directorate's effectiveness. What they may have done was lead to a somewhat messy filing procedure in the early days."

The Alvey Programme was a novel experiment that had not been carried out in this country before and that was bound to have difficulties of a great many kinds, Sir Brian told the committee. On the whole it had been a valuable program and it already had substantial achievements to its credit. "The NAO's report does not seek to appraise the technology that has emerged from the Programme, and this is a program about technology. It is perfectly fair to look at the administrative minutiae. . . . One ought not to ignore or lose sight of the basic aims of the Programme or the success which it has already enjoyed."

Sir Brian returned to this point when a committee member pressed him on the subject of value for money:

You said that the committee would look to value for money. I am very glad to hear it because the NAO report does not seek to make that comparison, it does not seek to establish the value of the Programme. This is a technology program; the NAO report does not try to assess the technology. It did not have a technology adviser, it did not interview the evaluators, it did not interview the project managers, it made no attempt to evaluate the outcome of the Programme.

What this program is about is helping British industry to be more competitive in the world market. If it does not have that effect, it is a failure. If it does have that effect, then we have secured value for money. You cannot measure that effect now. You can look at indicators of the progress being made in that direction.

On the question of small firms' participation in Alvey Sir Brian said that the Alvey Committee had expected two things: that small firms would be drawn into collaborative projects; and that they would have information disseminated to them which they would be able to exploit. "Small firms as a whole cannot afford to spend large sums on long-term research, they cannot afford to wait for the results, they cannot afford the initial investment. It may be that fewer small firms are involved in the actual research projects than might have been had we had 90-percent funding. Certainly the main participation of small firms was expected to be in exploitation, and in that area they have played a very significant part."

Clarifying the intellectual property rights position, Sir Brian said: "There is a condition of grant under this scheme which says that if the companies concerned do not exploit the results within three years of the completion of the project, then they have to make the results available to somebody who will. Some have said that three years is too long in this area, because the technologies are developing so fast, and if you wait for three years, you are out of date. There is some force in that, but we cannot change the rules of the game at this stage."

The most important criticism in the NAO report, Sir Brian said, was probably that the directorate did not get proper financial information procedures into operation more quickly. The directorate had had "two prolonged tries" with two different computer consultants, and neither had worked satisfactorily:

What they were trying to do was to produce a system which would meet the requirements of each of three separate agencies and of the central directorate, and it proved to be extremely complex. It is somewhat anomalous that a body which was concerned with advanced information technology should take so long to produce a computerized system for its own financial reporting.

The basic explanation for this is that they were too ambitious; they were trying to get too complex a system.... From February 1984, when taking the advice of Arthur Andersen consultants, they went in for the Al-Fin system and then decided to scrap it the following October because it did not work. The following year or later in that year they invited tenders for a new comprehensive system and gave that to a company called Starwest. That too proved to be unsatisfactory... and it was not until February 1986 that they began to establish a more limited financial management information system, using readily available and economical spreadsheet packages that would work on an IBM-compatible personal computer. That does work, and since the middle of last year it has been fully operational.... They really should have made up their minds to go for a simple system at the outset and got it into place within a year.

Evaluating the Evaluators

Not surprisingly, longtime Alvey evaluators SPRU and PREST also felt obliged to respond to the conclusions of the National Audit Office. In the June 1988 issue of *Alvey News* Ken Guy of SPRU spelled out their points of accord, and of discord. He made five comments:

1. He agreed that more was spent on academic research and less on industrial research than was originally intended, but disagreed with the implication that this would lead to less overall research (given the comparative costs of researchers in academia and industry) and that somehow this could and should have been avoided. The primary aim of Alvey was to increase the overall amount of research being conducted in the IT field, not to use public money to lever as much research spend as possible out of industry. Keeping to original targets for com-

parative spending on academic and industrial research was a subsidiary aim to the main task of maximizing the overall amount of high-quality research. Whether the directorate actually achieved this was a moot point, but there was little doubt that its selection decisions were in line with its priorities.

2. He did not agree that the Alvey Committee envisaged appreciable exploitation commencing during the early stages of the Programme. It was this committee that popularized the notion of precompetitive research and discussed the maturation of exploratory research into product development in terms of five-year and even ten-year periods. The NAO used a false benchmark when it decried the relative paucity of exploitable outputs by 1987.

3. He agreed that the Alvey Committee saw developments in software engineering providing great exploitation expectations, but the NAO had misunderstood both the nature of the outputs from the Programme and the timescales involved. The Programme set out to improve quality and productivity in the software life cycle and hence concentrated on long-term process innovations for use by software developers. It did not concentrate on short-term product innovations in specific end-user application areas. Great exploitation potential existed, but not as a result of the immediate sale of Alvey outputs. The rewards would be reaped when products developed using these outputs were marketed, and the timescales involved here extended well beyond the lifetime of the Alvey Programme.

4. He agreed that the number of early exploitable VLSI deliverables exceeded expectations, but did not agree that the VLSI area was expected to produce fewer deliverables at this stage than, say, the software engineering area. The VLSI program was more development oriented than any of the other enabling technology areas. The fact that most products being exploited by 1987 stemmed from the VLSI program was hardly surprising.

5. He did not agree that exploitation potential would have increased appreciably if non-project participants had earlier access to Alvey results. The attractiveness to nonparticipants of projects not exploited within the first year after project completion by participating firms was arguably as low one year after completion as it was three years after. From the point of view of nonparticipants, therefore, there were only marginal

advantages in giving earlier access to results. From the perspective of participants, shorter IPR protection periods could hasten the realization of exploitation potential by accelerating their development plans, but could also have the more extreme negative effect of dissuading firms from participating in projects in the first instance.

The SPRU and PREST teams' own endeavors were themselves the subject of much comment—particularly from within the Alvey Directorate. Among the commentators, David Talbot is less than enthusiastic:

> I have to say the evaluations that have taken place seem to me to have been splendid examples of how you snatch defeat from the jaws of victory, and very English, and very academic. Terribly academic. Appallingly academic. Academia at its worst. Academia at its very worst, on the basis that the thing you have to look for is something to say. When we saw the original proposals from the evaluators, all the industrial members of the team said "Bollocks!" We didn't take it sufficiently seriously and put the boot in sufficiently hard then, and that was a mistake. In the end it wasn't just uninterestingly unhelpful, it was positively dangerous and damaging to the Programme. It was very poor stuff.
>
> I think it was a nice idea but given to wholly inappropriate groups. It was fundamentally flawed. The European Commission did it better in the ESPRIT midterm review[24] by commissioning a small group led by a distinguished individual, Dr. A. E. Pannenborg, ex-Philips. The Alvey evaluators couldn't see the wood for the trees. We had a worry to begin with, and I have to confess that worry was fully fulfilled. If half as much effort and resource had gone into providing the infrastructure and management to the Programme as there has been on passing reviews by itinerant academics, whether they be in Whitehall or elsewhere, we would have had an even more successful program.

Professor Brian Randell picks up the NAO's exploitation point: "It seems to me that the recent attempt to bad-mouth the Alvey Programme and what it's achieved has been a classic case of moving the goalposts. The notion that at the end of a period of five years' research you would point to products already on sale is naive in the extreme. I would regard some of the reviews of Alvey as being almost offensive."

VLSE: Very Large-Scale Evaluation

The VLSI part of the Alvey Programme provoked argument and debate throughout the whole life of the Programme, and in 1985 was the subject of two independent assessments. One was written by Kurt Hoselitz, a visiting professor at SPRU and an ex-director of Mullard Research Laboratories, as an input to the total SPRU evaluation. The other was commissioned by the Alvey Programme Steering Committee from Professor Alec Broers of Cambridge University, one of the IT expatriates recently returned from the United States.

The overall Alvey strategy seemed excellent, Hoselitz[25] reported. But the final target, even if achieved on time, would leave the U.K. lagging in technology behind the leaders in the U.S. and presumably Japan. Thus critical questions arose about the validity of the Alvey approach and the part it could play in making the U.K. IT industry competitive in world terms. These were not purely technological issues; they were largely concerned with industrial and product policy.

Broers was asked by the steering committee to tackle two specific issues:

1. In the light of the current Alvey objectives and timetable to review the likely technological and competitive position of the U.K. in VLSI up to the end of 1988, relative to the U.S., Japan, and Europe, both overall and in particular aspects of the technology.

2. To consider whether any changes should be made to the VLSI part of the Programme, taking account of existing budget constraints.

Broers reported in April 1985. First, the good news: Alvey VLSI had provided a strong stimulus to industry and universities, and enthusiasm was high; the broad technical directions were correct, including overlapping projects; there was a good technical understanding by the directorate and contractors; the organization had achieved the desired collaboration; and the overall direction was respected by the contractors.

Next, the bad news. Resources were only marginally adequate to meet program objectives, and the full-process projects would not put the U.K. on a par with leading competitors in the U.S. and Japan. The funding level was very low—only about 5 percent of the U.S. VHSIC program, for example. Industrial funding of 1.5-micron fabrication facilities was small compared with the U.S., Japan, and the Pacific rim. Industrial funding of micron and submicron facilities was negligible. Overall facilities investment was about 5 percent of that of

Japan, about 20 percent of Korea, and perhaps 10 percent of the United States. Industrial development facilities were not competitive.

Broers went on to make recommendations for VLSI development and production. For development, the one-micron CMOS program should be accelerated by one year by improving existing fabrication facilities and increasing staff. (This would still leave the U.K. one to two years behind the leaders.) A competitive pace of development should be established by building and supporting two state-of-the-art development and low-volume production facilities for submicron technology, one for bipolar and one for CMOS. For production, three changes should be made. First, volume production of U.K. designs that use conventional technology should be brokered to the U.S., Japan, or the Pacific rim. Second, low-cost capital or an equivalent tax incentive should be provided to industry to build high-volume production capability where innovations gave a competitive edge. Third, the U.K. should enter the volume semiconductor business as soon as a technological edge was established.

Though the steering committee and the directorate absorbed the Broers message, neither of the two development recommendations was pursued. (The production recommendations were outside the scope of Alvey.) Three years later, as an invited speaker at the U.K. IT 88 Conference (in effect if not in name the final Alvey Conference), Broers reviewed Alvey VLSI progress. Alvey had established several competitive VLSI technologies on very modest resources, he concluded. But the extent of industrial exploitation was unclear, and Britain might prove to be the only nation not to help its semiconductor industry to overcome the capital cost problems of installing a sound manufacturing base.

Academic-Flavored IKBS

IKBS also was the subject of special attention from the Alvey evaluators. In July 1988 a SPRU report[26] by Erik Arnold noted that Alvey IKBS, unlike other technologies, had not had the effect of moving academic research toward the applied end of the spectrum. Alvey IKBS academic achievements included a strengthening of the established centers of AI research; world-class research, especially in logic programming, systems architecture, vision, and natural-language understanding; increasing the AI R & D community by between 150 and 200 professional staff; and the return of "key emigrés" to the U.K. Major industrial IKBS achievements included an expansion of the industrial AI R & D community; growth of AI resources in major companies; inclusion of small firms; and generation of short-term technical outputs in advance of the major developments expected later.

The Alvey IKBS strategy appeared to have suffered from six key weaknesses, the report said. It was a scientific rather than an industrial strategy. Where it did deal with industry, it did not take account of specific strengths and weaknesses. It suffered from technological isolationism, involving few ways to exploit U.S. AI developments. It lacked clear technological goals. It neglected research on key systems-building problems. And it was inflexible.

In general, Arnold concluded, the strategy was successfully implemented. But management monitoring of implementation was weak, administration was too complex, and the research infrastructure was inadequate. The task of the IKBS program was threefold: to strengthen the academic AI community, create an industrial AI community, and build a bridge between the two. A strategy geared primarily to the first of these tasks was adopted and adapted to meet the needs of the other two, with beneficial results. The program had important successes, but it might have been asked to take on more than was feasible at the time.

IT Users' Views

An alleged serious omission in Britain's IT strategy was pointed out in December 1983 by Professor Frank Land of the London School of Economics in a paper[27] presented to the Parliamentary Information Technology Committee (PITCOM). The emphasis should be on the *use* of the technology, he argued. The current strategy for IT was dominated by the interests of the profession and by the IT suppliers. The Alvey Directorate would provide strong technical direction to the Alvey Programme. "But there is no alternative view—no view which looks at the technology from the perspective of a user or a critic, or which can introduce economic or social thinking into the debate." He concluded: "A national strategy should aim at the building of a strong and competitive IT industry. We have a plan for that. But even more important, we need a plan to use the technology effectively."

As Land had noted, IT-using organizations were not involved at the start of the Alvey Programme (except in demonstrator projects). Not until March 1985 did they gain a collective Alvey voice, with the formation of the Alvey IT User Panel. This group aimed to provide "continuing user feedback and advice" to the directorate, promote awareness of Alvey among users, and stimulate user involvement in Alvey Projects. It excluded VLSI technology from its work, concentrating on IKBS, software engineering, and MMI. The panel was based on the National Computing Centre (NCC) in Manchester, and the NCC Director was ex-officio chairman of the panel. From mid-1986 the panel turned its attentions also to after-Alvey affairs, and in April 1988 it published its final report.[28]

In software engineering overall, the panel reported, there appeared to have been a significant mismatch between the Alvey Programme and the views and priorities of users, "perhaps because the Programme had been set up without formal user consultation"—though some of the large Alvey projects did relate to users' priority areas. In IKBS the panel had aimed to distill the lessons from Alvey projects for the benefit of new users of IKBS. (As part of the Alvey IKBS awareness program the NCC had produced and marketed a highly successful "expert-system starter pack" consisting of versions of four expert-system shells and supporting literature.)

Though it was not spelled out in the panel's brief final report, members clearly felt that users' views had not been taken aboard early enough for them to have had any major impact on the Alvey Programme. "Broadly, I think the panel felt that the involvement of users in the Alvey Programme was too little and too late," says Patrick Raymont, secretary to the panel. Certainly this lesson had been learned in time for the users to make a major input later, as plans for an after-Alvey program were being formulated (see chapter 14).

On the occasion of the publication of the final report John Aris, NCC Director and panel chairman, commented:

The use of IT is far more economically important than its supply, and industry, commerce and government has everything to gain—or lose—from exploiting or not exploiting IT. Users are therefore the best people to judge whether IT research and development are contributing against real-world problems, so they must be involved in establishing and evaluating IT R & D programs. That is why the Alvey Directorate set up the panel.

He added: "The need is just as strong today and in the future as it was in the past."

A similar point was made by a working group of the British Computer Society, whose membership consists of IT professionals. Dr. Peter Gray of the University of Aberdeen recalls: "This group was very critical of Alvey for its lack of impact on commercial data processing, which continues to be one of the biggest areas of economic activity in IT. It also criticized the lack of funding of database research, which then caused the software engineering projects to waste a lot of effort through lack of database expertise and help."

Cabinet Office Critic

An influential voice in U.K. government science and technology policy is that of the Chief Scientific Adviser in the Cabinet Office. The present holder of that appointment, on secondment from IBM, is John Fairclough. The Alvey Programme was well under way when he moved to Whitehall in 1986, but he has since taken an active interest in the Programme, in its evaluation, and in what should follow it. He gives his own assessment of Alvey as follows:

It's premature to draw any final conclusions. History will show it's had a major influence. One of the most important influences undoubtedly will be the cooperation that has developed between industry and the universities. That's generic, it's almost a cultural influence quite independent of the specifics of the work, and that has been a very valuable aspect of the Programme.

In Britain the physics-based industries such as electronics are not as well organized as those based on chemistry, in terms of R & D and relationships with universities. There are some exceptions, but generally the electronics companies operate under shorter-term goals and are not spending as much on forward-looking R & D. Alvey in part has played a role of helping those companies catch up, but I doubt whether that part of the Programme will be successful because in the fast-moving world in which we live you never catch up. Progress always is being made by your competitor, and so the most important part of Alvey will be the more advanced part of the research program. I fear that a lot of the VLSI work, as an example, comes into the category of catch-up, and I doubt whether that's going to be of any significance to us, either economically or scientifically.

It is essential that this new culture of collaboration is here to stay. As part of my role I decided that the focus should be that interface between industry and university. We have a record second to none in discovery. Our success in exploitation is below what it should be, particularly in the physics-based industries.

To an extent, Fairclough argues, Alvey distorted the pattern of university research:

A great deal of valuable work was done in Alvey, but I worry that part of Alvey has diluted the quality of the research we do at universities, inasmuch as there were these near-market pressures. Though the research was "precompetitive," probably the most difficult thing in getting projects started were the arguments between companies on intellectual property. If you're having arguments about intellectual property, that's a little incompatible with saying its precompetitive. A lot of the university work that was done in Alvey was more applied than it should have been. That is not a general comment, but there are many examples.

As chairman of the 1987 evaluation seminar organized by the Alvey Directorate, Fairclough had some critical things to say about the assessment of Alvey by the SPRU and PREST evaluation teams. He had expressed similar views the previous year. He amplifies his earlier remarks as follows:

When you embark on an R & D program, if half or even one-third of it is successful, you're doing very well. And so two years ago I was arguing that the Alvey projects should be critically evaluated and divided into three categories: first, those that clearly looked as though they were going to make a world-class contribution to research; second, those where it was too early to say—the work looked promising but a full assessment could not yet be made; third, those which had not come up to expectation.

Normally I would expect to see roughly equal numbers of projects in each of those three categories. But in Alvey there wasn't that commitment to identify that bottom one-third in order to find resources to do more effectively the top one-third. I would have cancelled some projects and transferred the money to the more promising ones.

The bulk of the Alvey evaluation was on the process rather than on the activity. It's so easy to evaluate the process, particularly if you get university policy people looking at it. I'm somewhat critical that there was not a businesslike approach to the Alvey evaluation processes. The other factor is that if you're going to do an evaluation of those sorts of projects, we are competing internationally and therefore you should bring in some international people to help you evaluate, particularly some Americans and some Japanese.

Returning to his three-category assessment point, Fairclough agrees that this would certainly have been the IBM approach had that company been running the Alvey Programme; projects would have been assessed against those three categories and resources reallocated from less attractive to more attractive projects:

> The general image of the community, as perceived by industry generally and by government, was damaged by not having that sort of philosophy to the management process. There are many senior executives in British industry who believe that IT has been given more than its fair share of government help.
> Another measure of success or failure at the end of the day would be for companies to form consortia or joint arrangements to begin marketing projects. I don't know how much of that is going on. But it seems to me that if there are companies now joining forces in a private development mode, that would be a very good measure of an output.

The Alvey Ethos

A perceptive study[29] of decision making in the Alvey Programme was prepared in 1987 by Leo Keliher, an Australian policy analyst, as his Ph.D. thesis in the Department of Government at the London School of Economics. Keliher's view as an informed outsider underlined the unconventional nature of Alvey policy making and management in the context of a large publicly funded program. In one part of his study Keliher looked at the Alvey style and ethos:

> An important aspect of the development of an Alvey ethos was the minimizing of disagreements (or the promotion of consensus). This took many forms. The most obvious were the large public meetings with industry and academics during the development of the individual program strategies and the removal of all contentious decision-making powers from the steering committee....
> It is apparent that the directorate set out to insulate itself from bureaucratic politics and the political process in general as well as attempting to achieve a consensus in most areas. These goals it largely

succeeded in meeting. There was another side to the Alvey ethos, however. This was the fostering of a spirit of camaraderie or community. One of the most striking features was the cordiality which existed between most of the civil servants, industrialists, and academics associated with Alvey and the esteem in which they generally held each other. . . .

With respect to the Alvey Directorate, the ethos manifested itself in the form of a pro-industry/anti-bureaucratic, independent organizational culture, a hardworking, friendly climate, and a relaxed administrative system. Other features included the burgeoning steering committee, a complex web of advisory panels and subcommittees, clubs, conferences, and workshops. It also involved complex bureaucratic negotiations with its public-sector "partners."

Keliher adds a wry comment on the early administrative problems:

While the Alvey Directorate was in the vanguard of Britain's quest for the fifth-generation computer, the directors were unable to produce statistics or forecasts for management information. Researchers might achieve the one-micron barrier on their VLSI project, but they could not tell anyone about it via their terminal; terminals did not talk to each other. At this point, the system/software supporters would point to the necessity for better software tools, the hardware proponents would claim that smarter machines are the answer, and the "soft science" MMI supporters would rest their case.

IV
Alvey and After

13
Meanwhile, in Other Places

Before moving on to discuss post-Alvey developments in Britain, a brief look at other nations' responses to the fifth-generation challenge sets the U.K. scene in context. In particular, new IT programs were mounted in the United States and in Europe as the Japanese effort got under way. Brian Oakley describes the ways in which these approaches both resembled and differed from the Alvey concept.

Precedents for Cooperative Research

The fifth-generation (5G) program announced by Japan in the autumn of 1981 was certainly not the first large-scale cooperative program. Pride of place for that must go to the initiation of the research-association movement by the U.K. government in 1917. This had come about under the stress of war, primarily because of the shock the U.K. had experienced in 1914, when it realized that the country was almost totally dependent on Germany to supply its optical industry. And this was not the only field of advanced technology of the day in which the U.K. was dependent on imports from what was now its adversary. British industry was, with the exception of the oil and chemicals field, where rationalization had been taking place in the previous twenty years, not only often technically backward, it was very fragmented and featured few large firms. (Today it is difficult to conceive that at the end of the Second World War the U.K. still had over a dozen aircraft firms.) So the government announced that it wished to see firms with a common technical or industrial interest together to share the costs of research.

The government was prepared to pump-prime this process by matching the costs of the work on a pound-for-pound basis. This led to the formation of the Research Associations (RAs). At its peak in the late 1950s there were some forty-seven RAs in the movement, the smallest of which was the Brush RA, the largest the Production Engineering RA (PERA). Some of the RAs still exist today, though the concentration of the industry into fewer and fewer units and the decline of the "smoke-stack" industries has decimated their ranks. Probably the most successful of the RAs were the technology-based ones such as the Scientific Instrument RA (SIRA), which has become renowned for its work in optics, and the Welding Institute, probably the most respected body in its field in the world.

Rather strangely, there were no RAs for the modern technologies of electronics and computing. This was probably because these industries were dominated by a relatively few large firms, though they also contained many smaller firms. It is possible that the presence of significant MoD funding for research and the large government research laboratories, such as the RSRE and ARL, played their part in inhibiting the development of RAs for these industries. The nearest approach to an RA was the National Computing Centre, but this was set up explicitly to serve the users of the technology rather than its generators, though both are in membership. The NCC does not normally concern itself with the generation of technology but with its application. However, it is true that many of the surviving RAs are more concerned with technology transfer than with its creation. The RA movement was widely copied in other countries, though with a few exceptions not with the same success. In Germany, presumably because of a philosophical objection to government intervention in industrial research, many centers of technology emerged, but these were largely at the lower end of the spectrum, like the world-famous Max Planck Institute. The more applied Fraunhofer Institutes seem to have made little impact outside Germany.

So it is probably fair to say that there was relatively little cooperative research involving industry outside Japan at the time of their 5G announcement. But this was not the first Japanese cooperative program. On some counting it was the eighth in the field of electronics and information technology. Only a few years before, the Japanese supercomputer program had been announced, with the simple objective of producing a Japanese machine with 1,000 times the power of the most powerful computer existing at the time of initiation of the program, the Cray 1. This eight-year program must be judged a success insofar as it enabled two Japanese firms to put supercomputers on the market, though at the time of writing Japan has not won the blue ribbon for computer performance, and their supercomputers do not dominate the market. Those honors still rest with the U.S.

If the supercomputer program was not an overwhelming success, the same can hardly be said of the silicon integrated circuit initiative. In many ways the 5G program was modeled on it. The participating firms seconded their workers to a new research center created for the role, in this case the Electro-Technical Laboratory (ETL). This very well-equipped laboratory attempted to emulate the best work and practices available in the West, primarily in the U.S. Within a few years it had done just that. That generation of research workers dispersed back to the firms that had been shadowing the work of the central laboratory with their own teams, at least as large if not of such high quality as the workers at the ETL. Within a few years the technology learned in the cooperative program, combined with the discipline of the Japanese workers and the firms' willingness and ability to invest large sums, had enabled the Japanese industry to dominate the world, at least in standard silicon VLSI components. Many hundreds of patents poured out of the program, and at least one new world-class process came out of it. But it is probably fair to assume that it was more a matter of emulating superbly the best that the world had to offer that led to their success. All the strands of this process can be seen in the pattern adopted for the 5G program.

The Japanese 5G Announcement

By 1981 the success of the Japanese cooperative program in integrated circuits was only just beginning to be apparent. So it is not entirely clear if this was a significant factor in the way the world reacted to the Japanese 5G announcement; probably it was an underlying important factor but not the dominant reason. The dominant reason was probably the way in which the Japanese made the announcement. Until then the nature of the Japanese programs was known in the West, but the Japanese had seen them as catching-up exercises and had not given them any special publicity. It was very different for the fifth-generation announcement, which was made with as much publicity as the Japanese could muster. The Japanese invited delegations from all the major research countries, most notably the U.S.

and the U.K., to their first 5G Conference, as well as sending personal invitations to many of the outstanding workers in the AI field in the West. They invited participation and cooperation from foreigners in their program while making it very clear that it was to be a Japanese program. But they also made it clear that the purpose of the ten-year program was to establish a world lead for Japan in the field of artificial intelligence and that this was to be an industrial as well as a technological lead.

The West certainly got the message. The Japanese announcement created a wave of anxiety in the U.S., Europe, the U.K., and elsewhere. To the extent that AI workers in the U.S. and the U.K. felt unloved, neglected, and underfunded, here were the Japanese accepting what they had been preaching for so many weary years. Books such as Feigenbaum and McCorduck's *The Fifth Generation* helped to fuel the concern, harping on the success the Japanese were achieving with their cooperative programs and on the importance of a response from the governments and industries of the West if this new and vital field was not to be dominated by the Japanese. After the successes of the Japanese in other industrial fields and with the camera, shipbuilding, and motorcycle industries of the western world already dominated by Japan it was a message that fell on fertile ground.

The U.S. Response

In the U.S. the most visible response was the formation of the MCC, but in the long run it may be that it was the increase in funding by the established agencies such as the Defense Advanced Research Projects Agency (DARPA) and NSF in the field of computing in general and artificial intelligence in particular that will prove of most significance in the long run. DARPA has had a long history of success in the information-technology field. In particular, the ARPA network, developed in the late 1960s and early 1970s, was a pioneering venture that put the U.S. in a leading position in packet-switched networking and remote computing, though perhaps their industry did not cash in on this technological lead in the way the Japanese industry would have, had they been involved. DARPA always runs on a relatively lean, high-quality team. Their response to the Japanese was the Strategic Computing Initiative (SCI), not to be confused with the Strategic Defense Initiative (SDI), which was announced somewhat later and thereafter has tended to gain all the headlines. The Strategic Computing Initiative was first announced in 1983, though DARPA had been canvassing for support for it since 1978. It was certainly not the first time that DARPA had funded AI research, for it had been by far the largest single source of funding for AI work in the U.S. since the early 1960s. Congressional support for an increased funding in AI was probably secured as a direct consequence of the Japanese 5G announcement. The SCI was planned to result in an increase in spending on AI from about $30 million in 1984 to $120 million in 1988, though the advent of the SDI would have dwarfed these figures, had it been funded as originally planned.

The Strategic Computing Initiative is heavily focused on what in Alvey parlance would be seen as a few large demonstrators. One of these is an autonomous robotic vehicle, the guidance and control of which is entirely based on a real time interpretation of visual signals derived from TV cameras on the vehicle. This is a most ambitious target, which will strain AI and parallel computing to its limits if it is to meet its demonstration objective by 1993. A second objective is the harnessing of AI techniques to help aircraft pilots and tank crews under battle conditions. And a third is concerned with the massive database and distributed computing problem of battlefield management. While these problems are derived from defense models, it would be a mistake to see them as of value purely to the defense community. Their successful demonstration by 1993 would have a vast impact on the potential market for the enabling technologies underlying them—VLSI, AI, and MMI—as well as for the specific markets, civil as well as defense, deriving from the particular applications demonstrated.

The SCI program is planned to cost $600 million in the five years from 1984 to 1989, and perhaps $150 million per year for the following few years. DARPA essentially provides 100 percent funding, about half going to universities in the early years but with industry getting the lion's share in the later years of the program. Because of the 100 percent funding regime DARPA does not normally explicitly call for cooperative project proposals but achieves cooperation by transferring the property rights from their university contractors to chosen firms. In the SCI, however, no doubt under the influence of the Japanese approach, a requirement for a degree of cooperation between firms, as well as between firms and universities, has been introduced.

In a sense it is unfair to compare the DARPA SCI program with the Japanese 5G program and the U.K. Alvey Programme, as the SCI program was not created in imitation of the Japanese program; rather, funding for it was obtained as a result of the Japanese program. The Alvey Programme was more the direct result of the Japanese program, and certainly in its organization it consciously sought to learn from the Japanese experience. Yet in many ways the DARPA program is more like the Alvey Programme, and not just because it involved more enabling technologies than parallel machine architectures and knowledge-based systems, though both are important. Like Alvey the DARPA program does not involve the creation of a single, ICOT-like research center. Like ICOT, and even more than Alvey and ESPRIT, it relies on a strong leadership from the DARPA program managers. It is very much a "directed" program. When ministers are wont to sound off about the inability of public servants to give a successful lead to industry about anything, they would do well to ponder the experience of DARPA, a notably successful body and one that was widely quoted by the Alvey Committee in the planning that led to the Alvey Directorate. But perhaps the main distinguishing feature of the SCI program in comparison with all other 5G programs stemming from the Japanese example is the strong lead and coherence given to the program by the use of the demonstrators. It remains to be seen if this model proves successful. It certainly takes the Alvey large-demonstrator concept to its logical conclusion.

An Industrial Research Cooperative in the United States

If the DARPA SCI program was the continuation of an American pattern of research support, spurred by the Japanese program, the Microelectronics and Computer Technology Corporation (MCC) was a revolutionary development for the United States. Not only was collaboration between firms contrary to the American ethic of standing on one's own two feet to fight in a free market in a caricature of Darwinian survival of the fittest, it was also against the antitrust laws. So the threat posed by the Japanese or more truthfully by the whole Japanese industrial process can be seen at its clearest in the formation of the MCC, a company founded in 1982 to carry out research in IT for its shareholders. At the time of its founding it had ten member companies. This rose in 1985 to over twenty large firms, though the number has fallen somewhat since then. Member firms pay a subscription to join a set of research programs selected individually from the seven or more on offer. These started with the typical 5G subjects of AI, KBS, and parallel processing but also included software technology, CAD for VLSI, and, rather strangely, semiconductor packaging and interconnect. (This last is not so strange when one remembers that virtually all members of the MCC would be sure to be members of the much larger Semiconductor Research Cooperative that deals exclusively, as its name suggests, with semiconductor and integrated circuit research, and not CAD and packaging.) New programs, such as a warm superconductor program and some work on neural networks, are added as the need arises.

The MCC is established in new laboratories on the land of the University of Texas at Austin. It has some 400 scientists, which makes it nearly ten times the size of ICOT, though probably not much bigger in the 5G fields if one takes account of the much wider scope of the MCC, and probably smaller if one takes account of the teams in the Japanese firms, each comparable in numbers to ICOT, who in some sense form part of the Japanese 5G program. One of the major challenges for the MCC has been to recruit good people. The original concept was that the staff would be recruited by secondments from the firms. But it was found early on that this approach would not work, so direct recruitment was substituted. In attacking this problem another problem for the MCC was made worse, since technology transfer is made much more difficult if it is not achieved by staff returning to the firms from their secondments.

Partly because of the property rights regime, which gives the participating firms a monopoly for three years after the end of the research program (a clear incentive to exploit rapidly) and partly because of the antitrust laws, work at the MCC sticks to research rather than following the DARPA model into demonstrators and development. There is much skepticism outside the MCC as to whether its unique approach will succeed; this remains to be seen. In contrast to Alvey, but like the Japanese program, the MCC works by concentrating scientists in a single research center. Yet it seems to neglect one of the supreme benefits of such an approach because since not all firms are participating in all programs it has been necessary to create "Chinese walls" between the different MCC research programs and teams. Like Alvey the MCC covers a wide spread of the enabling technologies of IT in its work, though some of the benefit of this must be lost because of the walls and because of the apparent unwillingness to go beyond the research stage. The MCC is, in organizational terms, one of the most interesting programs to have resulted from the 5G announcement. Of course to the British, acquainted for many years with research associations, this organization does not seem all that unusual, but on the American scene it is truly revolutionary. It remains to be seen if it will succeed, though the auguries do not appear promising. But one must always remember the remarkable U.S. capacity for exploitation. It would not be entirely surprising to find a new Route 128 springing up around the MCC in Austin, consisting of small firms founded by staff leaving the MCC to exploit their research work through start-up companies. In the AI field this already seems to have happened with knowledge based system software on the market stemming from work at the MCC.

Though the MCC is the cooperative venture of most interest to the Alvey Programme, it is worth noting that there have been a considerable number of other cooperatives in the IT field developed in the U.S. in recent years. Many of these, like the Semiconductor Research Cooperative (SRC), exist to fund academic research. The SRC has some thirty-five members, including virtually all of the firms with an interest in integrated circuit development in the U.S. Though it is not directly relevant to the Alvey Programme it is worth noting the emergence of the Sematech cooperative. Formed in August 1987, its avowed purpose is to enable U.S. industry to compete successfully with Japan in the semiconductor field. With an annual budget of about $250 million, it is expected that at least $100 million will come from government, inevitably via the Department of Defense. It will build a manufacturing center at Austin, like the MCC, but will also establish "centers of excellence" at various American universities. The origins of Sematech can be traced back to the same competitive fears of Japan that launched the wave of 5G programs. And like most of them its organization and structure owe much to emulation of the Japanese cooperative programs. What a complete turnaround from the time only a few short years ago when the antitrust laws and the country's ethos inhibited cooperation.

The European Response: ESPRIT

At the time that the Alvey Programme was being drawn up the European community was conceiving the ESPRIT program, which has turned out to be the largest of the commission's cooperative programs. In almost all respects it is similar to the Alvey Programme. The first five-year program was worth some 1.5 billion ECU (European currency units), or some $3 billion, of which half came from community funds. Like the Alvey Programme it was always envisaged that there would be a second five-year program, but unlike Alvey this has been established on a far larger scale than that of the first five years. The second five-year program will require some 3.2 billion ECU, half of that coming from the European bodies involved in the projects, the other half from community funds.

It was EEC Commissioner Viscount Davignon to whom the lion's share of the credit must go for creating the program through his "round table" of the twelve major electronics companies of the EEC in 1980. But it was the Japanese 5G announcement that made it respectable to use public funds on a large scale to bring the IT industry of Europe together. From the beginning this was seen as a major argument for the program, not an argument that seems to have played any part in the Japanese cooperative program! But the fragmented structure of the European industry has been a major weakness, made worse by the even more fragmented structure of the market. In comparing the Alvey and ESPRIT programs it is important to bear in mind this added dimension of the ESPRIT program; success can be measured not only by the technical progress and by the impact of this on the competitiveness of the individual firms but also by the extent to which the program has drawn together the European firms. By that last criterion, unlike the other 5G programs, ESPRIT can already be judged a success.

Inevitably, with the cost and time delays in traveling and with the cultural problems, the overhead of working in the ESPRIT program is very heavy—much more so than in the Alvey Programme, though the overhead there can be heavy enough. Nevertheless, very few of the firms do not consider the price worth paying. Like the Alvey Programme, but unlike the Japanese or some of the American programs, such as the MCC, ESPRIT is a distributed program with no center. Remembering the objective of bringing the firms together, the opportunity for meetings of the consortia held on each other's premises is very much part of the process. Like the Alvey Programme the scope of ESPRIT spans the enabling technologies, much wider than the AI and parallel architecture focus of the Japanese 5G program. Indeed, in the second phase of ESPRIT the AI work takes very much a back seat, though the parallel architecture work is significant because it features in one of the Technology Integration Projects (TIPs). These projects are in a way the equivalent of the Alvey large demonstrators or the DARPA SCI demonstrators. It is interesting to note that the ESPRIT parallel architecture TIP has a symbolic processing part directly equivalent to the ICOT parallel architecture work, but also a conventional numerical processing part. Virtually all of the firms concerned claim their architectures would be equally applicable to both! But it does illustrate the problems for Japan in treating the AI program as a thing apart. In Europe, knowledge-based systems are increasingly seen as part of the software engineering scene, albeit an important part.

In comparison with the other 5G programs one characteristic of the Alvey Programme stands out; it is the only program that truly embraces all parts of IT community in the country. Clearly the Japanese 5G program is rather special, as if the Alvey Programme were to be primarily restricted to the industrial AI community. The MCC is purely industrial, even if the center is located in an academic establishment and many of the works come from academic posts. The DARPA program is open to all parts of the American community but in practice is restricted to a relatively small part. Even the ESPRIT program tends to be less relevant for the academic community than is the Alvey Programme. Perhaps it is chance that the U.K. supports about the right size IT community to make that possible.

The Japanese 5G Program

Having drawn so many lessons from the structure and work of the Japanese fifth-generation program it is only right that this chapter should conclude with some remarks on that program itself. ICOT was set up in April 1982, following studies for the program started in 1979 and the announcement of the program at the first international conference in October 1981. The program is supported by the Japanese Ministry of International Trade and Industry (MITI) and the major firms in the IT industry. The staff of ICOT are typically on three-year secondments from the Electro-Technical Laboratory, NTT, and the eight major Japanese IT firms (Fujitsu, Hitachi, Matsushita, Mitsubishi, NEC, OKI, Sharp, and Toshiba). The program director, Dr. Kazuhiro Fuchi, comes from the Electro-Technical Laboratory and is respected throughout the AI world. It is difficult to pin down the number of Japanese research workers at ICOT, but it has probably grown slowly to about sixty. I know that Dr. Fuchi has had much the same problems as the MCC has had or as we would have in the U.K. in recruiting and retaining good workers on secondment from the companies. Each company has its own AI program loosely coordinated with that of ICOT through a series of research advisory committees or "working groups," as they are called. The top committee, the Project Promotion Committee, was chaired by the much respected Professor Tohru Moto-oka until his death in November 1985. He had been the committee chairman from its inception in 1981. He was the head of the electrical engineering department at Tokyo University, and it is entirely typical that the working groups are chaired by academics and indeed often dominated by them. This is often the way that academic work is coordinated with industrial, and their advice on technical matters seems to be an important factor in the direction the program takes. Their role is to provide a window on the world's activities so that the research work does not get too parochial. ICOT entertains a steady stream of overseas visitors, some of whom stay for periods of up to a year or more. The overseas visitors that ICOT attracts are frequently of very high quality, though most of those who have stayed for any period of time are relatively young, like the ICOT staff. Staff exchange schemes with the NSF in the U.S., INRIA in France, and the Information Engineering Directorate in the U.K. had been established by 1988—or at least seriously discussed. The general consensus is that, though ICOT has few names of world renown, the predominantly young workers are of good quality and very well informed about what goes on elsewhere in the world.

The Cost and the Staff

It is difficult to establish a clear picture of the cost of the Japanese 5G program, though in many respects they have been entirely open about what goes on there in technical terms. Any shortcoming in the West's picture of their program is more due to difficulties in comprehension through the language barrier. It is certainly not for want of published articles on the work of ICOT, for these have poured out. The cost of ICOT is probably about 5,500 million yen per year. (By June 1988 ICOT had spent 29,800 million yen). Changes in exchange rate make it difficult to evaluate this in western terms, though the figure of $500 million over ten years was widely bandied about in the early days. If that is correct (and it is probably a considerable underestimate), then the program will cost roughly what the Alvey Programme cost over its five years, a small fraction of the cost of ESPRIT over its ten years, and roughly half the cost of the DARPA Strategic Computing Program. But a more accurate picture is probably obtained by comparing numbers employed. The Alvey Programme employed some 2,000 people at its peak; ESPRIT some 3,500 or more in its first phase and probably 5,000 in its second phase; the MCC had grown to some 430 research workers in early 1988 and is still growing; and ICOT is roughly comparable in size and program to the European Computer Industry Research Center (ECRC) at Munich. By these measures ICOT is really not very large, when set against the world scene. But remembering that the scope of the ICOT program is much more exclusively concentrated around basic research in AI, or more truly knowledge-based systems, it is certainly a significant player in its field. There are always rumors that ICOT has lost favor with the Japanese government and industry because it has yet had little impact on Japan's commercial world, and certainly the ICOT budget has been cut back from time to time. But what research laboratory's budget has not suffered that fate?

The Initial Phase

The ten-year ICOT program was planned in three phases. The initial phase up to 1984 was focused on the development of the basic computer technology, the intermediate phase from 1984 until 1988 was concerned with the integration of the technology into small-scale subsystems, and the final phase is to be concerned with the development of the total system. In the original plan applications-system software was only to appear in this third phase, though this does not seem to have been vigorously adhered to. Indeed there has been a fair amount of criticism, particularly emanating from the U.S., about the rather rigid nature of this plan. In the West it is difficult to imagine such a detailed ten-year plan for basic research, though one suspects it is adhered to less vigorously in practice than is sometimes allowed to appear. One cannot constrain good basic research by detailed program plans.

It is perhaps not surprising that the first phase of the program was seen to be dominated by computer developments, both in the generation of the Personal Sequential Inference Machine (PSI) and the initial experimental work leading to the Parallel Inference Machine (PIM) and the Knowledge-Base Machine (KBM). Dr. Fuchi is on record as saying that the project is to develop computers for the 1990s. He probably meant computer systems, for from the beginning it has been recognized that much of the challenge would lie in the basic operating-system software (PIMOS) and machine and user languages—kernel language (KLD), core language (GHC), and user language. PSI and its operating system (SIMPOS) were seen as tools to help development of the program. They have been put into limited production essentially for the Japanese community. It would be quite wrong to judge the program by the quality of this initial work. Developments in the West in powerful personal computers and efficient compilers for inference computing languages have rather sidetracked the PSI, which will make no impact on the wider market if it is put into full production, which seems highly improbable.

The Japanese User Language

Much print has been expended to discuss the apparent choice of Prolog as the basis for the user language for the program.

In the U.S. this was seen as an error, since the AI community largely uses Lisp and recognizes the weaknesses in Prolog. In Europe the apparent choice of Prolog was greeted as a victory, since Prolog stems from work in France and the U.K. But ICOT never intended Prolog, a predicate logic language, as more than a starting point for the machine kernel language. For PSI the user language is ESP, a language incorporating modular and macro functions, though it seems probable that, like the PSI itself, ESP will not carry forward to the next stage. It does seem likely that the core language for the parallel inference machines will be based on Guarded Horn Clauses (GHC), a form of predicate logic. Concurrent Prolog, deriving from the work of Shapiro at the Weismann Institute in Israel, has also been a significant influence on the design of the core language.

In the intermediate phase of the program more effort went into natural-language processing, and it is interesting to see if this emerges as one of the main themes of the final phase. The study of practical knowledge information representation, storage, and processing only really started in the intermediate phase. In the original planning actual applications were not to be studied until the final phase, when matters like the user and machine language and the prototype hardware for the full 5G machine would be available. (By 1988 ICOT had developed a 64-processor-element Multi-PSI.) In the event it seems likely that more applications work has been introduced in the intermediate phase, and many research workers would feel this would be just as well in order to prevent the work's becoming too theoretical, too unrelated to the real problems of inference computing.

The Value of the Japanese Program

At this stage of a ten-year program it is both difficult and unreasonable to try to judge the value of the program. Probably in Japan as in the rest of the world its main achievement so far has been to raise awareness of the importance of AI, or of that branch of AI dealing with inference computing on which ICOT has been concentrating. The nature of the Japanese ICOT staffing process ensures that the work of ICOT gets well disseminated by the workers to their firms as they return at the end of their secondments. So whatever progress is made at ICOT will rapidly appear in the Japanese industry. It would be in keeping with the general Japanese industrial philosophy to expect them to want to exploit hardware, the parallel inference machine and the knowledge-base machine coming together in the fifth-generation system. With three different parallel architectures under investigation in ICOT in the intermediate phase, one can reasonably expect the Japanese to learn how to design efficient parallel systems. But if it turns out that there is no such thing as a single optimum architecture for the fifth generation, then they may not be able to gain such an advantage from the work of ICOT. In the West a wide variety of parallel architectures are under development and now coming on to the market. It may be that the fifth generation will see an age when machines are very much tailored for problems, with the universal machine becoming far less dominant than the general-purpose machine is today in the fourth generation. Perhaps the most valuable work of ICOT will lie in the very extensive work on system software, both parallel operating systems and language for the user and for the machine. The evidence from the past is that most unsatisfactory but widely used languages take a great deal of displacing by more elegant and efficient newcomers, so maybe the ICOT core language will not easily spread beyond Japan. But the Japanese society seems to be able to reach a consensus and then apply it with discipline across the whole industrial and academic spectrum. Maybe the Japanese will take up whatever core language for inference computing emerges from ICOT and implement it across their industry. Since it is clear that the Japanese have recognized the crucial advantages of the object-oriented approach, it may prove to be a very important competitive weapon if the ICOT work leads Japanese industry to standardize on a soundly based object-oriented language for inference computing, for it seems improbable that the West will do this for many years to come.

As far as inference computing as a whole is concerned, one wonders if ICOT has left the real problems too late. The problems of knowledge representation in a form that provides for the domain expert to be able readily to validate, amend, and extend the stored knowledge do not seem to have occupied much of ICOT's time, at least so far. Yet this is seen as one of the major challenges for inference computing. And despite the publicity in the early days relating the program to the problems of society, little attention seems to have been given to the end-user interface. Yet it is becoming clear that a useful knowledge-based system must provide for an easy dialogue between the end user and the system; the end user must be able not only to receive advice but to ask why that particular advice has been given, what part of the knowledge has led to the advice, and what happens if the parameters of the problem are somewhat amended. Maybe we will see the emergence of many, if not all, knowledge-based systems having an adaptive user interface that can tune the output to match the particular needs, skills, and state of mind of a particular user. It would appear that ICOT is doing little work in this field, but maybe that will emerge in the final phase, just as natural-language work has been seen to play a larger part than appears to have been originally envisaged in the intermediate phase. The ICOT intelligent interface work may be the forerunner of much more work on the end-user interface.

One thing we have learned over the last twenty years or so: never underestimate the Japanese. If today we see the Japanese fifth-generation program as largely contributing to the world through its announcement, through its very existence rather than through what it actually achieves, maybe we will live to regret the day when we could not see anything of great significance emerging from the program. Anyway, those of us in the U.S., Europe, and elsewhere who have been engaged in fifth-generation work will always be eternally grateful to the Japanese for the way they have focused the world's attention on the opportunities.

14

A Son of Alvey?

The question of what should follow the Alvey Programme surfaced publicly in 1985. Following the Alvey precedent another committee, chaired by Sir Austin Bide, was set up to consider what should be done. In November 1986 the Bide Committee duly produced an ambitious plan for a follow-up program that would concentrate heavily on the application of information technology, and would involve IT users as well as suppliers and researchers. The government bided its time in responding to the Bide Report. In the 1987 general election Mrs. Thatcher's government was reelected, with a significant change of ministers at the Department of Trade and Industry. Not until January 1988 were the government's intentions made clear. Kenneth Owen describes this phase.

First and Future Task

Within the Alvey Directorate Brian Oakley and his deputy Laurence Clarke disagreed on one major issue: the timing and manner of promoting a follow-up program. Clarke wanted to waste no time in getting things moving. He quotes the director of a major U.S. software collaborative program who, given a five-year supply of funds, said "My first task is to ensure the second five years' funding."

Clarke accepts that the Alvey Programme Director had other first tasks. "To have said that at the beginning of Alvey might have been a bit difficult; nevertheless I'm sure that Brian should have started much, much earlier on the trail of saying 'This is a ten-year program at least.' I know he was up against the fact that Maggie was very reluctant in the first place, but I think that we should have made a much stronger effort."

The Alvey Programme Steering Committee also raised the question of an Alvey continuation quite early in the Programme. At the committee's third meeting, in November 1983, members discussed whether the Programme should be planned on the assumption that it had a five-year life, or longer. They decided to assume the Programme would continue beyond five years but noted that the continuation question would need to be considered in about two years' time.

In fact they considered it just thirteen months later. At their December 1984 meeting it was suggested that an Alvey 2 committee might be set up in the summer of 1985. The DTI fired a warning shot by way of a sharp comment by Oscar Roith, Chief Engineer and Scientist, that a more DTI-based system might be a more appropriate continuation; the title "Alvey 2" would be a misnomer. Colin Fielding of the Ministry of Defence agreed with his Whitehall colleague that the second phase should be distanced from Alvey, so as not to leave the impression of a program set to run forever.

Academic Action

It was the academic community, acting at the instigation of the SERC Engineering Board, who first got together to discuss and recommend what should follow the Alvey Programme. The board decided in April 1985 to consider the SERC's participation in an extended program and set up a working party chaired by Professor Eric Ash, by then Rector of Imperial College, to address the subject. Other members of the working party were Lord Gregson of Fairey Holdings; Professor Cyril Hilsum, GEC Director of Research; Professor Roger Needham; and Dr. David Thomas, as SERC IT Director; with Dr. Mark Wilkins of the SERC acting as secretary.

The working party wrote its own terms of reference: to review the role of the academic sector in Alvey; consider requirements for a follow-up program; consider relationships with European programs; and report to the engineering board. A draft report was written and presented for discussion to over 300 members of the academic community at a "town meeting" held at the Mermaid Theatre, London, on 22 October 1985, and that discussion helped to shape the final report[30] published in April 1986.

The case for undertaking a major IT research program was convincing three years ago when the Alvey Committee reported, the Ash report noted, and it was even more convincing now. The intense worldwide competition was not confined to products and markets but was just as vital in the area of core technologies. It was clear that this was an activity that the U.K. could not abandon if it had any intention of maintaining, let alone enhancing, its relative industrial strength. The issue was how to organize Britain's effort to the best advantage of industry.

One of the lessons of the Alvey Programme, the working party said, was the acceptance of the need to establish common goals across a broad band of research activity. There was a degree of enthusiasm for this approach that must be built-on for the future. Despite difficulties in finance and administration there was little dispute on the success of the central objectives. It was inconceivable to consider returning to an unstructured means of support. U.K. IT research should be integrated with that of Europe.

Despite the success achieved in collaboration with industry, the report noted, some academics did not accept the need to collaborate. They perceived a loss of academic freedom. But the choice for the community was clear: participate in a major European and national enterprise or carry out independent research on a small scale with very inadequate funds. "In truth, the academic community need not fear an excessive degree of unwelcome direction, since experience has shown that its own contributions have been vital in program definition in the Alvey Programme; the community should continue to enjoy a substantial degree of influence in this sense in the future."

On the thorny topic of the arguable need for academic research to be more market-oriented, the Ash working party said it believed there was scope for both long-term and shorter-term research but that these must be kept in an appropriate balance. Too close an identification with the market and too great an emphasis on short-term work would be dangerously stultifying to creative academic work.

In any future program much remained to be done in the Alvey enabling technologies. Possible new enabling technologies included optoelectronics and III-V compound semiconductors. Alvey technologies should be applied to other areas of academic research. The working party was less convinced of the need for a continued major involvement of the academic sector in large demonstrator projects. Advanced network research should continue to be pursued.

The group's conclusions and recommendations are summarized in appendix 3. Their overall objective was for wholehearted academic participation, rising to £25 million per year, in a broadened after-Alvey program integrated with European programs. Significantly, and based on Alvey experience, they also urged that a six-months planning period should precede the program itself.

Commenting on the report at the time of publication, Professor Ash said: "In one sense this debate about After Alvey is too early, and in another sense it is already almost too late. It is too early because we cannot yet know the full benefit of the existing program. It is too late because in a technology of such vital economic importance to the U.K. a firm, consistent, and vigorous long-term commitment to research is a crucial factor in ensuring our future industrial competitiveness."

Edinburgh 85 and IT86

The first annual Alvey Conference was held at the University of Edinburgh from 24 to 27 June 1985. On the final day Geoffrey Pattie, who had succeeded Kenneth Baker as Minister of State for Industry and Information Technology, invited industry to assemble a working group to consider future policy. Important decisions would soon be required, he said, not only on the future of the Alvey Programme but also on the ESPRIT and Eureka programs in Europe. "To assess what needs to be done, industry must play a leading role. I hope that one of the results of this conference will be to set up an industrial working group to which officials of my department as well as the Ministry of Defence and the Science and Engineering Research Council will be prepared to contribute. I welcome signs that industry has already started thinking about the issues." The minister was skillfully equivocal in declaring the government's view:

I am sure the government will want to encourage the continued cooperative endeavor in the U.K. Whether such support is needed in the form provided by Alvey, and with a U.K. focus, is not so clear. Industry cannot expect financial support to continue indefinitely.

In some areas at least it is likely that programs like Alvey and ESPRIT will have fulfilled their pump-priming task of stimulating cooperation which can now continue without government assistance. In other areas there may be a case for continued assistance. In these areas the question has to be asked whether the assistance should be coordinated at a European or at U.K. level. Perhaps Europe should focus on a few large, market-oriented projects where the scale of effort is all-important to cope with the competition from the U.S. and Japan. Perhaps the U.K. should concentrate nationally on some of the fundamental technologies.

Mr. Pattie's hoped-for group emerged on 4 February 1986, when the Alvey Directorate announced that Sir Austin Bide,* Chairman of British Leyland and past Chairman of Glaxo, was to form and chair a committee to be known as the IT86 Committee to look into the question of what should follow the Alvey Programme. The committee had been organized by Sir Robert Telford, and members were to be drawn from the IT industry, IT users, and academics. Welcoming Sir Austin's appointment, Mr. Pattie said that he hoped that the new committee would be able to produce a report by October.

The Directorate's announcement stated:

The Alvey Programme has been running for nearly half of its five years, and most of the funds are now committed. The committee will wish to consider the scope, balance, and development of U.K. national and European collaborative research programs in information technology following the Alvey and ESPRIT 1 programs, and the exploitation of the advanced technology stemming from programs like Alvey and ESPRIT. The committee will pay particular attention to the needs of users of information technology and to the markets that the new technology will open up.

The committee's terms of reference were:

1. To consider and recommend cost-effective ways and means: (1) to improve the international competitiveness of the U.K. IT industry and of users; and (2) to enhance and improve the provision and application of IT within the U.K. The study would have regard to the need for awareness throughout U.K. industry and commerce of the results from current programs such as Alvey and ESPRIT as well as from new programs. It would also have regard to the special considerations and potential ad-

---

*Sir Austin had been chairman of the Confederation of British Industry's Research and Technology Committee. Sir John Hoskyns, Director-General of the Institute of Directors, founder of the Hoskyns systems house, and former (1979–1982) Policy Adviser to the Prime Minister, was invited to chair the IT86 Committee but declined because of pressure of work.

vantages arising from U.K. membership of the European Community.
2. To consider and recommend cost-effective ways and means of exploiting internationally this improved competitiveness.
3. To consider and recommend on the scope, balance, and development of U.K. national, EEC, and wider European collaborative IT programs.
4. To consider and advise on the manpower and training implications of the above recommendations.

Workshop Time

Meanwhile, in the months between the Edinburgh conference and the IT86 announcement, Laurence Clarke was at it again. Impatient at the delay in forming the after-Alvey committee, he decided to repeat the pre-Alvey workshop exercise, this time with industrial participation only. Horseracing, not cricket, provided the national inspiration this time around, as the Berystede Hotel, Ascot, was chosen as the location for twin workshops on research and exploitation. Clarke convened the meeting, which took place on 6–8 January 1986 and produced recommendations for a combined after-Alvey program. The starting point for the workshops was clear: the Alvey Report had foreseen the need for research continuing beyond five years and for a second phase of work to improve the exploitation of U.K. research.

Dr. Nigel Horne of STC chaired the exploitation workshop at Ascot. The objective of the program that his group recommended was to improve the effectiveness and competitiveness of the U.K. through the exploitation of IT in key sectors, while developing a strong U.K.-based IT manufacturing industry. The aim was to create closer links between IT users and suppliers in order to exploit national strengths in IT-using enterprises and achieve pull-through into the U.K. IT industry to produce effective world competitive systems.

The main thrust of the proposed exploitation program was toward a number of beta-site demonstrations where leading IT users worked closely with suppliers to exploit the results of Alvey 1 and Alvey 2 research, together with U.K. application expertise. A £2 million "bridge" activity over eighteen months would identify potential partnerships in strategic areas and conduct feasibility studies. The total cost of the exploitation program would be £1–2 billion over five years, with an average 25 percent coming from public funds.

Dr. F. G. Marshall of Plessey chaired the research workshop at Ascot. His group concluded that Alvey had led to a general improvement in the U.K. position in IT research, but three facts were important. First, Britain's competitors had also progressed and new fields needed exploring. Secondly, Alvey had revealed the importance of topics not sufficiently understood to obtain the appropriate slice of funding and attention in the first round. Thirdly, though Alvey had established good channels of collaboration between firms, universities, and government R & D establishments, the workshop believed that these links would not survive if funding were to be withdrawn. It was essential to establish the strong national foundation needed for the U.K. fully to exploit European opportunities and to retain adequate national capabilities should European collaboration fail to achieve good results.

The suggested research program would cost £500 million—about the same as Alvey 1, allowing for inflation. There were revised priorities and some new topics among the enabling technologies. Sensors and peripherals should be added; software engineering and IKBS should be merged. Computer integrated manufacturing and gallium arsenide should be added. Optoelectronics should be left to the JOERS program. An interim research budget of £25 million support should be sought immediately, to enable a further £40 million of projects to be launched. This would maintain the Alvey collaborative momentum until a decision on the main program was taken. University participation in the research program should be increased to £100 million.

The combined program recommended by the industry workshops at Ascot would result in costs to the taxpayer of £500 to 750 million over five years, representing £250 million for research and £250 to 500 million for exploitation. As the deliberations of the IT86 Committee got under way, the Ascot workshop papers proved to be a significant input.

Research and Applications

In particular the research and exploitation categories explored at Ascot were reflected in the Bide Committee. At the committee's first meeting, in March 1986, Sir Austin set up three subcommittees: on ways and means, which he chaired; on research, chaired by Cameron Low of PA Consultants; and on applications, chaired by Nigel Horne.

"On the ways and means subcommittee I had people who were what I would call very broad gauge," says Sir Austin, "and they were specifically of my own choosing—including Lord Gregson, Professor John Ashworth, and my right-hand man, David Speake of GEC. The broad aim of the subcommittee was to coordinate and make quite sure that things were moving in the right direction and moving at the right sort of pace and that the right kind of things were being done. It was not concerned with how the money might be raised for any program we might propose; it was an internal coordinating group."

The work of the applications subcommittee marked a major departure from the pattern set by the Alvey Programme. Nigel Horne had joined the IT86 committee specifically to pursue the concept of applications. He explains the idea behind his subcommittee's work:

The idea is a very simple one. Alvey had encouraged collaborations among IT professionals, and its big contribution was to link academic professionals with industrial professionals. But one thing it did not do was introduce strong market pull. For various reasons the British are excellent at research and will go on happily researching forever and won't pull through hard products unless necessity forces the issue. Also, Alvey—enormous step though it was—involved predominantly IT professionals. The user is interested in IT only as a tool to solve a problem. But nine times out of ten IT on its own won't solve the problem.

So I wanted to do two things. One was to get collaborations vertically, that is, between users, industrial suppliers at various levels, and academia. Secondly, to make it more multidisciplinary. Government, as one of the big users of IT, has a major role to play. I felt that there was great scope here in reducing duplication and in greater coordination in things like office products, networking, security, reliability, and standards. Also, I felt the government could use IT as a weapon—in tackling unemployment, for instance, by using interactive distance learning to train IT and other professionals. All I was trying to do really was to focus minds on some of the things that needed a catalyst to make them work.

The government's view of the proposed applications effort was to become a key issue in the after-Alvey debate. What was Horne's perception at the time? "I think they were anxious to take IT through to examples of applications. The government did not discourage applications at any time. As far as I was aware, there was great enthusiasm for an applications program at that time."

Cameron Low recalls his surprise at being asked to join the IT86 Committee—and his even greater surprise at being asked to chair the research subcommittee. (As head of PA Computers and Telecommunications he was no scientist but an experienced consultant and manager.) He says:

> I was naive enough to believe that there was a real chance of a proper successor program—provided we did not let what I will call "the more skilled manipulators of HMG funding" spoil the true arguments. I was aware of the risk of a "con job" taking advantage of my ignorance of matters hardware technical. But not aware enough? Maybe that is harsh on the guys who worked so hard; they are passionately interested in the work itself. One of my main memories is of an awful lot of paper. Many new filing cabinets were bought in various offices.

Outlining his subcommittee's approach at the 1986 Alvey Conference Low said the work sometimes felt like performing a balancing act on n orthogonal tightropes, where n was at least three:

- National/European.
- General/specific: general enough to be on the right scale; specific enough to be acted upon.
- Majority/minority: reflecting majority opinion for support; qualified minority opinion for insight and foresight.

The aim, he said, was to produce recommendations on research that preferred effective selectivity to ineffective "fairness," where that was the choice, and that spurned quantitative precision but strove for qualitative rigor.

Bide's three-subcommittee structure spawned a rather substantial collective effort. The research subcommittee set up working parties on human interfaces, systems, software, and hardware and components. The applications subcommittee established a working party for each of eight identified exemplar applications. The Alvey IT User Panel represented the users' views, and a two-day users' workshop also formed part of the IT86 exercise. The number of people participating in these groups totalled over 200 (though some names were repeated in more than one group). Eric Ash doubts the wisdom of this scale of activity: "My SERC After-Alvey Committee consisted of five people. The Bide Committee, complete with subcommittees and working parties, consisted of something approaching 180 people. The idea of having these vast numbers of people to discuss what essentially was a fairly clear-cut, well-defined problem, I thought, was exceedingly odd."

Like the Alvey Committee before it, the Bide Committee solicited the views of all interested parties. They received written contributions and/or took oral evidence from forty-seven organizations, ranging from the British Psychological Society to the Trades Union Congress, and from forty-six individuals, including thirteen professors. In June at Millbank Tower they discussed the European dimension with Jean-Marie Cadiou, Horst Hüncke, and John Elmore of the European Commission's ESPRIT staff.

Following the sporting theme begun with the pre-Alvey meeting at Lord's and the pre-Bide workshop at Ascot, the Bide Committee chose a more general-purpose sporting location, Wembley, for their weekend get-together to finalize their thoughts on 5–7 September 1986—not Wembley Stadium (which might have been appropriate, if all the IT86 subcommittee and working-party members had attended) but the Ladbroke International Hotel.

The Bide Report

The IT86 Committee published its report[31] in November 1986. In his foreword Sir Austin acknowledged the SERC after-Alvey report and the industrial workshop report as "the foundation upon which we built our study." The summary section of the report is reproduced as appendix 4; the main recommendation was for an IT plan of action consisting of a scheme of collaborative IT applications; a supporting scheme of collaborative research; and measures to promote technology transfer, the widespread adoption of IT, and the development of IT skills.

For the applications scheme, £125 million should come from public funds, with the funding rate related to project risk. This would stimulate a much larger investment by industry and generate a total applications program of £500 million or more. For the research scheme, costing £550 million over five years, £300 million would come from public funds, but this would include

Britain's contribution to ESPRIT 2 as well as the national program.

In arguing for such a billion-pound program the committee's starting point was the general industrial background. World competition was rapidly intensifying, and nobody owed the U.K. a living. While the IT revolution was widely recognized, its depth and pervasiveness was not. We were only in the foothills of what advanced IT could do to drive down costs. Alvey and ESPRIT 1 had played a significant part in helping the U.K. to maintain its position, but the hectic pace of IT development would continue well into the 1990s, and unless the U.K. and its European partners recognized and accepted this challenge the adverse results would be far-reaching.

In seeking to improve its competitive position U.K. industry faced a number of obstacles. The U.K. market base was small; high interest rates and the short-term outlook of financial organizations did not encourage a high rate of R & D investment; and the market was distorted by the substantial assistance given by foreign governments to their own industries. The rate of technological change was dramatic; international standardization moves were welcome but exposed U.K. industry to even greater competition, and restraints on access to technology were an increasing problem. Deregulation in the U.K. posed problems as well as benefits, and issues of intellectual property rights became more complex as companies grouped together.

For whatever reason, the U.K.'s excellent record in research and invention had not been matched by excellence in developing invention into products, in manufacturing and marketing those products, or in applying them to create further wealth. It was crucial to add exploitation to invention and "market pull" to "technology push." There was a mutual interest between IT users and suppliers that could and should be developed further. Hence the key elements of the proposed plan:

• An integrated national/European approach.

• Coordinated action involving both users and suppliers.

• Government involvement, including financial support for specified projects.

• A major thrust to create awareness of IT and its potential.

• A substantial education and training program.

• Opportunities for the best U.K. academics to work on exploitable research programs.

- Maintenance of the collaborative culture established in the Alvey Programme.

The aim of the applications scheme was to stimulate the development of new products and services by the exploitation of IT research and to demonstrate how this could be done effectively. It would involve a series of projects in which IT users and suppliers would collaborate, to their mutual advantage, in IT systems development. These projects would draw on Alvey, ESPRIT, and other technologies. Eight possible projects had been studied as examples:

- Security and control of services and systems in domestic and commercial premises.
- Clinical data and process models for health care.
- Interactive distance learning as a teaching aid.
- Distance learning for senior management.
- Control of the manufacturing process in mechanical engineering.
- A practical project support environment.
- Electronic funds transfer at the point of sale.
- Provably safe systems for railway signaling.

The proposed research effort would be focused on perceived future market opportunities and would help to support the development of IT applications. Part of the research would be generated by the applications projects and part would be longer-term work based on an analysis of market trends, user problems, and potentially significant technical advances. Details of the research effort outlined in the IT86 report reflected the committee's research subcommittee structure, with sections devoted to human interfaces, systems and software (software; IKBS; systems architecture; and speech, signal, and image processing), and hardware. The suggested allocation of resources between research areas was:

Human interface	£25 million
Systems and software	£200 million
Hardware	£250 million
Demonstrators	£75 million
Total	£550 million

This, in essence, was the Bide Report—the case for a billion-pound, government-supported, market-oriented program based on applications (involving financial contributions from IT-using organizations, including government departments, as well as from IT suppliers) and supporting research. The Alvey Committee's report had led to the Alvey Programme; would the Bide Committee's report lead to a follow-up Bide Programme? The committee and the community were hopeful.

The Long Silence

On 21 November 1986 the DTI press notice announcing publication of the Bide Report quoted Mr. Pattie as saying: "I intend to pursue the government response to the report as a matter of urgency." Mr. Pattie's urgent pursuit was to take a further fourteen months (and, indeed, he was to hand over the baton in mid-pursuit as he failed to survive a political reshuffle). Nigel Horne echoes a point made by Alvey committeemen: "They were pressing us for the report and wanted it early. That's one of the reasons the report was not as adequate as it might have been. The irony was, it then took about fifteen months for the government's response."

About halfway through this period an interim response was made by Kenneth Clarke, newly appointed Minister of Trade and Industry at the Department of Trade and Industry under the new Secretary of State, Lord Young of Graffham. In reassembling her government after the general election of June 1987 Mrs. Thatcher had chosen not to reappoint a Minister for Information Technology as such—not the most hopeful of messages for the IT community. On the occasion of the 1987 Alvey Conference at Manchester University Institute of Science and Technology (UMIST) the IT spokesman was Mr. Clarke. As an IT spokesman, he was an excellent political stonewaller.

Clarke told the conference that the unification of the British IT community was one of the major achievements of the Alvey Programme so far. The IT86 Committee had been concerned that the momentum that the Alvey Programme had generated should be maintained. "Obviously it is important that the momentum that has now been acquired is maintained," the minister said, "both by suppliers and by users throughout the economy. I certainly agree with the committee that the full benefits of information technology R & D can be realized only when they are translated into IT products and these products are applied by users in the commercial world." On the IT86 report the government had consulted widely, and this consultation process had produced substantial support for the committee's recommendations. "What we have to do now is to examine critically the justification for further government funding at a time when there are huge demands for the taxpayers' money."

Clarke added: "I can confirm that the government are in principle quite prepared to accept that there is a case for continuing to fund collaborative programs in some way." But the government was at the moment reviewing public spending priorities. "If we do join in supporting and building on the collaborative spirit that the Alvey Programme has so far helped to nurture, we have to decide how we can best concentrate government support on application projects, promoting the application of information technology to improve the competitiveness or efficiency of user and supplier and the general health of the economy." And the closer one got to the marketplace, the minister added, the more the government would expect industry to bear a considerable part of the cost: "No sector of British industry can ever look upon government as the prime or only source of finance for essential research and development on which the industry's own health depends. . . . Nevertheless I and my colleagues recognize that there is a case for government support. . . . I certainly accept that support is justified, especially for research and innovative applications where early users experience extra risks and higher costs." Delegates had expected the government's response that day. Toward the end of the session at which the minister had spoken, announcement of the question-and-answer period was greeted with total and eloquent silence.

Enter Enterprise

At long last, in January 1988, the government's response to the Bide proposals emerged—not as a discrete announcement in its own right but as a minor part of a major repackaging job on the DTI itself. Lord Young, Secretary of State for Trade and Industry, had announced new objectives for his department the previous October, and the revised policies and organization intended to implement these objectives were now detailed in a government White Paper[32] that presented the DTI as "the Department for Enterprise." Publication of the White Paper marked the launch of a £5 million advertising campaign for the restyled department at which Lord Young commented: "Government programs are like cornflakes. It they are not marketed, they will not sell." Alas, the Alvey Community discovered that the government's IT cornflakes were not the crisp and nourishing Bide brand but a rather weak and soggy substitute.

Overall, the White Paper aimed to describe the role of the DTI in encouraging enterprise. It declared:

The central theme for our policies remains the belief that sensible economic decisions are best taken by those competing in the marketplace. The responsibility of government is to create the right climate so that markets work better and to encourage enterprise. The aim of our policy is thus to encourage the process of wealth creation by stimulating individual initiative and enterprise and by promoting an understanding of market opportunities combined with the ability to exploit them.

One of the ten chapters in the White Paper addressed the subject of "Innovation, Using Technology," and it was in this chapter (see appendix 6) that the response to the IT86 Report appeared. The government noted that "the Alvey Programme has provided a good focus for the IT research community" and accepted that "some resources should be devoted to a national initiative complementary to ESPRIT" but went on to reject any "specific program of support for applications in IT."

The DTI had decided to change the balance of existing innovation policies in order to move away from near-market R & D support, the White Paper said. Greater emphasis in collaborative programs would be given to longer-term research between companies, and collaboration between universities and companies would be encouraged. Greater emphasis would be attached to technology transfer. Industry would be encouraged to spend more on R & D and to apply new technology more effectively.

Against this background the White Paper included a one-sentence rejection of the applications scheme recommended by the Bide Committee. On research, the U.K. was contributing £200 million to ESPRIT 2; the DTI had earmarked £29 million over three years for national IT research programs; and the

SERC planned to devote some £55 million over five years to related academic research, mainly in partnership with companies. The DTI was to bring together all its collaborative IT research activities into a new unit.

The White Paper had some kind words to say about Alvey, but as indicated above the response fell far short of what Bide had proposed. Arguably it matched the overall total for research, but with a greater European share. Bide had envisaged £300 million from public funds over five years, including an estimated £135 million for ESPRIT 2. The White Paper also indicated a likely five-year total of about £300 million, but based on an ESPRIT contribution of £200 million. As for the £500 million applications scheme, the heart of the proposed IT86 program, this was rejected out of hand on political grounds. The other element inherent in the response was the rejection of a named after-Alvey program as such in favor of a "new unit" (discussed in chapter 15) that would succeed the Alvey Directorate and would run a variety of IT programs.

15

The New Era

The government had rejected the applications scheme proposed by Bide, placed even more emphasis on European research, and agreed to mount a modest national research program. Sir Austin took the news calmly, others less so. Alvey was subsumed into a new directorate, headed by one of the original Millbank Tower team, which aimed to apply the results of the Alvey experiment in a new, permanent IT research structure. In mid-1988, Kenneth Owen records in this chapter, a new post-Alvey era of SERC/DTI collaboration was born.

Responses to the Response

The Alvey Community had been hoping for a clearly defined "Son of Alvey" program to carry forward the spirit and achievement that Alvey had pioneered. They had argued that it would be ridiculous to stop after five years, for reasons that the Alvey Committee had indicated. They had believed that the government would favor taking the Alvey research a stage further toward exploitation. Perhaps they had assumed too much. One might expect that in commenting on the government's response they would rise in unanimous protest against it. But reactions are mixed, and none is more surprising than that of Sir Austin Bide, who appears remarkably relaxed about the government's total rejection of his committee's proposed applications scheme.

First, with hindsight, does Sir Austin believe his committee got it right?

Yes, I do. We produced some figures about government involvement, but to me that really wasn't the fundamental point. Government at the end of the day would make up its own mind on whether they wanted to do these things and, if so, on the magnitude of doing them.

I never regarded the actual figure as fundamentally important. What to me was fundamentally important was whether or not the concepts were pursued. Industrialists with the backing of the researchers came to a conclusion that there were certain kinds of applications of a broad importance that would require a coordination of effort. If that fundamental concept is true, then it seemed to me that that was something that ought to be done. Whether government put up the money or not is not by any means the fundamental question.

Hence Sir Austin's equanimity at the government's negative response:

People have asked me "Were you disappointed?" No, I wasn't disappointed—nor fundamentally was I surprised, because government obviously had to take a view as to where it was going to place its resources, and we are now a committed partner in the European Community. I guess they took the view that they would have to put the major effort into ESPRIT. Even for applications it lies within the competence of the Community structure to do those things. If it's not done there, it ought to be done somewhere. On applications it was always my personal view that they could be Eureka projects, but whether that would be other people's view I don't know.

The thing that would surprise me, disappoint me, and worry me would be for the industry, having said that this is a worthwhile thing, just to drop it flat. I would expect them either to seek Eureka partners or to do it within the framework of a U.K. effort without government funding. I would be most disappointed if these projects did not now take place on some footing or another.

We shall see what we shall see. But I think that government may have missed a trick. If government had chosen to put in an amount of money, whatever the figure, it would then be very difficult for the people who have made these observations not to pursue what they have claimed to be important. People keep talking about monetary incentives. I would regard that as a monetary spur.

Sir Austin clearly distances himself from the views of his committee. His position is that he was a "neutral" chairman, told by his committee of experts that these things were fundamentally important and believing them. This perception extended into the next stage, that of waiting for the government's response—a time when, many people have suggested, the Bide proposals should have been lobbied hard: "At the point where they'd done the report I stood back. It didn't seem to me that it was any part of my role to go out and proselytize, to be lobbying. If anybody was going to lobby, that was for other people, people who contributed material to the report. I was not asked for a view by government. I took the view that if I was a neutral chairman, it would be quite inconsistent with that view if I then started lobbying all over the place. I'm a logician."

Sir Austin appreciates that others may be less relaxed in their reaction to the rejection of the IT86 report: "I think I understand the situation. Those who are closer to it in the technical sense and have a vested interest may have felt a degree of outrage. I didn't, because I was taking a much more detached view." He denies that, in the event, the enormous amount of effort that went into the IT86 exercise was wasted. "If industry will do for itself what government won't assist in, the effort won't be wasted. That's my point. If industry really believes in these applications, industry should do them. If they told the truth, they should just do it."

Nigel Horne, not surprisingly, feels more strongly than his IT86 chairman on the subject:

It was a very inadequate response—only three paragraphs on the IT86 proposals buried in the White Paper, including a single sentence rejecting the applications scheme. I felt that to be dismissed like that was not very polite to the many people, users and suppliers, who had helped me to write the applications program. I was naturally disappointed. The thing that disappointed me was not so much the refusal of the program, as the fact that there was absolute deathly silence on it after we had submitted the report. Given a little more time, I believe we could have made the applications scheme almost self-funding, largely through the sharing of programs.

Turning to the implications of the response, Horne says: "The biggest gap is this: What is the U.K.'s IT competitive advantage? Sooner or later, the U.K. has to balance its books. In the world of IT you can't do that by attacking everything in the whole domain. You have to narrow down and decide on something at which you're going to excel. I felt that by means of user/supplier collaboration we could start to focus in on things where we could excel and satisfy real needs. In my view the government has a positive role to play in this."

As for Sir Austin's suggestion that if these applications are worth doing, industry, possibly with users, should go ahead and do them anyway, Horne has reservations:

I have some sympathy with that view, but not total sympathy. If a user has an internal problem, I should expect him to go ahead and solve it. In no way would I ever suggest that a government should become involved. But when it comes to something like an EFTPOS system, where you need national standards and there is no mechanism for setting the standards, there has to be a catalyst. Somebody has to get in there to make it happen.

That is one prime reason for the applications program. There is another: on many occasions, a user will buy IT equipment for reasons that are not necessarily logical. He may, for example, decide to buy a piece of French equipment. Once he's bought that equipment he keeps on buying it, at least for a while. So the other argument for having an applications program is that on some of these initiatives if you can start the buyer on British equipment, there's a fair chance he'll keep it rolling for a while. And that does benefit the U.K."

Eric Ash does not share Horne's opinion:

Applications appeared to be the flavor of the month at the time, and there was a lot of talk about things being too researchy and too far away from the marketplace. That appeared to put a shadow on the Alvey kind of approach, which in general was further back from the marketplace. I think the Bide Report implied a level of commitment to applications collaboration between firms—firms funded at only 50 percent—which would have been difficult to implement. I also think that their request for research funding was too modest; it was about half what we suggested in our report.

Nonetheless, Professor Ash regrets the absence of an Alvey 2 program. "I would have liked to see an Alvey follow-on program. We recommended that in our after-Alvey report in 1986, and on rereading it I think we got it about right."

Cameron Low's interests in IT86 were not confined to his subcommittee's research proposals; he speaks of lobbying, applications, and the rules of the world electronics market:

I proposed that we should set up a carefully structured lobbying campaign. I wrote papers on this and worked it up with Rob Morland (Secretary to the Research Subcommittee). It got support from a lot of folk, but I think Sir Austin got a tip that it would be counterproductive. Certainly we could have done with more "supporters" from outside the IT industry.

The delay in the response was very damaging in itself. I wonder if it was caused by superhuman attempts by the knowledgeable to bash some sense into politicians' heads? If so, I'm glad they tried so hard. It will be interesting to see whether the new scheme pays any attention to the strong recommendation we made on the need for a sensible approach to funding of overheads. If that got some action, then my time on IT86 was worthwhile to me. To be fair to HM Treasury, if you've been conned sideways for years, you are going to be pretty suspicious.

However untidy our plans would have looked against a backcloth of "The City is the best judge" and "Whatever other countries do is their business," I still think it is silly to pretend that the rules of the world electronics market are how Maggie would like them to be rather than how they are. Of one thing I am certain: we missed a huge trick as a country by not adopting the applications scheme. Given rigorous vetting of proposals, we could have had all the benefits of creative public procurement à la U.S.A., plus ideas synergy and development by multiple good minds. For good minds we have in the U.K.

The SERC Council supported all three elements of the IT86 proposals, Tony Egginton says: the European dimension; the research program, continuing in an Alvey-like mode; and the applications area, which the SERC regarded as very important. "So we were disappointed in the government's overall response. We accept that the DTI is worried about the applications area, and the SERC is now exploring the possibilities of promoting a better dialogue between IT and engineering, with the aim of making IT a generic technology that all engineers working on SERC projects would regard as just part of their way of life. That is not in breach of the near-market argument; it is saying we want U.K. engineering academics to take IT very seriously."

Professor Brian Shackel also is among those who regret the government's decision:

The rejection of the IT86 applications scheme was very disappointing. Much of the benefit of Alvey has been the experience of collaboration and how to pull things through toward the market, and now we're throwing it all away. The Bide applications would have capitalized so much on Alvey. The U.K. still has a leading position in human factors. Above all, the human interface is part of the market appeal of a product. If the government had supported the Bide applications scheme, that would have put a lot more HI into our products, and that would have given British products the market edge.

David Talbot, former Alvey Software Engineering director, describes the decision not to mount an Alvey 2 program as another classic English example of "snatching defeat from the jaws of victory." Professor Feigenbaum of Stanford (whose Alvey criticisms are reported in chapter 10) suggested[33] in 1983 that the British have an alarming propensity to "shoot themselves in the foot." Talbot adds: "In both feet, actually. Colleagues of mine in the U.S. and on the continent are perpetually amazed at our ability to do this. This lack of any long-term view worries me. It's the difference between running a corner shop and running a major chain of stores."

Laurence Clarke clearly was in favor of an Alvey 2 program and bitterly regrets both the government's decision and the long delay in reaching it. The adage that a prophet is not without honor save in his own country applies to Brian Oakley and the Alvey Directorate, he says. "All the other nations thought Alvey was bloody marvelous, and Her Ladyship thought it was useless."

Others who were also in at the beginning share these feelings. Reay Atkinson speaks with "infinite sadness" of what has followed Alvey. "We were presented as a country with a great opportunity and a very effective embryonic organization. Because of a totally inadequate approach to funding and lack of awareness of the situation we are in danger of losing that. I simply do not understand how the government can ignore the analogues of other nations."

Alvey Committee members differ in their views in 1988 as they did in 1982. "I was opposed to an Alvey 2," says Iann Barron, who would prefer government incentives for IT industrial investment combined with a tighter monitoring of academic research. "I was not really in favor of the Bide proposals," says Philip Hughes, "though the way they were treated is little short of scandalous. To me the idea of putting money into user projects is not really a sensible one. As for the White Paper, I read it and said 'There's the sandwich, where's the meat?' The only meat in it is £29 million over three years."

Derek Roberts says he would have supported the government if it had not wasted people's time on the IT86 exercise but declared a commitment to ESPRIT 2 and then gone on to fill any serious strategic gaps with national projects. That would have been rational, he says, and would have broken the unfortunate synchronization between the European and national programs. As for the IT86 recommendations, Roberts says:

> I would have preferred the applications side to have been completely divorced from the concept of the follow-on to Alvey. Precompetitive research collaboration implies a ten-year or even fifteen-year program. The applications emphasis in Bide came from a school of

thought that seemed to believe that Alvey had done all the research. It was not adequately recognized that the research had to be continued at the same time as one was growing the applications; it should not be one or the other. I would have regarded the applications thrust as a good thrust but one that should be pursued through Eureka.

A Political View

Sir Geoffrey Pattie, former IT Minister, places the Bide Report in the context of wider industrial, political, and European issues:

There were three areas in the Bide Report. Training was starting to come through to the sort of apple-pie status that it now enjoys, so that was OK; there was applications; and then there was the question of continuing the research program. That included a lot of money for ESPRIT and RACE. So what was clear to me was that there was quite a significant amount of funding in the DTI's budget in the forward years which took account of the research activities that Bide was talking about.

The problem was exacerbated to some extent by the fact that we had this awful wrangle about the European Framework R & D program, including ESPRIT and RACE, a wrangle for which I was supposed to be totally responsible. This went on for months, and people began saying the Framework program is being called into question by Britain. In a sense Bide and his report started to get caught up in the Framework business. In due course the Framework program was signed off, in a somewhat mutilated form.

The applications thrust of Bide was really to say, first, as cynics might argue, "We need more of the same." But the committee also said, I thought very correctly, that the way that these programs could really score would be if there were some practical appreciation across different government departments of the application implications of programs such as Alvey—to accept that technology was not something that went conveniently into one bag and happened to coincide with the accepted view of governmental responsibilities. Aspects of technology have an impact across different government departments—but usually either one department would lead to the exclusion of all the others, or several departments would pursue parallel and totally non-intercommunicating programs. One was left saying there must be a better way of doing this.

A lot of that thinking went into the Link schemes involving government departments, universities, and industry, and so in a sense Bide struck several important and timely blows which were noted and, perhaps to a more significant extent than he and members of the committee appreciate, were acted on.

But had not Pattie been arguing the importance of the exploitation of research results at the time of the Bide investigation?

Yes, and it is coming out in the Link schemes. There is a belief that at the center of what is a really rather complicated question about why our industrial performance is not as good as it should be one gets down to the exploitation factor. It is agreed in virtually every pub and public hall in the land—not with a great deal of substance to support it, though it certainly was true once—that we in this country are the innovators of the world but, having got Frank Whittle in the outer office with a brown paper parcel with the jet engine in it, we then sit there saying "We're not so sure about this, Frank." This has fascinated me for quite a while. It doesn't do any more than fascinate me, because I don't know what to do about my fascination.

I'm not a macropsychoanalyst; I can't put the nation or the nation's leaders on the couch, and in any case it's certainly not a Thatcherite phenomenon. If one is keen on the exploitation factor, one says: "If we have got ideas, we must find ways of bringing them into the market quicker." In a governmental sense you can take that process only so far. You can make certain that industry are talking and checking out ideas with universities and research institutes, research institutes are checking out practical viability, feasibility, and production techniques with industry, and all are working together. But fairly soon you arrive at those points, in the railway sense, where you either go into a storage siding to check again because of the expense or you go down the main railway track on a journey which is high-cost and rather hairy as the train starts to gather speed. At that stage, on this government's philosophy, the decision as to which way to go should be a commercial one.

The former IT minister stops short of maintaining that the government has been consistent all along. "It is frightfully difficult to be precise about these things. I believe that a certain amount of government support activity is right and proper, and if I'd been still in government I would have weighed all things in a way that ensured that Alvey 2 went on through the various different forms."

Including applications? Well, yes, he admits.

The sums of money are not that enormous, when you chop them down. They always sound good in ministerial statements, but that means they have been aggregated over five years and spread over four programs, so you divide by four and divide by five and get down to £8 million a year. As we had had those sort of sums around, the problem would have been the applications side—and I would have supported that, and that was at the back of the statements I was making at the Alvey conferences. I actually did this at the MoD, where it was a little bit easier because one had more money available. We put it to industry in 1982, for example, that we would support something called the Experimental Aircraft Programme if industry would put some money into it.

They took an awful lot of awakening to the fact that we actually meant it. However incredible that may seem six years on, it then appeared as a sort of revolutionary statement. It took me three meetings to convince the then chairman of British Aerospace that I meant what I said, that we weren't going to fund it at 100 percent. We agreed we would build the aeroplane and embody in it all the developing technologies, then fly the thing and find out exactly how it worked. That to me is a Bide-type demonstrator program.

It is important to wean companies away from excessive dependence on the defense or telecommunications authorities. Companies like GEC and Plessey were virtually ruined in technological development terms by excessive dependence on public procurement over many years. They developed some quite good technology as well, but I don't think their international position was enhanced in the process.

The New Era

The new unit mentioned in the DTI White Paper of January 1988 is the Information Engineering Directorate (IED) of the Department of Trade and Industry. The manner of the Alvey Directorate's transformation into this new unit merits a brief mention here. Brian Oakley retired from the civil service on 10 October 1987, to be succeeded by his deputy, Laurence Clarke. Only six weeks later, on 23 November 1987, Dr. Timothy Walker, the DTI official who had been the first Alvey Administration director, returned to the directorate to take over from Clarke, and on 12 January 1988, coinciding with the publication of the White Paper, the Alvey Directorate was absorbed into the new Information Engineering Directorate.

Laurence Clarke describes his brief occupancy of the Alvey Director's office: "When I was appointed Director it was on the clear understanding that when a new program went ahead, it was not a foregone conclusion that I would continue to be the Director. There would be a beauty contest, as Alastair Macdonald put it, in which I would be one of the contestants. I was content with that." On November 6 Clarke, in Brussels on business, received a message to telephone Macdonald. This he did on his return that night, to be told that it had been decided that the future program was to be run by a civil servant.

"I immediately wrote to Brian Hayes saying why I thought it was wrong, quite regardless of whether or not it was me, and he called me to discuss that note with him. On 16 November I saw him again, and he told me that Timothy Walker was to be appointed. I still believed that such a directorate would have been better headed by somebody from industry."

The Science and Engineering Research Council, partner with the DTI in the Alvey Programme, received even less notice than did Clarke of the change of Alvey Director. Macdonald told Tony Egginton and Mark Wilkins, SERC IT Director, of the decision on Wednesday 18 November, just five days before the appointment was to take effect. The signs were that the decision had been taken abruptly by the Secretary of State with scant regard for the normal process of consultation. Certainly its implementation appeared inept.

The Information Engineering Directorate opened for business on 12 January, taking over the Alvey Directorate's responsibilities and also a number of new areas, including optoelectronics, gallium arsenide, the Link program, molecular electronics, advanced semiconductors, and superconductivity. As the new directorate settled down, it regrouped the Alvey technologies into three broad areas:

- Devices, including VLSI and CAD.
- Systems architecture, including parallel processing, speech, vision, and distributed systems.
- Systems engineering, including software engineering, IKBS, and the human/computer interface.

Rob Morland of Alvey VLSI became the initial IED devices director, succeeded at the end of September by Brian Nuttall of British Telecom. David Morgan of Alvey software engineering became director of systems engineering; and Chris Cheetham was recruited from ICL to be director of systems architecture. In addition, Mark Gibson was appointed director of administration, and a new post at this level, filled by Dr. Andrew Wallard, embraced international, education, and optoelectronics affairs. Keith Bartlett of Alvey Infrastructure and Communications continued as IED director of standards and infrastructure.

During 1987, as the government's response to the IT86 Report was awaited, the Alvey Directorate had commissioned discussion papers intended to help in the planning of a future program. These outline technology strategies were based on the assumption that such a program would follow the IT86 recommendations. Revised versions of these strategies—now grouped under Devices,[34] Systems Architecture,[35] and Systems Engineering[36] and described in ESPRIT parlance as "workplans"—were drafted in the wake of the DTI White Paper and distributed at the U.K. IT 88 Conference at Swansea in July 1988. In a keynote speech at Swansea John Butcher, Minister for Industry and Consumer Affairs at the DTI (deputizing for Lord Young), invited outline proposals for projects under what he described as the government's new national IT research program.

A major feature of this program, and one which may prove to be the most significant organizational change to stem from the Alvey Programme, had emerged during the first half of 1988. The SERC and the DTI, having not been on the closest of terms at the time of the unilateral DTI decision to appoint Dr. Walker as Alvey Director, agreed to come closer through a unified approach to their IT research planning and implementation—not just for a specified period but indefinitely.

The new deal was announced jointly by the DTI and SERC on 6 May 1988: "The work objective is to establish a unified framework for the support by the SERC and DTI across the whole spectrum of IT research, ranging from fundamental work in Higher Education Institutes through collaborative Link programs to industry-led activities, often in collaboration with the academic sector," the announcement stated. "A new advisory structure will be set up, drawn from the academic sector and industry in roughly equal numbers, and headed by a single advisory body, advising both SERC and DTI on research programs and resource allocation, and on individual applications for support. . . . Other government departments will be encouraged to join those programs of interest to them."

Lord Young and Professor Bill Mitchell, SERC Chairman, both welcomed the integration. "This reorganization will further strengthen the links between industrial and academic researchers," declared Lord Young, among other things. Mitchell expressed himself "delighted"; the new set-up would enable the SERC to maintain a proper balance between fundamental and strategic research. Later it was announced that the chairman of the top-level strategic committee would be Dr. Nigel Horne of STC, proponent of the rejected IT86 applications scheme.

Alastair Macdonald, now the DTI Deputy Secretary whose responsibilities include the IED, explains: "We had a tremendous number of advisory committees covering electronics in the Department, and Tim Walker and I felt that with the new program and with changes in the structure of the Department it was best to start with a clean sheet of paper. From that clean sheet of paper, building upon the Alvey experience, has come the notion of the SERC and DTI having one committee to oversee IT research and development. In a sense this joint committee has taken over from the Alvey Programme Steering Committee."

Nigel Horne summarizes the main features of his SERC/DTI committee:

First, the committee is advisory; we will not be assessing projects. I would expect to assist in laying down broad directions, which after all is what I was trying to do via the IT86 applications scheme. The second point is that there are users on the committee, which I think is crucially important. And the third point is that it involves cross-departmental coordination in government. The last point is: the amount of money is very small, but I hope we will be able to make it strategic investment.

Certainly there will be a problem in trying to strike the right balance between long-term research and short-term development. If there isn't a problem, we haven't got enough bright ideas. We all get hung up on it far too readily, without really knowing what we're talking about. Academics love to believe that they need the freedom. Give them tuppence, and they'll forget all about freedom and get on with the work. And industrialists are no different.

The Oakley View

As Director of the Alvey Programme Brian Oakley was reluctant to take a major part in the IT86 activity, though the Alvey Directorate provided support services for the committee. He confirms the general view at the time that an applications program was perceived to be politically desirable. "We believed that ministers were in a mood to say 'We have research coming out of our ears,' and since the emphasis on exploitation was very strongly in the air, everybody believed that ministers would be keen on an applications program. That was the perceived wisdom of the time; it was a general consensus led by Nigel Horne."

Oakley did suggest to the IT86 committee an alternative form of organization for a follow-up program: one that would be outside the government machine:

> They came down against what I was saying, and I think I understand why they did, but in retrospect it is just possible that they would have done better to have followed this alternative. I suggested that what we had done under Alvey was to find a forum for sampling the views of the IT community that was under the direct umbrella of government. I argued that it would be perfectly possible to organize such a forum outside government, in a new body, probably a nonprofit company. There was a precedent among the research associations: the Construction Industry RA had no central laboratory; it acted as a forum for the community, it received funds from members and from the government, and it allocated those for research which was done in the community. That could have been an appropriate model for running the Bide program.

This approach, Oakley argues, could well have appealed to ministers—and not only for political reasons. An additional practical reason concerns small firms, which suffered from delays during Alvey caused by government vetting regulations. "If you took that outside government, bureaucracy should be much reduced due to lack of direct parliamentary accountability."

Also, with hindsight, Oakley believes that the applications part of the Bide Report could itself have been presented in a way that could have been acceptable to ministers. As he notes in chapter 13, applications are regarded as of prime importance in the DARPA strategic computing program in the U.S. and also in the Technology Integration Projects in ESPRIT 2. The IT86 applications scheme could have been presented in terms of applications that were needed by government departments, he says.

In proposing to introduce IT-using organizations as cost-sharing partners in the applications scheme the Bide Committee was taking a step into the unknown. Was there any evidence that the user organizations would contribute their share? Oakley admits to doubts on this point:

> If you think back to 1982–83, when we were discussing collaboration between firms, there was a real element of doubt as to whether this

could be made to work. Many people didn't believe it. Many of us believed that the time was ripe for that to happen, and in the event we were proved right. If the IT86 applications scheme had gone ahead, there would undoubtedly have been uncertainty as to whether the users would join with the IT suppliers in a partnership. I believe they would—and that the benefits to them and to industry would have been proved over and over again. I have been involved in my public life in many battles to persuade reluctant users to take the British products, and the key difficulty was that the British supplier didn't get alongside the user early enough. So I believe the scheme would have worked, but you can't be absolutely certain.

As for the new national IT research program, Oakley warns that a scrutiny of the small print in the terms of the research contracts "must put a very real question mark over whether the program will succeed in being a true descendant of Alvey." The Link rules that apply differ from the Alvey rules, he points out; the new terms cover public funding of 50 percent of total project costs (academic and industrial). In Alvey, academic partners received 100 percent of their direct costs. The new regime thus places a heavier financial load on industrial partners, says Oakley, and this is "a crucial difference."

The new joint SERC/DTI committee structure is "a very healthy development," the former Alvey Director says, though there is a danger that academics could dominate on the joint committees—not in numbers but in influence:

My experience is that academics tend to dominate in joint committees. That could be very dangerous, and in particular it could lead us back into what I consider the bad old days when a great deal of research work was put forward which was not related to industrial priorities. Depending on the way the new structure is organized, it could be that the whole thing will get the very academic bias that Alvey was often accused of having—which I personally believe was not true. The new scheme is a great opportunity. If handled with extreme care, it could be an enormous strength for the U.K. in the long run. If I were running the IED program now, I would be putting a great deal of effort into getting the balance of representation right—with a very light touch, trying to ensure that the opportunity is properly seized. It won't be easy, because there will be all sorts of forces working on it to pull it one way or another, and accidental things such as the Link terms, if one could call that accidental, could sweep it off course. But it's a great opportunity.

The Persuader

John Fairclough, the government's Chief Scientific Adviser, sees Alvey and the after-Alvey era in clear-cut and consistent terms:

I've been very instrumental in persuading government that government ought to stay away from near-market subsidy; they should not subsidize product development. They should identify resources that are associated with product development and move those resources upstream to the higher-risk end of the activity. I felt there was a lot of product development associated with the Alvey Programme.

The phrase "precompetitive research" implies that the research is upstream. I believe the way to separate the roles is to say: "Government should not use public money to subsidize product development; but in technology—taking a piece of science and fleshing it out to the point where it becomes exploitable—government and industry have a partnership role." And there was a lot of that in Alvey. But there was also a lot of product development.

The rejection of the Bide applications scheme, it is generally accepted, resulted from the ministerial changes of 1987 and the restyling of the DTI. But Fairclough points to a basic misconception on the part of industry:

Quite independent of any change of government policy, the thought that one needed to subsidize industry to pull through some of the Alvey work into application areas was asking for trouble. The prime minister was led to believe—and this was all done before I arrived on the scene in 1986—that if government supported Alvey as a fixed program, that would produce some capability that industry would agree to carry forward on their own resources. Alvey was regarded as a one-shot, five-year exercise.

The message that it was a five-year program really wasn't driven home. Companies didn't act like it was a five-year program. If there was one error that occurred, and it's probably on both the government and the industry sides, it is that there is absolutely no doubt the government felt it was a five-year program, whereas programs of work were put in place that were ten-year research projects. Before projects were launched, the question ought to have been asked: "How is the ongoing work going to be financed?" They all assumed they were going to talk government into an Alvey 2. Not only that, but they built programs that were viable only on the assumption that there *was* going to be an Alvey 2, which I found remarkable, with a lot of commercial money going into it.

No, Fairclough says, he would not have favored an Alvey 2 program; he accepts that Alvey was a one-off, five-year project intended to give a stimulus to the community. "To follow on from Alvey with a European bias was very appropriate. In many areas of science and technology, national activity really is a precursor to establish a capability which will make us a more effective international partner—or international competitor, as the case may be. I suspect history will show that we've fared a lot better in Europe because of Alvey."

Fairclough develops a point which he touched on earlier (chapter 12) and which Geoffrey Pattie also noted (this chapter):

> The physics-based industries really do have an entirely different perspective on R & D than the chemistry-based industries. I think it is the cumulation of many years of government procurement policy, where industries, particularly the electronic industries, have built businesses and organized companies to serve the needs of the nation. Those companies have got used to government paying for their R & D. We're in an environment now where companies are making better profits, and one of the key questions is: Are they going to spend some of those profits on R & D and create a relationship with the City where that is expected of them, to be internationally competitive, or are they going to continue to run their companies on the basis of serving the nation? I don't think the latter option is there.
>
> It has to do with confidence. In terms of making a case for an effective R & D program to the City, it has more to do with credibility, confidence, ability to deliver, and a record of delivering than anything else. If ICI said short-term pressures are going to reduce our R & D program, their share price would be marked down. If other companies did that, their share prices would be marked up. It is primarily up to the companies to achieve that City understanding. In terms of government policy in continuing to provide subsidy for those sorts of companies, I don't think there's any doubt that it is perceived that they're earning more profit, and their future destiny lies with their own actions and not with continuing government subsidy. Government's help must be upstream, at the boundary of discovery and science and its emergence as exploitable technology.

After-Alvey Directions

The new Information Engineering Directorate has retained the flavor of the Alvey Directorate in many ways, including the principle of seconding staff to the directorate from industry and academia. Timothy Walker outlines his view of the relationship between Alvey and the successor national program, and his approach in establishing new directions for IT research in Britain:

What I've tried to do is to build a closer, more intimate relationship with SERC. That could not have been contemplated without Alvey. It is the logical next step. Alvey was an experiment. Having had the experiment you decide whether you implement the experiment, or you go further, or you go back. What we are trying to do is go further. We are working with SERC in an integrated way, and we're aiming to involve MoD and other government departments as well. If you're going to have a permanent structure, it has to be different from something that is an experiment. An experiment can try things which no one would necessarily want to make permanent. In building what is intended as a permanent structure it has to be more firmly bedded in to the parent organizations.

In DTI there was always a tension between the Electronics Applications (LA) Division and the Alvey Directorate. I now have the former LA people in my directorate. The new structure has brought the two together and integrated them in such a way that they are now one team, rather than two teams competing. The single DTI/SERC committee structure is very important. All these developments are building on the Alvey experience. We are now better able to help people in ESPRIT, because we have staff who now concentrate on that. And SERC want their IT education and training budget handled by the new structure. All those are things that are being pulled together in a way that could not have been contemplated before.

On the subject of the government's decision not to mount an Alvey 2 program as such in favor of a continuing but smaller national IT research effort, Walker argues that this brings practical advantages. "When a big program comes to an end everyone expects another big program, but there are many political and logistical difficulties in starting big programs. I'm trying to develop a framework in which there are a number of programs. Then the decisions you have to take are not whether to have another £200 million program but whether to have a £20 million program or a £10 million program or whatever. Those decisions are easier to take and easier to manage."

What does the IED director see as the main lessons to be drawn from the Alvey experience?

There was and still is a real need to stimulate and cultivate collaboration between industry and universities, and attitudes to that on both sides have changed radically over the past five years. One now has to ask the question: How much government money is needed to continue that collaboration? The economic argument always was that people didn't know about collaboration and its benefits, so they had to be helped over the barriers. Obviously, you can't continue to use that argument. Either the Alvey Programme helped to reduce the barriers, or it didn't. If it didn't, trying again won't help. If it did, what else are you going to do? We have to look for the more difficult things now, which is why one of the new emphases is on interdisciplinary research.

The Alvey Programme created the communities in individual technologies. That was good, but it's been done. Now what we have to do is get the various communities to talk to each other and work together. That is a much harder task. Also, after five years' experience one is now in a better position to say what ought to be done in Europe and what ought to be done nationally. Those are issues that I'm trying to get people to face up to. We need to see this directorate as moving its emphasis away from being just a grant-giving body toward providing a service to the IT research community. There's a great danger that if a program has been a success you institutionalize it. In fact, if it's been a success you need to do something else. I don't mean stop it entirely. You build on what you've achieved; you don't just repeat it. It is a different program now. It covers a wider range of activities.

Overall, Walker says he believes the Alvey experiment was a success. It has given a lot of confidence to the research community. They are more aware now of their strengths—and, indeed, their weaknesses—and are better able to plan for the future. He argues that it is too early to say how successful the Programme has been in economic terms, because that will depend on the exploitation. "The self-confidence of the community arose in part because of the international recognition of what has happened in Alvey. Everyone knows what the Alvey Programme is, and that helps to build up confidence. It has a very high profile, which people like. Again, it's easier for an experiment to have a high profile, and to some extent I've deliberately reduced it, because we now want something that's permanent."

Tony Egginton gives the SERC view of the new togetherness:

We wanted to construct a relationship with the DTI for the next period which maintained the collaborative culture of Alvey and which maintained the directorate mode, but which also drew in rather more peer review than in Alvey. In other words, there would be a greater involvement of the community and consultation with them than perhaps had taken place in Alvey. An important point now is that the funding balance between DTI and SERC has become more equal. So how to combine the directorate culture with the somewhat more cumbersome nature of the peer review system is the task ahead of us. It isn't going to be easy; the natural way of working is at one end of the spectrum or the other.

The new joint program will be wider than Alvey, in that it will cover basic research as well as precompetitive research. We now have in our grasp a strategic overview of the whole field—basic and applied, every single bit that we call IT. DTI and the SERC are tackling the task now, and if MoD comes in later, so much the better in some parts of the work. An important point is that we envisage the SERC funding for IT research continuing at about the same level beyond the next five years, subject only to periodic review. We want to try to break this terrible five-year block, at the end of which there has to be a major upheaval. So it's a steady-state situation, subject to review but with no major discontinuities.

Exit Alvey, Rather Quietly

The transformation of the Alvey Directorate into the IED in January 1988 marked the beginning of the end of the Alvey Programme, though some projects were set to continue into 1989 and 1990. The Alvey community might well have expected some celebration of the end of a successful program—at the final Alvey Conference, for instance—but this was not to be. Indeed, the name of the conference was changed to U.K. IT 88, after having been announced as the Alvey Conference, and an Alvey amnesia appeared to have afflicted most of the official speakers at that event.

This also marks the beginning of the end of our story of the Alvey Programme, as the research emphasis shifts into Europe and the U.K. Government takes a tougher line on support for near-market applications. Certainly the collaboration culture is planted and has taken root. Key elements of Alvey have been adopted and adapted to fit what is intended to be a continuing structure for collaborative research in information technology, as outlined above. Some of the key issues and achievements have been discussed in previous chapters. In the broadest sense, was it all worthwhile?

The final answer will depend on U.K. industry, since the aim was to improve the industry's competitive edge—and that will happen only if industry takes up what Alvey has delivered. In the meantime, the question is whether Alvey has delivered the right technological goods. Brian Oakley brings our version of the Alvey story to a close by addressing this question in the next and final chapter.

16
Was it All Worthwhile?

An assessment of fifth-generation approaches and achievements in key areas of technology shows positive results from the Alvey Programme. An assessment of government approaches to the public support of R & D shows fashions and cycles. The impacts of Alvey were complex, as this chapter by Brian Oakley illustrates, and there are hard lessons to be learned. So, was it all worthwhile? Yes, indeed, says Brian Oakley.

The Evaluation of Research

It is an unfortunate but seemingly inevitable consequence of research programs directed to an economic end that they should be judged too soon. This seems partly the natural desire of those responsible for committing the funds that some evaluation of their investment should be made with a view to optimizing the use of financial resources. In the modern western world there are never enough resources to fund all the research work that some interests would like to see carried out. Indeed it is a poor research team that does not feel that it could produce great work if only more resources would be invested in its particular specialty. There are always pressures for reallocation of resources, and indeed without those pressures it is not obvious that a proper mechanism for allocation of resources can be operated; there must be many who have looked at certain lavishly funded defense research programs with a sense of despair that such third-rate work can get support simply because the funds are available. Pressure for more funds for research may sometimes be more sensibly understood as pressure for better reallocation of resources. It is probably true that the limitation on good quality research staff is always a more real barrier to progress than limitation on funds at the more basic end of the research spectrum; at the applied end to some extent ready availability of funds may sometimes be a more real barrier.

For programs that involve public funds the demand for early evaluation tends to be exacerbated by the requirement of the politicians to demonstrate the wisdom of their investments to the voter, or by the bodies who receive public funds wishing the politicians to recognize that continuing or more usually increased investment is justified. Unfortunately the political horizon tends to be all too short. With an election cycle geared to a period of less than five years, the period from the time when a decision to invest is made to the time when the same politicians need to show benefit tends to be less than three years, frequently far less.

Incidentally, there is one other instability in this political cycle that influences public investment in research, and that is that politicians understandably want the sort of results that can be readily explained to voters. Now it is generally accepted, and acceptable in political circles, that it is an appropriate charge on the public purse to fund fundamental or basic research, just as it is accepted that it is the responsibility of the state to fund defense research. But to fund applied research raises all sorts of problems in the political mind. Why should the general public pay for some investment that would appear to bring financial benefit, at least preferentially, to one particular firm or group of firms? There are, of course, situations where that is desirable for the public good, normally the long-term public good.

The policy of Colbert,* in the time of Louis XIV, provides perhaps the first clear example of successful public investment in industrial prosperity for the public good. To a large extent this chapter is an attempt to evaluate whether the Alvey Programme met the particular arguments used to justify the investment in an applied program. But the general point is that governments find it easier to justify investment in basic re-

---

*Jean-Baptiste Colbert, who as Louis XIV's chief minister used public funds to create and strengthen many industries in France by recruiting expert craftsmen from abroad, doubling tariffs on imported manufactured goods, improving internal transport, and creating export companies. This laid the economic foundations for France's greatness.

search at the time that they make the investment and then very rapidly demand applied results from that investment.

Inevitably evaluation of benefits will be required within a few years of the inception of a program, yet the closer the program is to the basic end of the spectrum, the longer it must be expected to take before economic benefits can be demonstrated. This is the dilemma that introduces an element of distortion, even propaganda, into all efforts at evaluation of programs where the participants are involved in the evaluation process. It is, of course, true that incidental benefits may and probably will stem from attempts at premature evaluation. Matters of administration and allocation of resources may be improved by the attention given to these parameters in the success of research programs. And, at least in the U.K. environment—in contradiction to the situation that apparently pertains in Japan—an emphasis on exploitation that stems from the attention of the evaluators may not come amiss. Times change, but the time when perhaps this century's greatest collection of research workers in the U.K. could toast their work with the codicil ". . . and may it never be of use"* is still a living memory. The fact that their work changed the face of the world more than any other class of research activity up to that time adds a certain piquancy to their attitude but does not lessen the justification for pressure to achieve exploitation.

There is much force in the argument that major players are not the best critics of the game. Evaluation of research programs does require truly independent people, preferably those with experience and knowledge of the evaluation process. Yet is it possible to find evaluators who are both independent and informed? The historian does not have to have been a political player to throw light on his subject, yet it is often the case that the player turned historian can illuminate events in which he has been involved in ways that will prove valuable to subsequent, more dispassionate inquiry. It is in that spirit that this chapter and indeed this whole book is written, not as a balanced evaluation of the Alvey Programme but as a contribution from

---

*Toast said to have been made at dinner for Rutherford's team at the Cavendish Laboratory, Cambridge University, in the 1900s. The work of this team led to the creation of the electronics industry and the development of atomic energy.

the inside, from the players, to that dispassionate evaluation that it is hoped and expected others will carry out.

Scale of the Programme

It is perhaps worth pointing out that the Alvey Programme was on a scale that deserves, requires, and indeed demands evaluation. Though £350 million is not a large sum by the standards required to bring a major product to the market, it is a significant sum by U.K. standards for investment in more basic research. It must not be forgotten that the Alvey Programme was directed at precompetitive research, a term not always easy to explain or define, as those involved in the allocation of resource decision making often found. There were those, including at times the Director of the Programme, who tended to consider that it embraced any work where effective cooperation could be achieved. But there is no doubt that the Alvey Committee intended and that those who decided to commit funds to the program believed that it implied applicable or applied research at the basic or generic end of the spectrum, because it was felt that with the limited experience of cooperative research in the U.K. in the early 1980s it was essential to start cooperative research where it had more chance of being successful. The Alvey Committee believed that the Alvey Programme would roughly double the number of research workers in those fields. With over 2,000 workers engaged in the program at its peak, it is probable that the size of the community was increased by at least that factor. Other influences also tended to increase the numbers involved, though undoubtedly the Alvey Programme was the biggest single cause and it indirectly influenced some other factors, such as the creation of many new academic posts and new industrial research laboratories. Because the distribution of these increases in research workers was uneven across the program, there were some fields, such as software engineering and IKBS, where the influence was much larger, especially in the industrial world. Whole new teams were created where few existed before.

Yet it is not only the scale of the Programme that justifies attention to its performance and input. The changed nature of the Programme—a cooperative one where cooperation had hardly existed before—deserves examination. The directed nature of the Programme did not break new ground for most industrial research, but it was unusual for a publicly funded program outside the defense field. The directorate mechanism, bringing industrialists and academics to work with civil servants on the administration of public funds broke new ground, at least in terms of the scale. And the reality and perhaps more importantly the sense of a national effort involving all parts of the U.K. IT research community had not been attempted outside wartime in any other field, save perhaps atomic energy. So there is some justification other than self-justification inspiring this book.

Progress toward the Goal of Artificial Intelligence

Though Alvey was never seen as purely a fifth-generation program, and it would be wrong to look on it purely in that light, there is no doubt that it embraced one of the various western attacks on the fifth-generation that resulted from emulation of the Japanese program. It is not unreasonable to look at the worldwide progress of the fifth generation as background to progress in the U.K., as this was an important aspect of the founding fathers' conception of the Alvey Programme. In 1988 we seem to be going through a period of disillusionment with artificial intelligence such as has regularly beset the field since its inception after the Second World War. This is partly the fault of enthusiasts of the field who make such exaggerated claims for its potential that inevitably a sense of disillusion sets in when goals prove more difficult to achieve. It is not so much that the goals are unattainable as that the timescale for economic reward tends to be much longer than the protagonists allow. They let their vision and enthusiasm override their judgment about how long it will take.

This time the sense of disillusion seems somewhat unjustified. The Japanese saw their fifth-generation program as a ten-year program beginning in 1981. By 1991 it seems highly likely that at least two substantial markets for so-called AI products will have been created. One is in the field of parallel computers. Though it can be argued that this development owes little to the attack on AI research, the fifth-generation programs have been instrumental in driving forward the work on parallel architectures, because AI tends to be a power-hungry field. Though perhaps not the first field where large markets will be achieved, pattern recognition is one where it is clear that without the benefit of massive power at cheap prices little progress can be made, in research or in application. Though less evident, the same is probably true for the first major AI applications field, so-called expert systems, better expressed as knowledge-based systems or, as one author prefers to characterize it, "inference computing." There seem to be two reasons why the promise of expert systems has not been fulfilled and applications have only begun to find their place in the spectrum of commercial computer work in recent years. One is the lack of sufficient power at acceptable costs to handle the power-intensive work of the tree searching of the knowledge bases inevitably involved in almost any application in the real world, where it is difficult if not impossible to structure a knowledge base that avoids the dreaded "combinatorial explosion" liable to result from the search for rules relevant to a particular set of circumstances. At the inception of the fifth-generation programs special machines that could run list-processing languages (in particular Lisp) efficiently were just beginning to come on the market. But these were expensive and though suitable for research there was no economic solution to the system delivery requirement, if a widespread market was to be achieved. Today the situation is very different, partly due to the availability of powerful yet cheap personal computers and partly due to the development of highly efficient compilers for the languages, such as Lisp and the logic languages like Prolog, best adapted to this type of inference computing. Today we are about to see the ready availability of parallel computers that will take much further this process of providing inference computing tools at market prices, for example mechanisms for the parallel searching of knowledge bases as well as for conducting many logical operations in parallel. There can be little doubt that the fifth-generation programs, if they did not initiate these computer-tool developments, vastly accelerated the emphasis on them and so the rate of progress of AI applications.

The Human Interface in AI

The other factor delaying the application of inference computing was attention to the human interface. Rather paradoxically, this has not usually been seen as a fifth-generation topic but one stemming from the concurrent drive for office automation.

The breakthroughs in this field were achieved (preeminently in Palo Alto, at the Xerox PARC Laboratories) as the fifth-generation programs were first being formulated in the late 1970s. It was the dissemination of these advances, largely through machines such as the Apple Macintosh, that first drew general attention to what could be achieved in presenting a more human-adapted computer interface to the general public. Of course there was a heavy potential price to pay in machine time and complexity, and again it was the revolution in cheap computer power that made this accessible to the mass computer user. While such good interfaces are still not universal, the Alvey years revolutionized user expectations. If the fifth-generation program cannot claim responsibility for this change of attitude, since the human interface was not a major ingredient of it, the concentration on AI had its part to play, since a good human interface is an essential ingredient of a successful inference computing system. A proper analysis of the fundamentally different nature of inference computing from the conventional algorithmic computing, based on arithmetic and Boolean logic, that has constituted the vast mass of computer applications over the first forty years of practical computing, might have led the authors of the fifth-generation program to recognize the significance of the human interface in most AI computing. (There is a class of AI computing, such as image processing, where no human element appears, employed for example in industrial robotics, normally characterized as an application of AI. Though in the long run this class of application may become very important, it seems likely that for many years to come human intervention, and so the significance of the human interface, will remain essential for most applications of AI because of the incomplete scope of the knowledge bases. AI systems may be well versed in the rules for a limited domain of knowledge, but they always lack "common sense" in their ability to relate that specific knowledge of a larger frame of knowledge in the real world.)

It is the uncertainty, imprecision, incompleteness, and indeed contradictory nature of a real-world set of heuristic rules that leads to the need for an adequate interface for an inference system, one that enables the user not just to obtain advice from the system but also to understand the reasons that have led to that advice, the particular rules that have played the prominent part in the decision, and the sensitivity of the advice to changes in the input assumptions. This is in direct contrast to the result from a conventional computer program, where the certainties of the laws of mathematics normally lead to only one, unambiguous answer. This type of computing is acceptable with a simple human interface, whereas in inferencing computing the quality of the human interface becomes a crucial element in the acceptability of the system

In announcing their fifth-generation program the Japanese placed great emphasis on the significance of the results of their program for society, though rather surprisingly they made little of the importance of the human interface in the work of the program. (It is noticeable that the implications for society do not seem to have played much significance in the execution of the program, demonstrating that propaganda to achieve public funding support of programs is as well understood in Japan as in the West.) This is surprising, because the importance of the human interface is all too readily recognized in Japanese computing in general, presumably because of the sheer difficulty of communicating through their language, depending as it does in part on a large number of essentially Chinese ideograms that are, at best, fiendishly difficult to enter quickly. This has resulted in a concentration on the data-entry problem, especially through speech-recognition research, with different programs concentrating on this before and after the fifth-generation announcement. So it may be the very existence of that work that led the Japanese to play down the human interface aspects of their fifth-generation work. This can only be considered a weakness likely to affect public acceptance of the fifth-generation program in the future, if it has not already done so.

By contrast the Alvey Programme, from the deliberations of the Alvey Committee onward, always acknowledged the need for a human interface segment, though one seen as one of the generic enabling technologies of computing that formed the basis on which the Alvey Programme was built rather than as a vital component of the AI, or fifth-generation, part of the Programme. Because the Programme was handled as an essential unity, this was not necessarily a weakness, though in retrospect it would have done no harm to have placed a greater emphasis on the human factor aspects of the IKBS work, rather than treating this as a separate subject. But the activity in one part of the Programme inevitably rubbed off on other parts, and indeed specific efforts to bring this about were made in the interdisciplinary aspects of the Alvey conferences. The Alvey Programme was not the only one with strong fifth-generation aspects that included human factors, but perhaps it can claim to have taken these aspects most seriously. Whether it did this well and effectively will be discussed below. But it is appropriate to add that the Xerox PARC work, directed as it still is more to office automation than the fifth generation, remains the biggest single contribution to the development of the human computer interface.

Parallel Architecture Work in Japan

On the other important aspect for the acceptance of AI application in general use, parallel architecture and related tools, the Japanese fifth-generation program has always had a heavy emphasis. Indeed in the early phases of the program this seemed to dominate the work, as it almost certainly did. Of course, this plays, in a typically Japanese manner, to the strengths of their industry. It seems rather old-fashioned in computing to place emphasis on the hardware. After all, in a modern computer system the hardware component of the cost is small compared with the software element, which will typically take 80 percent or more of the costs of development. But the Japanese industry has always thrived on the hardware aspects, as witness their domination of the standard computer peripherals field and their success in the silicon semiconductor integrated circuit field. Perhaps their computer systems hardware industry has not expanded as fast as many in the West expected—and feared—that it would. It remains true that IBM continues to dominate the world's markets—everywhere except in Japan. The Cray company remains dominant in the supercomputer market, even if the Japanese supercomputer program has resulted in some impressive but not widely adopted machines from two stables (adopted, that is, outside Japan, where Cray sales remain dominant, though of course the Japanese buy their homegrown product if they possibly can).

The Japanese fifth-generation work on parallel architectures often looks more like trampling a problem to death than inspired architectural genius. However, it can do no harm to have three very different parallel architectures to compare, as the

Japanese have at ICOT. Perhaps only at the Edinburgh University Crystal Computer Architecture Laboratory, where machines stemming from the Alvey architecture work tend to go, can such a diversity of experience be sampled under a single roof. The early phase of the Japanese work concentrated on producing a sort of Japanese Symbolics inference computing machine, and this PSI machine was produced in some numbers (sixty machines?) for deployment in the Japanese fifth-generation community. In its final form, when full advantage was taken of their expertise in miniaturization through VLSI, it looks like a competent machine. But it has made no impact on the market (the Japanese would say this was never intended), perhaps because the onward march of conventional architectures, combined with vastly more efficient compilers for the inference languages, has resulted in the ready availability, primarily from U.S. sources, of conventional PC machines every bit as efficient as inference computing, at a fraction of the cost because of large-scale production for a wide variety of applications beyond inference computing.

It remains to be seen if this is the fate of the Japanese parallel machine work under the ICOT banner. It is reported that there are now over 100 companies in the United States offering some version of parallel architectures, of course only some of them directed to inference computing. No doubt the field will thin out rapidly, but we may well see an age in which it is so easy to develop a special, normally parallel architecture optimized to handle a specific class of problem and sometimes a single problem, that a thousand flowers will continue to bloom. The development of these parallel architectures in the U.S. probably owes more to the investments made by DARPA and the NSF than to any specific fifth-generation program such as the MCC, in which machine architecture is one of the major themes.

For any modern computer system the system software can be and usually is a more important element in the economic success of the system than the actual architecture (hence the rise of RISC architectures). The Japanese claimed that they were concentrating on logic programming for their fifth-generation work, as least in ICOT. This was normally interpreted as using Prolog, the language widely used in Europe for this type of work, rather than Lisp, the list-processing language widely used in the U.S. In practice the Japanese seem to have developed their own language based on the form of logic known as guarded-horn-clause (GHC) logic. It is probably more important to be able to compile and run a program efficiently than to have the optimum language for the construction of the system. In the interests of compiler efficiency the Japanese apparently have had to use a restricted form of GHC logic. This may have diminished the advantages of GHC over Prolog, and work in the U.K. now suggests that an efficient compiler for pure GHC logic could be produced. To some extent the emphasis on the particular language employed seems excessive. In the U.K. a variety of languages are employed, and if it turns out, as well it might, that inference computing takes its place as one element of a computer system, appearing where appropriate in the system as nuggets of KBS work embedded in a properly software engineered system largely using conventional computing, then it may well be that a variety of languages will be employed to build the system, the appropriate language being employed for specific parts. What will matter is whether the system architecture and system software can readily and efficiently make use of a variety of languages. It was in this field of system software that the Japanese seemed particularly keen to tap the undoubtedly strong U.K. expertise. But it would be wrong to suggest that the Japanese have a weakness in this area of their machine architecture work. It might be more true to say that they have not yet demonstrated any very wide or deep creativity in the field. They may yet do so.

Parallel Architecture Work in the U.K.

As has been pointed out in chapter 6, the Alvey Programme was always intended to have an architecture component, and indeed the strategy for the dominant fifth-generation section was actually entitled a Strategy for an IKBS Architecture. But it was not until after the first year of the Programme that a major element of the Programme, devoted to architecture work, was introduced. Perhaps because of the previous work carried out in the universities under the leadership of the SERC Distributed Computing Programme the U.K. universities were particularly strong in architecture ideas at the initiation of the Alvey Programme. The Alvey architecture program served to transfer these ideas from the academic world to industry, to build on them, and to test and develop them. This was a fruitful part of the Alvey Programme. Without question the depth and diversity of the work can be compared to the best that is available anywhere in the world, which essentially means with the best available in the U.S. Because of the creation of the Alvey community, strengthened in this field by the architecture club, the ideas and results generated in this part of the Programme rapidly spread through all relevant parts of the U.K. IT community. If ICOT had its three or more different parallel architectures, the true parallel in the U.K. was not Edinburgh University, where so many of the advanced architectures could be compared, but the whole Alvey architecture community, where the variety of machine and system software ideas were discussed, compared, and subject to peer criticism. It is important to emphasize that this community was not simply academic, but open to any firm engaged in research in the U.K. It well demonstrates the strength of the Alvey Programme.

Unfortunately it also demonstrates the potential weakness of the U.K. IT environment. It is not enough to have ideas; one must have the industrial will and resources to exploit them. The question is, will the U.K. be able to do so? Among the dozen or so firms taking part in the architecture part of the Programme, firms such as GEC and Plessey can be relied upon to use their research for defense related work, if MoD requirements provide the financial incentive to carry out the development. A similar incentive might come from telecommunications requirements, essentially provided by British Telecom and involving the joint GEC-Plessey telecommunications company GPT or STC.

It is not surprising that this part of the Programme was dominated by ICL, for STC/ICL is the one major British-owned computer company. In many ways that term no longer has much meaning as all the large computer companies become more linked in larger groupings, become multinational. The cost of developing a new generation of computer systems and the shrinking lifespan of a new generation means that large markets have to be secured in order to recover the investment. Both to share the R & D costs and to guarantee a wide market firms have consolidated into larger entities or formed partnerships with what had been their competitors. In the U.K. this process took place in the 1960s and 1970s for the main business-computer firms, leading to the emergence of ICL as the national champion. For some years ICL has been encouraging partnerships in Europe, first in matters like standards and then in research. It is interesting that though the Japanese fifth-generation research center, ICOT, is well known throughout the computer world, it is not widely known that ICL, Bull, and Siemens, the champion computer firms of U.K., France, and Germany respectively, created a joint research center, the European Computer Industry Research Centre, at Munich in the early 1980s—at about the same time that ICOT was formed. The work of the center is similar to that of ICOT, and is comparable in size. So it is natural that the three companies should link together to develop the next generation of "fifth-generation" computer systems. The single largest project of the Alvey Programme, the Flagship project, aimed at the early stages of developing a computer system for inference computing. This was based on the work of Imperial College and Manchester University, with other teams such as that of the University of East Anglia also involved in the software development. Plessey was also initially involved, but when in 1986 they decided not to continue the project for which they needed the parallel computer, a speech-driven word processor, ICL looked around for another partner and naturally turned first to Bull, which brought in the French national computing research center, INRIA, and then to Siemens. In 1988 the three firms applied to ESPRIT for continuing support of this computer system, each company concentrating on a different part of the system based on a common architectural and software system approach, and with the Joint Research Centre work brought to bear on the development.

It is too early to say if this system development will prove successful where it really matters, in the marketplace. But in many ways the progression from a national project supported by the Alvey Programme to a multinational project supported by ESPRIT can be seen as a supreme justification of both the Alvey and ESPRIT programs; each of the national champions' computer developments involving internal collaboration have led to multinational cooperation. In many ways the Alvey contribution was to facilitate cooperation and to teach the key U.K. players how to work together effectively. This lesson is now being used on the wider and inevitably more difficult multinational scene. Ideas generated in universities were brought first to the national champion and then through ICL to the international stage. It is difficult to believe that much of this would have happened without the Alvey Programme. Even the coming together of the best of the British universities' work is improbable without the catalyst, through funding and an element of mild direction, of the Alvey Directorate. And, similarly, the ESPRIT program has a crucial part to play in lubricating the next stage of cooperation.

What would have happened without the Alvey catalyst? It is, of course, impossible to say, but precedent suggests that the teamwork involved in bringing the key players in the U.K. together was most unlikely, some would bluntly say impossible. It is probably safe to assume that the work of the Flagship project provided ICL with a valuable counter in the negotiations with what have emerged as her European partners, even if the specific technology is not the only, or even the key, thread of the final system. The work will certainly illuminate the decisions on the nature of the final system and must serve to improve them. One can, of course, take the view that without the intervention of the Programme, the process of merging international partners would actually have been accelerated. More likely, remembering the history of the difficulty of European partnerships, collaboration would have been delayed until one or more of the partners was essentially eliminated from the game. The remaining partnership would have been weakened, both by the narrowing of the technical talent brought to bear on the development and by the reduced market that might be expected to be readily available, especially the government-dominated element of the market—a significant element in the market because of its size but also because of its ability to carry through early developments and its trend-setting nature. Against this must be set the problems of multinational partnership management, which might be simplified if one or more partners was in a minority position. That such partnerships can be made to work is demonstrated in Europe through Airbus Industrie and the space consortia, both proven successes in the marketplace. And one could cite the way in which the largest multinational of them all, IBM, has welded together the contributions from its many national components. The contribution of the U.K., through the Hursley development laboratories and, perhaps more surprisingly, the very efficient production lines at Greenock and Havant to the overall prosperity of IBM has been significant. (Even if the world chooses not to notice the IBM work in the U.K., it can hardly have failed to notice the outstanding research developments coming out of the multinational IBM laboratory in Switzerland.) In the long run the contribution of the Alvey Flagship project in helping to teach ICL how to manage the difficult process of multipartner collaboration may prove to be a key, perhaps the key, benefit.

Small Firms

It would be nice to be able to claim that the Alvey architecture program played a key part in helping the small parallel computer firms to emerge and grow. It certainly played an important part in demonstrating that the transputer is an ideal element for the creation of parallel computer systems. Many, probably most, of the Alvey architecture projects used transputers, including Flagship in its Alice prototype. Inmos was directly involved in only a few of these projects, but of course they benefited indirectly and directly from all the transputer projects and from the widespread use of the low-level system-building language Occam that Professor Tony Hoare and the Programming Research Unit at Oxford University had developed especially for the transputer. Their parent company, Thorn-EMI, through these developments and work initiated under the Alvey Programme and developed under ESPRIT, was helped to put a parallel machine on the market in 1988. It is difficult to evaluate the contribution of the Alvey Programme to the fortunes of the transputer and of Inmos. But it does seem likely that it was considerable. The dissemination of information about the transputer in machine building and prototype use must have been accelerated by the Programme. This occurred not just in the U.K., for the Alvey Programme attracted worldwide interest. Dissemination of information was certainly accelerated in all major fifth-generation centers and wherever else parallel architectures were being developed. The Alvey Programme cannot claim credit for the conception and development of the first generation of transputers; that distinction rests largely with Iann Barron, a member of the Alvey Committee who always played a very active role as informed critic of the Programme's development. Without his encouragement the U.K. academic architecture community would not be such a vital element in virtually all of that part of the Alvey Programme. Yet the Programme can claim a significant role in using the transputer and in providing ideas for its subsequent development.

Various small firms have now been formed in the U.K. to carry forward the exploitation of the transputer in computer systems. Most of these emerged too late for the Alvey Programme directly to involve them, though many of the ideas and individuals owe something to the Alvey projects. In 1983, at the start of the Programme, the small computer company Acorn, which produced the BBC micro and was aiming at the schools market, was in ascendancy. They joined half a dozen of the projects and played a valuable role, with their chairman Herman Hauser as an EARB member in the Alvey Programme Steering Committee and subsequently on the ESPRIT Advisory Committee, after Acorn was taken over by Olivetti. Unfortunately, Acorn's first rise proved to be a rocket, though their subsequent resurgence under the Olivetti banner means that their Alvey work has not been lost to the European family. But few of that generation of British microcomputer firms were able to participate in the Alvey Programme, and of course most have now disappeared with the thinning out of the industry. The fact is that very few of the small start-ups in the computer hardware industry make it through to the big time. In this a distinction from the small software firms can be noted, where most survive, merge, are absorbed, but in general grow. The one distinguishing feature of the scene, and this applies equally to the large firms, is that those ventures that require significant capital for development and perhaps above all marketing have great difficulty in doing so in the current U.K. climate. Indeed this has been true for many years and in most high-technology fields, in contradistinction to the U.S. but perhaps like the Japanese and certainly like the German scenes. A few exceptions emphasize how rare such developments are in the U.K. It does seem that there is no shortage of initial venture capital now on the U.K. market, but it would appear that the scale of initial start-up is just too small to overcome the problems created by the limited size of the national market for even the best national developments. It is surely significant that interest rates in the U.K. have almost always tended to be much higher than in other countries, notably Japan or Germany. This probably acts as a disincentive to deployment of capital on a significant scale in risky, high-technology ventures when ample returns can be made from investments in areas such as property or the retail industry. What seems to be needed is initial investment on an adequate scale to tackle international markets from an early date, when the development is still at the forefront of the technology. This will call for a change in attitudes of both entrepreneurs and investors. There is no evidence that U.K. management is incapable of handling the larger-scale problems involved, though few of the technologists have the experience or willingness to face these challenges. The importance of the current convergence in Europe, both in opening up the market and making it easier to obtain an adequate return in a shorter period of time and in opening the eyes of the U.K. technical community to opportunities beyond these shores, can clearly be seen. It must also be true that the coming together of financial institutions in Europe and the creation of a larger and more stable exchange rate for sterling will lead to lower interest rates and longer periods before new ventures must show growth significant to satisfy their backers. It is not obvious that cooperative programs such as Alvey have much to contribute to this scene, except that the creation of a climate conducive to cooperation and management lessons in cooperation that stem from experience of such programs have their part to play in easing and accelerating the movement to successful cooperation in Europe.

Before leaving the architecture scene, mention should be made of one other way in which the Alvey Programme provided direct assistance to the computer industry. ICL first developed the Digital Array Processor (DAP) back in the early 1970s. It is an example of the single-instruction parallel machine, ideally suitable for problems where the same operation can be simultaneously carried out in a large number of elements. There are many such problems in the real world, but the DAP was slow to take off, perhaps because of the wrong marketing strategy, which linked it to large computers instead of seeing it as a valuable tool linked to a variety of processors of all sizes, especially for particular operations where large power to carry out some repetitive operation was needed. Due to the help of the Science and Engineering Research Council, the DAP has been used for a large variety of problems, until recently mostly in academic environments. This has provided it with probably the largest body of applications software available for any parallel computer in the world. Toward the end of the Alvey Programme ICL floated the DAP off into a new venture company, Active Memory Technology (AMT), attracting new funds from the venture capital market and a forceful and entrepreneurial management. The Alvey Programme was too late to help in the development of the concept of the DAP, but it could help to pioneer various advanced development projects using the AMT machines. The last Alvey project was of this type, where the research lay in the advanced applications rather than in the machine itself, though, of course, such developments become inextricably mixed up with the creation of the ideas that go into the next generation of machines. The Alvey Programme had its part to play in stimulating advanced applications that might otherwise never have seen the light of day. This is of value both to the users and to the system developer.

Market Penetration of Knowledge-Based Systems

To return to the analysis of the fifth generation, it seems appropriate to say something about the state of market penetration and the part that the Alvey Programme and the other fifth-generation programs have played in this. In practice this is at this time largely a matter of the market for knowledge-based systems or, as the market calls them, expert systems. It has already been pointed out how the fifth-generation programs have helped to tackle the twin problems of machine power, through the assault on parallel architectures, and (at least as far as the Alvey Programme is concerned) work on the human interface. There are many other problems before the great promise of knowledge-based systems can be fully achieved, not least in knowledge elicitation and in knowledge representation and organization in the computer memory. But, at least outside the U.S., a crucial problem in the early 1980s was to acquaint the market with what could be done with such systems. To that end the Alvey Programme, perhaps more than any other fifth-generation program, set out to educate the market, not just to develop the technology. This was a key element in the Alvey IKBS strategy and proved a material success. Through the Alvey clubs and demonstrator projects some hundreds of firms were given the opportunity to experience the techniques and appropriateness of the technology, the problems, and the opportunities. Of course it could be argued (indeed it was at the time) that the awareness program need not form a part of the Alvey research program, that it would be more appropriate to use the funds for further research, perhaps mounting a separate awareness program. Actually, the awareness program was quite cheap, and there were benefits from carrying it out under the Alvey banner. This gave the program a certain cachet and ensured that the U.K.'s key experts were deployed where necessary, if only to give advice. Nevertheless the point remains that this aspect was different from most of the Alvey Programme and could have been mounted quite separately. What is perhaps less in doubt is that it was very desirable at that state of appreciation of the potential of the approach in the market. Whether a separate awareness program sponsored by government would have been forthcoming is not clear, though at that time it probably would have been. Its effect was to provide the U.K. with a general understanding of the potential of expert systems in advance of that elsewhere, except in the U.S. A somewhat similar, though probably less effective, awareness program was mounted in the human-factor field, largely through creating and initially funding three national advisory centers. A strong case can be made that a large proportion of the Alvey funds should have gone into awareness by mounting such programs in other parts of the Alvey field, such as software engineering. Certainly awareness programs tend to be a very cost-effective way of using public funds to create a general understanding of the attributes and potential of a new technology. But it may be much more difficult to implement them successfully if they are carried out without the infrastructure and the advantages of being seen as part of a wider advanced technology program.

Perhaps because the Alvey Programme was able to take a more relaxed attitude to the definition of research and the stated reasons for which public funds were provided, only the Alvey Programme out of all the fifth-generation programs had a significant element of awareness in it. The time was ripe for the spread of knowledge-based systems, so that by the end of the Alvey Programme the use of such systems was as much talked about in the U.K. as in the U.S. The technology is now rapidly rising, and if it still remains more an experimental technique than a widely used approach, there can be no doubt that at least that part of the fifth-generation work will fulfill its promise in the coming decade through widespread use. It needs the work of the fifth-generation programs to bring about its cost-effective deployment in many areas, and much development yet remains to be done, for example in tackling large knowledge bases, linking separate knowledge-based systems together, fully integrating the technology into conventional software engineering, and perhaps above all learning how to structure and represent knowledge effectively. The Alvey Programme played its part in accelerating the understanding and use of the technology. To that extent its widespread application in the years to come will owe something to those in Japan and the U.K. who had the vision to initiate the fifth-generation and Alvey programs. It remains only a matter of time before inference-computing applications far exceed today's so-called conventional uses of computers.

Achievement in VLSI

There are two other parts of the Alvey Programme that deserve some consideration, both falling outside the normally conceived boundaries of a fifth-generation program, namely VLSI and software engineering. Yet both are so fundamental to progress in information technology that one could argue that without progress in them the fifth-generation work is doomed to failure. Certainly no one argued that these two topics were not an obvious part of a program of "enabling technologies of IT," as Alvey was conceived to be. While there was no argument that software engineering should form part of the Programme there was a minority on the Alvey Committee that would have been happy to have seen VLSI left out of the Programme. In one sense this stemmed from the rather separate nature of the work. Though the impact of progress in VLSI work on other aspects of IT is vast, the way that the systems designer handles the VLSI product, the integrated circuits, is through an interface and a specification; the details of the technical work within the VLSI product is of little interest to the systems designer. Probably a more influential reason with its critics on the Alvey Committee was the feeling that the subject had always attracted considerable public funding and would continue to do so, whether it was part of the Alvey Programme or not. While this was probably true at the time, the case for supporting VLSI work within the framework of the Alvey Programme was strong if Alvey was truly to cover the enabling technologies. The clinching argument was that the MoD was a significant source of funds for the Programme, and the MoD wanted VLSI to be a part of it. Yet it has to be admitted that we had little success in integrating the VLSI work and workers with the rest of the

Alvey Programme. Except in the CAD part of the VLSI program the VLSI workers kept to themselves on occasions such as the Alvey conferences. They are a different breed of men from the rest of the IT workers, often physicists and chemists with little interest in IT. So it must be doubted if it would have made much difference to the progress of the Programme had VLSI been treated separately. It might have had an impact on the large firms' attitude to the Programme, since their research labs were accustomed to receiving support from public funds and so were attuned to cooperate with, and influence, the source of such funds, in this case the Alvey Directorate. At the time there was no strong lobby from the large firms for other parts of the Programme.

In technical terms the VLSI part of the Alvey Programme achieved virtually all of its objectives. It always proved easier to find quantitative objectives for VLSI, since one could describe objectives in terms of the chip geometry—i.e., one-micron line widths—or in terms of circuit speed. And a quite remarkable degree of cooperation developed between the technologists in virtually all of the VLSI research teams, with the notable exception of Inmos, though this may have been due to the fact that in the early years of the Alvey Programme most of the Inmos VLSI technology came from its laboratory in the U.S. It is when one looks at the position of the U.K. VLSI chip manufacturers in the world that one wonders if the VLSI program was a sound investment. By the end of the Programme, the large capital cost of keeping the VLSI production lines at the forefront of technology had resulted in most of the U.K. production being merged into the one remaining major U.K. player, Plessey. The other firms in the Alvey VLSI program tended to retain some production capability for their internal requirement but abandoned a general market presence except in niche markets. By contrast Inmos abandoned its U.S. production line and consolidated in the U.K.

The critics of the Alvey VLSI program were virtually unanimous that we should have concentrated our support on fewer process technologies. If this had had the result of increasing the concentration of the industry on fewer technologies, it would certainly have been right to have reduced the number of different technologies we supported. But would it have had this effect? Two considerations make it seem doubtful: the investment in R & D is only a fraction of the cost of putting a process on the market, and the Alvey support was itself only a relatively small fraction of the industry's investment in R & D. And for a firm with a large investment in R & D there must be a degree to which the public contribution on one topic simply enables the firm to invest more of its own funds in another topic. If we had concentrated more resources on one process, would the firms have chosen to put more resources into the chosen technology, or would they have simply transferred more of their resources to the deprived technologies? Who can say? What one can say is that, in contrast to other parts of the IT field, the firms' VLSI research directors formed a very cohesive team adept at optimizing the government contribution to their work. This, of course, stems in part from their long experience of working with the MoD, but the Alvey environment certainly helped to bring them together.

Perhaps the key question in the VLSI field is whether it was predictable that the U.K. players in the field would be reduced over the Alvey years from the five or more players at the start to the one or two at the end. And if it was, should that prediction have influenced the Programme? It was certainly apparent that the investment that the U.K. industry was prepared to make, was capable of making, was far smaller than that of its competitors in Japan and the U.S., perhaps by an order of magnitude. In Europe the failure of any U.K. company to join the significant Philips-Siemens investment for the development of VLSI was a clear indicator to the way things were going. It would have required a very determined Alvey Director to have stood out against the barons of the large electronic firms. And I can plead that there were more important targets in my sights that required the active cooperation of these firms—which, incidentally, was unstintingly given. But the writing was on the wall for the industry. It was a Greek tragedy with a predictable end, but one the players could not avoid even if they behaved somewhat differently. The main accusation to which I plead guilty is that it should have been possible to predict the way the industry was going and redeploy the public investment elsewhere. That that course of action was almost certainly impractical does not change the desirability of having tried to make the change.

Of course one has to ask what has happened that the U.K. semiconductor industry should have found itself so depleted, so concentrated? It is not only in the U.K. that this has happened. No doubt the picture has been repeated in industrial history on many occasions in other fields, for example when the oil, chemical, and steel industries went through rationalizations or, in more recent time, the automobile and aircraft firms. The big difference is that at the turn of the century British firms led in rationalization and concentration. Even in the more recent industrial rationalizations the U.K. has retained some players in the world league. It would appear that our ability to lead such concentrations in the electronics industry has disappeared through lack of the willingness to invest the capital required, through lack of the top-management drive. Nothing that the Alvey Programme could have done would have changed this. It is interesting to speculate on whether a more interventionist government could have persuaded the U.K. electronic firms to pool their investment in VLSI, so that a U.K. world force could have emerged. It would certainly have required a substantial government investment to sweeten the pill. That such intervention by government can sometimes prove very successful is demonstrated by the emergence of ICL as the U.K.'s computer flagship company in the 1960s, under the influence of government intervention and support. Whether that success could have been repeated in the 1980s is an issue on which people will divide on party political lines. All is not lost; the U.K. remains a player on the world VLSI scene, albeit with a tenuous grasp.

Integrated Circuit CAD

It is easy to see now that two peripheral aspects of the Alvey VLSI program should have been moved center stage, namely the CAD and instrument industry aspects. A VLSI CAD awareness program, combined with a CAD research program based on trying to produce a national CAD approach, to integrate the existing tools, to fill in the gaps, and to proceed to the next generation would have been highly desirable. It would have required considerably more resources than we put into the CAD aspects. And it would have been necessary to have drawn experienced software engineers into the VLSI CAD work. This could and should have been done, if necessary using resources from the VLSI technology program. It is certainly not too late to do this. The emphasis in planning the program would have to be on the needs of the users of VLSI CAD, who of course would include the large electronic firms but not be dominated by them.

Integrated Circuit Instrument Industry

For the VLSI instrument industry the picture is less clear. It is a fragmented industry, with under-capitalized firms but with several having world-leading products. For such firms public funds to support expensive R & D programs are crucial. Co-operation among themselves is not welcome, but cooperation with their potential customers is highly desirable, if that helps to get the specification correct and the customer fully involved in taking the prototype, helping to clear the initial bugs, and then demonstrating to the world markets what the instruments can actually achieve. Cooperation with universities is particularly valuable in this field, since so many of the developments are based on work first researched in the developments needed for quite basic science, such as fundamental particle research work. Though this would require rather careful evaluation, it seems probable that putting increased resources into this industry would have paid increased dividends. But one has an uneasy feeling that the undercapitalization of the firms puts a barrier to their ability to dominate the world market, as they seem quite capable of doing in terms of their technology. It is very much a field that deserves study. Interestingly, though CAD for VLSI is part of the EEC programs (though it did not feature strongly in ESPRIT), only DARPA of the other fifth-generation agencies seems to have featured CAD and the instrument industry in its programs.

Software Engineering

The first time that software engineering featured as a major feature of a support program was when it was made part of the Alvey Programme. Since then several of the other programs have featured software engineering, notably the Department of Defense Software Technology Advanced Research Program (STAR). There is a marked similarity between the contents of these programs and the Alvey software engineering program, with much the same priorities and even the use of terms like "integrated project support environment" and "software factory." Alvey may not have invented them, but the publicity given to the strategies for this part of the Programme certainly served to propagate and popularize the terms. If the strategy proved trend-setting, it also proved difficult to set firm targets, and perhaps for that reason evaluators like the U.K. Parliament's National Audit Office found it difficult to assess the value of this part of the Programme. Perhaps it is hardly surprising that they seized on the apparent situation that the Alvey Report had promised some deliverables from the software engineering part of the Programme within a year or so of its inception, and none was on the market. Within another couple of years most of the tool sets were on the market, though it remains to be seen what market they attract. Probably the usual British defect will arise that the investment, especially in overseas marketing, will not be adequate to achieve a satisfactory return.

Yet the deliverables were not really the right factor by which to assess the value of the software engineering program. Judged by an admittedly partial evaluation of the progress on the projects it was slow, at least relative to other aspects of the Alvey Programme, in particular VLSI. On the other hand the targets were probably more difficult and the value of progress greater. What we were trying to do was to put software engineering on the map, to achieve respectability for it, and to improve the quality of the development and maintenance of the software constructed in the U.K. It is difficult to overestimate the value of doing that, for software has become the dominating cost in virtually all IT systems. Most software has been inadequate in its design, construction, documentation, and ease of maintenance and further development. Unfortunately the investment in unsatisfactory software in the past is so massive that we cannot just scrap it and start again, though a few brave organizations have done just that. But we can hope to produce better software now that the techniques are becoming available, so that gradually the quality of our stock of software will rise. The Alvey software engineering program was really all about improving the techniques and propagating better methods in the software-writing industry, both in the electronics firms and in the specialist and software companies, the so-called "software houses." In this the Programme was very successful. Firms that had never invested in "research" in software engineering set up internal teams. Cooperation with the outstanding U.K. academics, who are among the world leaders in much of this field, especially in formal or logical methods, was strengthened and broadened. The software engineering scene in the industry was markedly better after the five years than it was at the beginning. These changes in attitude will not be reversed; a real step forward has been taken.

Yet there was one respect in which more, perhaps much more, could have been done in software engineering. The Alvey Programme was conceived and executed very much as a support program for the IT industry, the electronics firms, and the software houses. Indeed there were occasions on which we actually turned down projects where we felt that there was no adequate firm in the industry to exploit the work of a project where the key players were users rather than from the industry. With the funds available we had to concentrate, and we argued that helping to improve the industry was in the interests of the U.K. users too. Only in some of the awareness programs, especially in expert systems, did we directly address the users—though we did always encourage user firms to join the consortia, provided they were not the major players. In software engineering, not addressing the users was a mistake. To have addressed the large user firms would have helped to improve the quality of specification and the impact that they can and do have on the software industry—quite apart from their value as generators of major software in their own right. Of course the resources required to support a user-oriented program would be significant, unless it was severely restricted in size. It might have been sensible to mount a program to support the production of high-quality specifications, when user firms were setting out to commission work from the industry. It might have had to be restricted to certain crucial fields like safety-critical software and secure systems. A program to raise the quality of specification writing, at the same time helping to cement the bonds between software user firms and their U.K. suppliers, would have paid considerable dividends. It was not part of the Alvey Programme, maybe it should have been. It is not too late to mount such a program.

Speech Technology in the Alvey Programme

As a final illustration of the strengths and weaknesses of the Alvey Programme it may be useful to look at the speech technology program. This was not a large program, consisting of some twelve projects in all. Only a handful of firms were involved, for there are only a few firms in the market. Virtually everybody working in the field in the U.K. was involved. One influence of the Alvey demonstrator directed at producing a speech-driven word-processor was to build up a large (by U.K. standards very large) team at Edinburgh University. The partnership with the lead firm in that demonstrator, Plessey, was never very satisfactory (as described by participants in chapter 10), though technology certainly did flow one way, and an understanding of the market and costs of capturing it flowed the other way. While it is technically a very difficult field it is such an applied field that it would be wrong to mount a major program without strong industrial involvement. When the partnership does not work well there are increasing problems for the academic team. In this case they culminated when Plessey, quite sensibly, reassessed their situation and decided to pull out. It is tempting to say that having started on the project, Plessey should have seen it through. But this is quite unrealistic in the real industrial world, and in any case research projects have as part of their objectives educating the participants. In this case Plessey decided that the investment before a large enough market would be established to give an adequate return was just too large. The technology was not ripe for exploitation, and this particular part of the speech market would be better addressed by the large word-processing equipment firms. So Plessey pulled out. What was the Directorate to do with the project at this stage? Another industrialist might have been found to pick up the project; that happened with other Alvey projects when the prime industrial partner dropped out.

In this case we eventually found that a part of GEC was prepared to join a speech program involving the Edinburgh University team, but it was not the key project around which all other parts of the Alvey speech program could hang. Good management considerations suggest that the project should have been brought to a halt at that point. But the Edinburgh team had been built up, many members of which were on several-year contracts, some having come over from the U.S. especially for the program. It seems likely that the solution should have been to put the Edinburgh work into a loose consortium, a club, containing all other members of the U.K. speech community. Perhaps an opportunity was missed to unite all the relatively few U.K. speech workers on one team. This had certainly been our intention, but the large-demonstrator program was seen as the focus for this club. With that project in disarray it seems likely, but not inevitable, that though cooperation in the individual project teams was usually successfully achieved, total cohesion of the community was not. There was one other respect in which the Alvey Programme had an impact on speech research in the U.K. It has been recognized for some time that continuous speech recognition is most unlikely to be achieved by waveform analysis alone. It will require the ability to parse the sentence to provide some semantic assistance in interpreting the sounds. But because the traditional speech scientist is an expert on waveform analysis but knows little about natural-language research, it is necessary to bring the two types of scientist together in cooperation. This seems obvious, but within the rigid departmental structure of universities it is often quite difficult to achieve. The collaborative nature of the Alvey Programme made such cooperation seem natural, albeit with a bit of pressure from the Directorate. Such cooperative programs are ideal for encouraging multidisciplinary research, which lies at the heart of future progress in so much of advanced information technology.

The Wheel Turns

There are fashions, even cycles, in public support for research and development. From the First World War until well after the Second World War it was the fashion for public funds only to be put into cooperative research where the outcome of the work could enter the public domain for the general good. When it was recognized in the 1960s that this tended to help our overseas competitors and perhaps led to the failure of any one firm to exploit the work, the fashion changed to single-company support, the beneficiaries being selected through what Tony Benn called the "principle of maximum unfairness." Underlying this trend was the belief that the U.K. was good at inventing things but bad at exploiting them. This led to a concentration on short-term development projects and to the encouragement of universities working closely with industry. During the 1970s in information technology it became clear that ever-increasing R & D costs and ever shorter product cycles was leading to market domination by the big battalions—almost always U.S. firms but with the increasing threat of Japan. It became fashionable to look at Japanese industrial growth and seek the secrets of this success. So when the Japanese announced their fifth-generation program the time was ripe to learn from their experience—or at any rate to think that we were—and to adopt at least some of their approaches, in particular cooperation in research followed by tooth-and-nail competition in the marketplace.

Those were the circumstances that led to the Alvey Programme. If it seemed uncharacteristic in the U.K. at that time to build a program around cooperation, it was acceptable because of the perceived lesson from Japan. Five years later the wheel had turned further: the idea of a national program based on cooperation and substantial government support was unfashionable and unacceptable. The climate surrounding academic research also was beginning to change, with a renewed emphasis on basic research in academia and a weakening of academic/industry ties.

At the same time the focus of Britain's IT research was shifting toward Europe—though a cynical observer might regard the U.K.'s European Community research contributions as a small price to pay for evidence that the British are good Europeans, and for softening the blow caused by the reduced support for a national IT program. But let us not forget that no change in Britain's affairs is ever total, ever absolute.

The Lessons that Remain

Such cycles are an inevitable part of life for those who have to or choose to seek public support. Perhaps the big question to ask about the Alvey experiment is whether it has left the community better able to cope with the whirlwind, better able to look after itself, better able to seek support anywhere other than the national purse? There may be two clear lessons to be learned from the experiment. First, cooperation can be made to work beneficially for all involved—if the right steps are taken to select partners and programs with an eye to the long-term outcome, if the right management techniques are learned and assiduously applied, and if all the partners really have the will to succeed. Secondly, because the wheel will turn again, government has a role to play, not in setting the detailed agenda for industrial and academic affairs but in serving as an active and intelligent catalyst to bring about ends that are difficult if not impossible for industry, even with the close backing of the academic world, to achieve on its own. A partnership of all the interested parties lies at the heart of the successful modern state; government cannot avoid its role as one important partner.

If the Alvey age, however imperfect it was in conception and execution, was a form of Camelot to those of us who have long believed that cooperation is an outstanding goal for civilized man, then we must believe that, like Camelot, the age of cooperation will come again. Maybe next time it will take the form of a truly international attack on the immense intellectual and practical problems we face before we can claim to have harnessed artificial intelligence for the good of all society.

Appendix 1
A Program for Advanced Information Technology

Executive Summary, Report of the Alvey Committee, 1982

• There should be a national program for advanced information technology (AIT). This would cost £350 million over five years. Government should contribute three-quarters of the direct cost of this program. Industry should provide the remainder, as well as the much larger sums needed to translate the results of the program into marketable products.

• The aim of the program is to mobilize our technical strengths in IT. This is essential to improve our competitive position in world IT markets. Our present technical effort is fragmented and fails to exploit fully our current strengths.

• The program should be a collaborative effort between industry, the academic sector, and other research organizations, in order to improve the harnessing of our technical strengths to industrial objectives, to get the best value from government support, and to allow the widest possible involvement and exploitation.

• Some £57 million should go to support research and training in academic institutions. This should be 100 percent government-funded. The rest of the program should be carried out by industry. Where very wide dissemination of the results is required work should be funded 90 percent by government. Other work should receive 50 percent funding. The overall ratio of government funding for the program in industry would be roughly 60 percent.

• A high level of government support is essential. Without it collaboration is not possible, nor full dissemination of the results of the program and their exploitation, particularly by the small-business sector.

- Technically it is a broadly based program covering four key enabling technologies: software engineering, very large-scale integration (VLSI), man/machine interfaces (MMI), and intelligent knowledge-based systems (IKBS). The U.K. IT industry cannot compete in world markets unless we have a strong domestic capability in each of these technologies. Urgent action is needed to generate this capability. We have achievements and potential in each of the enabling technologies on which we can build.
- A broadly based program is needed but with specific technical targets and coverage of the important interactions and overlap between the enabling technologies. We have defined a program to meet these needs.
- The program roughly doubles existing U.K. activity in the enabling technologies. It aims to improve the coordination or "gearing" of our current effort and to raise the total level of activity. Achievement of both objectives is needed; they are interdependent.
- The program covers precompetitive activities, i.e., basic research, design tools, and a communications infrastructure to link researchers. It also includes capability demonstrators to test the emerging technology and assess its potential commercial application. In all of these areas collaboration is feasible and vital, if we are to make the best use of limited technical resources. Collaboration is more difficult the closer one gets to the market. It will be for individual companies to translate the results of the program into marketable product in a wholly competitive mode. This is fully compatible with collaboration at the precompetitive stage.
- The program includes measures in the areas of education and training to provide the human resources to mount the technical program, particularly in IKBS, where the number of skilled practitioners is very low, but also in software and MMI.
- The program must be run as a U.K. effort. Foreign multinationals should participate only where they can contribute a particular asset vital to the program, where the results of their involvement will be available to the benefit of U.K. industry as a whole, and where it is guaranteed that valuable technical information will not leak from the U.K.

- Industrial property rights should be handled to encourage collaborative participation and full exploitation by U.K. industry.
- The program will have to be firmly driven to achieve effective implementation. We propose that a new directorate be set up within DoI charged with implementing the program. It must be dedicated to this task and have the necessary powers and resources to act speedily and flexibly. In charge should be a director hand-picked for the job. He should be accountable for his broad strategy and overall operations to a modified form of the EARB and through existing DoI control machinery. But he must have enough autonomy to get on and run the program and be supported by a small but carefully selected team.
- SERC and MoD should also be directly involved in the management and control of the program strategy. They should provide some of the government funding.
- Exploitation of the program can start at an early stage. This should be actively encouraged by the directorate. Exploitation can occur throughout the duration of the program and beyond. Exploitation should in no sense be restricted to organizations which have participated in the program.
- Though broadly based, the program does not cover all possible areas of IT in which collaboration is necessary. Other areas need to be considered as part of an ongoing review of our technological capability in IT. Arrangements must be made for this. We would expect the directorate to be closely involved in this.
- We have drawn up a detailed and costed program lasting five years. Collaborative activities will be required beyond this period, particularly in IKBS, for the full benefits to be yielded.
- The U.S., Japan, and countries in Europe are now all mounting programs comparable to the one we propose for the U.K. These rival programs present a serious challenge to the U.K., which we must face. The EEC ESPRIT program is complementary to the program we propose.
- Implementation of the program above is not sufficient to secure a competitive position for the U.K. IT industry. Action is needed on other fronts too. There must be continuing support from government for product development; effective use of public-sector procurement; and an expanded program to pro-

mote the application of IT, particularly in the service sector, to provide follow-up to IT82.

- Also vital is a substantial program to generate more human resources to develop IT products and to apply them in all areas of industry. The supply of skilled manpower in this respect is totally inadequate for current and future needs.
- Unless there is action to implement the AIT program and in these other related areas, the prospects of the U.K. competing successfully in the world IT market will be sharply reduced. The spread of advanced IT applications in the U.K. will also be constrained. Both of these would be extremely damaging to employment prospects, to our industrial efficiency as a nation, and to our general economic position. Money put into the program would be money well spent.

Appendix 2
U.K. Government Approves Alvey Plan

Statement by Patrick Jenkin MP, Secretary of State for Industry, in the House of Commons on 28 April 1983

The Alvey Committee was set up last year at the request of the IT industry to investigate the scope for a collaborative research program in advanced information technology in the light of mounting concern in the industry at the increasing threat of overseas competition. I am most grateful to the committee for their extremely valuable report. After detailed consultations with industry I am now able to announce the government's response.

The future competitiveness of our IT industry is a subject to which we attach the utmost importance. The report outlines the key areas of technology in which the IT industry must maintain and strengthen its competitive position in world markets. Its theme is the need for collaboration between industry, academic institutions, and other research organizations in order fully to mobilize our potential in advanced information technology. The task is beyond the resources of any single enterprise. The central purpose is to pave the way for IT products, IT processes, and IT services which can be sold in the market in competition with the rest of the world.

We therefore accept Alvey's recommendation to establish a program of collaborative research concentrated on the four main areas of technology set out in the report. These areas are software engineering, very large-scale integration, man/machine interfaces, and intelligent knowledge-based systems. Industry has realized the need for collaborative research in these areas, and it is ready to take part in such a program. This positive involvement of industry in the funding, management, and execution of the program is crucial to its success, if we are to turn successful research into marketable products.

The key feature of the program will be collaboration between companies, government research establishments, and academic institutions. Work carried out in academic institutions will as usual be funded 100 percent by government. In the case of work carried out in industry, Alvey recommended that most of this should be 50 percent government-funded but that some projects should attract 90 percent funding. We have considered this last recommendation closely but have decided that 90 percent government funding does not secure a sufficient industrial commitment and could lead to the program becoming divorced from industry's needs. I have, therefore, decided that all industrial work should be 50 percent government-funded.

Companies taking part will be required to release know-how and to share results with their project partners. They will also be expected to license results on reasonable conditions to others in the program and to organizations outside the program where this is needed to secure exploitation.

The report estimated that the research would cost about £350 million over five years. The government stands ready to support a program of research on this scale. However, the extent of the government's contribution to the program depends upon industry making its contribution and upon the program's technical progress.

The report proposed that academic institutions should carry out some £50 million of research over five years and industry the remaining £300 million. The full cost of this to the government would be around £200 million. This money will be provided by the Department of Industry, the Department of Education and Science, and the Ministry of Defence and, over the PES (Public Expenditure Survey) period, will not add to existing allocations. The Department of Education and Science will fund research through the Science and Engineering Research Council, mainly in the universities. The Ministry of Defence will fund research of particular importance to our future defense industry. The Department of Industry will provide the major portion of the government's funds and will carry overall responsibility for the management of the program.

A new, small directorate will be established in the Department of Industry to coordinate the program. It will be headed by Mr. Brian Oakley, currently Secretary of the Science and

Engineering Research Council. It will be staffed by people from industry and supported by the government departments concerned and the SERC. The directorate will report to a small supervising board of industrialists. Sir Robert Telford, who has substantial experience of the electronics industry, has agreed to serve on a part-time basis as chairman of the board.

This is the first time in our history that we shall be embarking on a collaborative research project on anything like this scale. Industry, academic researchers, and government will be coming together to achieve major advances in technology which none could achieve on their own. The involvement of industry will ensure that the results as they emerge are fully exploited here in Britain to the advantage of our economy. Information technology is one of the most important industries of the future and therefore one upon which hundred of thousands of jobs in the future will depend. Collaboration will ensure that the results of the research are widely disseminated, particularly to small firms which have such an important contribution to make to the industry. No one can guarantee success, but the government is convinced that this program will ensure for British industry secure access to the new technology and to the products and processes on which our future prosperity depends.

Appendix 3

Academics Favor After-Alvey Program

Conclusions and Recommendations, "After the Alvey Program—Academic Research in Information Technology" report by a Working Party of the SERC Engineering Board, March 1986*

Our main conclusions are as follows:

1. The Alvey Programme in the main represents a successful attempt to strengthen the IT industry through a major collaborative research program.

2. The academic sector has an indispensable role in the program.

3. There is clearly a need for a follow-on program closely integrated with European activities.

4. A follow-on program should continue work on the existing enabling technologies, including communications research, and add new areas.

5. A follow-on program should not be responsible for applications activities but should cooperate with them.

---

*In an introduction to the report David Shore, Chairman of the SERC Engineering Board, noted the working party's recommendation for support of £25 million per year, but commented: "It is not yet evident whether resources of this magnitude can be made available." In a preface to the report Professor Bill Mitchell, the SERC Chairman, added: "Council has been impressed by the academic/industrial collaborations which have been set up in the current program. However, before making its definitive judgment on any increase in resources to be deployed in this area, Council will wish to see evidence of achievements resulting from its current investment. It also hopes that there will be applications of the current work and it envisages that these may, in many cases, be suitable for joint funding between SERC and industry. Furthermore the funding demands in the whole field of IT and its applications are likely to require a sharing of projects and collaboration on a European scale."

6. The U.K. should determine its strategy for the contents of European and national programs as a matter of extreme urgency and preferably before seeking to agree these principles with our European partners.

7. A number of changes should be made in administrative arrangements for a follow-on program.

We therefore recommend a follow-on program on the following basis:

1. The academic community participates wholeheartedly in a program which is broadened and integrated with European activities.

2. The program is extended to include additional areas.

3. The national funding of the academic component should rise to £25 million per annum.

4. The University Grants Committee and the National Advisory Body for Public Sector Higher Education should participate from the outset in the plans for a follow-on program.

5. The program should be preceded by a realistic planning period, allowing particularly for conclusions to be reached on the strategy for U.K. and Europe.

6. The arrangements for supervision of the program should be revised and strengthened particularly in terms of European involvement.

7. Adequate staff for the program should be recruited and staff for liaison with Europe should be employed, if necessary located in Brussels.

8. The arrangements for intellectual property rights should be standardized.

Appendix 4
A Plan for Concerted Action

Summary Section of the Report of the IT86 Committee, 1986

1. Enhancement of efficiency to compete successfully in the world market is a vital need of U.K. industry and commerce and hence of the U.K. economy.

2. The manipulation, storage, and communication of information have become pervasive elements of modern society and are key to the efficient operation of both manufacturing and service industries. More effective development and use of information technology (IT) will improve the competitiveness of industry in general. Failure to respond fully and swiftly to the opportunities it offers would seriously damage that competitiveness.

3. The size of the U.K. market for IT, and for the many products which depend on its effective use, is inadequate to pay for the research, development, and marketing resources required to create and sustain international business. Strenuous efforts should be made to take full advantage of European schemes for collaborative work in the IT field.

4. There is a mutual interest between suppliers and users in IT which should be exploited to the benefit of both and in the interests of the nation. IT suppliers need a U.K. home market from which to develop international markets. Users stand to gain from a world-competitive supply industry which understands their needs.

5. A Plan of Action for IT is proposed, founded on: (1) a scheme of collaborative applications; (2) a focused collaborative research effort to support application needs; and (3) measures to promote technology transfer, widespread adoption of IT, and the development of IT skills.

6. The applications scheme will involve an active partnership between IT users and suppliers which, in addition to the intrinsic value of the projects, will encourage understanding by both of how to transfer technology and to exploit research by developing and testing specific IT systems based on emerging technologies. Government itself is expected to play a major role as IT user in relevant projects.

7. The research effort will be geared to perceived future market opportunities and to supporting the development of IT applications. It will consist of work specifically generated by application projects and longer-term work based on enabling technologies perceived as useful to the creation or improvement of IT systems.

8. Additional measures to promote IT awareness are also proposed: in particular, the further encouragement of education and training measures to provide the manpower and business skills which will increasingly be necessary as more advanced IT systems are installed in all sectors of the economy.

9. Participation in European programs such as ESPRIT, RACE, and Eureka is an integral part of the proposed plan of action. In particular, many of the research projects are expected to be carried out as part of the second phase of the ESPRIT program.

10. The government should play an important part in the plan of action by stimulating and helping to finance the proposed work. Industry is expected to play the major role, but individual companies would unsupported be unlikely to make such risky collaborative work a first priority in their own business plans.

11. The government contribution to the scheme of applications should be £125 million, with variable funding rates according to the assessed risks incurred in each project; it would be planned to stimulate a much larger investment by industry and to generate a total program of £500 million or more. The scale of the proposed research effort should be £550 million (over a five-year period) of which the government is expected to provide £300 million (including £50 million for academic research), a part of which would be its contribution to the second phase of the ESPRIT program. The basis of funding would be 50 percent to industry and 100 percent to academic participants.

12. Government spending on education and training and on support-for-innovation schemes are outside the above figures and should be maintained, but we are convinced that these activities should be closely coordinated with our program.

13. Features of the Alvey Programme which have proved to be particularly successful should be preserved. They include: (1) a close partnership between universities and industry; (2) effective coordination of spending from a number of government departmental budgets; (3) an integrated approach to problems involving industry and more than one government department; and (4) a strong focal point for the IT community to share expertise and discuss common problems.

14. Industry should play a major part in the organization and management of the proposed programs, within a DTI framework. The prime mechanism for determining strategy and taking major decisions would be a board chaired by a senior industrialist, supported by an executive group within DTI, whose head should be a member of the board. Both board and executive group should include representatives of government departments which in addition to being users themselves, are sponsors of user industries.

Appendix 5

Evaluators Report on Alvey Programme

Conclusions Section, "Evaluation of the Alvey Programme: Interim Report," October 1987

Implementation

1. The system of seconding industrial staff to the Alvey Directorate worked well in principle, but some areas did not have enough staff to cope with the workload and delays ensued. All areas had insufficient support staff. In future, staff numbers should be front-end loaded in line with the peak of work imposed by processing proposals.

2. The lack of administrative procedures and management information systems during the early part of the program could have been alleviated by a preparatory working group during the period between the announcement of the program and its commencement.

3. The lack of a deadline system for proposals was not popular with participants but allowed for flexibility in refining projects in consultation with the directorate.

4. In most cases, projects were found which covered the strategies prepared by the directorate and advisory committees. This was facilitated by the use of strategies which were indicative, rather than by identifying specific projects and calling for bids.

5. Alvey funding was concentrated in the large firms which account for most of the U.K.'s IT research. The concentration was most marked in VLSI and least in MMI, reflecting the industrial structure and degree of maturity of those fields.

6. The administration of Alvey by a directorate has been beneficial in providing a cohesive program and a focus for the community. The most serious failing has come in the interfaces between DTI, MoD, and SERC—caused by the split in contrac-

tual administration and reflected in varying administrative practices within the directorate. Efforts to improve these interfaces should be continued and procedures should be consistent for all parts of the program. A single budget should apply for the whole program to avoid repetition of the SERC funding problem which has led to delays and partners working out of sequence with each other.

7. Most participants have reacted favorably to collaboration. Alvey has tended to upgrade existing links more often than forge new ones. Information transfer within consortia is generally good. Interproject links are more important in specific cases of linked work than in the clubs.

8. Collaboration agreements have been a major source of delay to the program. The problem could be substantially reduced if the basic principles required were embodied in the contract and all supplementary items left to participants to agree among themselves. This could be greatly facilitated if participants had free use of their collaborators' results.

9. Careful attention will need to be given to the implications for intellectual property rights of regroupings of collaborators in subsequent U.K. or international programs. Very complex ownership patterns may arise.

10. After a slow start, the project monitoring system appears to be working well in Alvey. In future, it is important that the monitoring officers are involved with projects as early as possible.

11. Central institutes have a role to play where closely managed, goal-oriented research on issues of wide interest is required, for example, in standards research. Separate funding regimes may be necessary to establish the institutes. They should not be allowed to persist beyond the completion of their mission.

12. Closer coordination with the ESPRIT program is required.

13. A rolling program with scope for committing funds throughout the life cycle would have allowed better scope for updating strategies and building on strengths as they emerged. The funding system militated against this.

Progress and Impact

1. VLSI: In both the academic and industrial sectors, Alvey has accelerated and expanded research activities and improved

links. Monitoring officers report good progress, and the main technological targets appear to be on schedule. All the whole-process projects are showing evidence of exploitation and will provide a route for exploitation of some layer-processing projects.

2. IKBS: Monitoring officers again report satisfactory progress. The main achievement has been to strengthen the community in academia and industry. The community clubs have been one of the major successes of the program, linking users to development projects in a technology transfer mechanism. These and other expert system projects have shown the most exploitation progress. Some other areas are much further from the market, as one would expect of a program largely geared to academic research and the consolidation of a research community.

3. Software Engineering: There are indications that progress toward the ambitious program goals is behind schedule. However, Alvey has again expanded and accelerated U.K. activity, with Alvey projects representing a high proportion of participants' research work in this area. The collaboration engendered between firms was rare prior to the program.

4. MMI: This area was the slowest to start. Once under way, projects appear to be keeping to their schedules, though monitoring officers do not rate highly as many projects as in other areas. In the speech area, a coherent research community predated Alvey, but in the other areas one of the main tasks has been to consolidate a fragmented national effort. Advances have been made, but the goal is yet to be achieved. Problems with the speech demonstrator may jeopardize exploitation of linked MMI projects.

5. Large-Scale Demonstrators: After delays at the beginning of the program, these projects have proceeded well, with the exception of the Speech-Input Word Processor and Workstation, from which Plessey has withdrawn. The Mobile Information Systems project appears closest to exploitation.

6. Alvey funding provides a substantial proportion of academic research funds in the areas it covers. It has led to an increase in the pace and scale of research and to a substantial increase in collaboration with industry. The academic community is particularly vulnerable to interruptions between funding, causing teams to break up. Continuity is thus essential.

7. It is too soon for Alvey to have had major discernible impacts on firms' strategies, but it has had significant impacts on the rate, scale, and direction of research. Alvey funding appears to satisfy additionality criteria by increasing the rate and scale of research and by fostering collaboration. The program has also broadened the strategic horizons of firms in a way which may pay dividends in the longer terms.

8. Apart from directly realizable impacts through the exploitation of products, improved processes and techniques, and the development of standards, the Alvey Program has facilitated future collaboration, created awareness of new technologies, unified research communities, and had beneficial effects on manpower.

Appropriateness

1. VLSI: The area is a core technology and deserved to have been included in the program. Technical targets were sufficient given the niche markets in which U.K. firms operate, but the absence of a standard product component in the overall U.K. context is regrettable. The choice of six whole-process projects was correct for an ASIC strategy, but the CAD area should have been larger. The main problem is that there has been no rationalization of the U.K.'s fabrication capability. The realization of structural goals of this kind was beyond the capacity of Alvey.

2. IKBS: It was correct to concentrate on strengthening the academic research base as a prerequisite to technology transfer, but the overall strategy did not give enough thought to the eventual transfer process. The choice of established software and large systems firms as the most appropriate vehicles for eventual exploitation was justified, but the success of the community clubs should not disguise the fact that they linked development rather than research activities to the market. Further coupling of research to the market—a vital component of a successful program—would require additional foresight and resources.

3. Software engineering: The inclusion of software engineering in Alvey was beyond contention. Questions have been raised over whether a database development component or shorter-term work on fourth-generation languages should have been included. While these areas were probably beyond the resources of the program, its concentration on longer-term process innovations for use by software developers may mean that

the industry is insufficiently supported in current-generation areas before it has the opportunity to exploit next-generation research. An expanded remit of support is necessary.

4. Man/Machine Interface: The evidence suggests that the advantages of collecting the areas of speech, image, human interface, and displays under a single generic and administrative heading have been slight. On the other hand, the areas involved are of critical importance, often providing the main product differentiation features in the market. Continued support should involve a matrix structure which stresses intellectual links (such as those with IKBS) and the application of MMI techniques to other areas (especially human-interface work) as much as it involves support for the present groupings.

5. Large-Scale Demonstrators: The goals of providing exploitation-led targets and of demonstrating the results of Alvey research were admirable in principle, providing a link between product development and the enabling technology areas. In their implementation, however, although they may prove successful as projects in their own right, the demonstrators will not meet these goals. The two main problems concern phasing and the lack of a clear framework within which other projects pass results to the demonstrators. More fundamentally, as the speech demonstrator seems to suggest, market choices are more vulnerable to change in company policy than technology choices, and hence the projects are more risky. These factors require careful consideration in the context of the IT86 Committee's recommended applications program.

6. Infrastructure and Communications: At least one of these projects is of a high calibre with good exploitation potential. This research area was not intended to be part of Alvey yet has consumed substantial resources. A clear decision is necessary as to whether communications research is to be supported. The high-speed network appears to have been expensive in relation to the use it has been to the program.

7. International comparisons suggest that the scale of world activity and government support for this type of research means that British industry would have been substantially disadvantaged without a national program. The choice of technologies in Alvey is in line with world thinking.

8. Equivocation about the balance between short-term and long-term R & D in collaborative programs is counterproduc-

tive. Programs should attempt to maintain a dynamic balance between both.

9. The manner in which Alvey was formulated and implemented satisfies some of the criteria of successful policies and policy making. However, it still remains to be seen whether continuity and coherence characterize the way in which Alvey links with future initiatives.

10. It was correct to undertake a program of precompetitive research in the U.K. in the early 1980s, but there was also a need for other complementary policy measures aimed at tackling the problems the U.K. encounters in exploiting its research.

11. The evidence supports the choice of technical areas in the Alvey Programme, and for precompetitive research the funding was adequate. It was inadequate to conduct the full range of activities which the program has shown to be necessary for successful coupling of such research to the market.

12. It is beyond the remit of the evaluation to comment on whether there should be a follow-on program to Alvey. However, delays in decision making have strong implications for the current program. The present uncertainty is already breaking up research teams. Much of the research requires follow-up work to reach an exploitable form. Without a follow-on a substantial part of the potential benefits of Alvey will be lost. This does not exclude a rigorous consideration of which lines of research should be continued and which terminated. Selectivity should be aided by experience, but the timing of decisions concerning a follow-on program is becoming critical.

Appendix 6
U.K. Government Responds to IT86

Extract from Innovation Chapter, "DTI—The Department for Enterprise," White Paper, January 1988

Collaborative Research

8.15 New technologies can transform products, processes and services in remarkable and often unfamiliar ways. The U.K. has particular strengths in some of these technologies in scientific research and industrial application. But exploiting those strengths often requires new collaborative arrangements both between companies and between companies and researchers in the public sector. DTI can encourage and facilitate the development of collaborative arrangements with other departments concerned; this is particularly important where technological risks are high.

8.16 Technological strengths can be exploited on a collaborative basis internationally within Europe. Few European countries can compete with the scale of resources available to the U.S.A. and Japan but collaborative research can maximize the strengths of industries and researchers in different European countries. DTI will encourage the participation of U.K. companies in technological collaboration with other European firms and research communities, including programs such as ESPRIT and RACE.

8.17 There are four main ways in which DTI, with other government departments in some cases, will encourage and finance collaborative research:

• *LINK* encourages companies to undertake joint research with Higher Education Institutions (HEIs) and Research Councils. The research will be precompetitive but industrially relevant. Programs currently under preparation include new technologies such as nanotechnology and industrial measurement systems.

• *EUREKA* encourages industrially led projects with European Community and other European partners. These should both strengthen European technological capability in world markets and contribute to the completion of the single European market.

• *National collaborative research programs* promote longer-term, industrially led collaborative projects between U.K. companies in advanced technologies. These research programs in new technologies will often involve mixed scientific and technological disciplines. Such technologies are likely to have a pervasive impact on economic activity of all kinds, often characterized by high entry costs and/or technological risks, usually some distance from the market but offering a good prospect of market exploitation. DTI's role is to help establish the collaborative links both between firms and between firms and the research community at the precompetitive research stage. Once these links are established, decisions on further collaboration and commercial exploitation should be taken by industry itself. DTI, with advice from its Technology Requirements Board, is currently running collaborative programs in such advanced technologies as advanced robotics and gallium arsenide. A new program on superconductivity is now being launched, linked with initiatives by the Science and Engineering Research Council.

• *General industrial collaborative projects* encourage collaboration through a variety of projects. Some foster R & D serving the interests of fragmented industries where small firms typically do not have the resources for advanced technological projects; research associations which pool resources can meet those needs. Some encourage the adoption of technology originating in the science base, particularly in the government's research establishments. Some are collaborative projects only involving industrial participants in joint research for companies with similar interests especially small and medium-sized companies.

8.18 Research covered by the collaborative program will change over time. In the future DTI will only contribute funds to research which would not and could not go ahead without some support from the taxpayer. It will normally be DTI's policy to fund any particular project or area of work only over a specific time period and where appropriate to reduce the rate of funding over time. Companies themselves are expected to become aware of the benefits which collaborative arrangements can bring and to undertake collaborative research without any government funding.

8.19 Within the context of the policies outlined above, the government have considered whether the proposals in the report of the IT86 Committee should be included amongst the national collaborative research programs.

8.20 The government have already agreed to support ESPRIT 2, for which there will be a U.K. contribution through the Community budget of the order of £200 million. The government also recognize that the Alvey Programme has provided a good focus for the IT research community, which has helped to bring together different parts of industry as well as industry and HEIs. The involvement of secondees from industry, academia, and the government departments involved has also proved successful and has assisted U.K. organizations to participate fully in ESPRIT.

8.21 The government nevertheless accept that some resources should be devoted to a national initiative complementary to ESPRIT, within the framework of the national collaborative research program set out in paragraph 8.17. DTI has earmarked £29 million over the next three years for programs in this area and SERC has plans to devote some £55 million over five years to related academic research, mainly in partnership with companies. Together with ESPRIT 2, and with other programs in this area, this provides very substantial support for collaborative research in IT. DTI will bring together all its collaborative research activities in information technology into a new unit which will continue to use people seconded from industry, HEIs, and other government departments to allow better coordination of support for European and national work in this area. The government do not, however, intend to provide a specific program of support for applications in IT.

Appendix 7

National Audit Office Audits Alvey

Summary and Conclusions Section of National Audit Office Report on the Alvey Programme, March 1988

1. Information Technology (IT) is concerned with collection, storage, processing, transmission, and presentation of information by electronic means. It is essential to the competitiveness of virtually all manufacturing and service industries and has a fundamental impact on society.

2. This report records the results of an examination by the National Audit Office (NAO) of the management and attainments of the Alvey Programme for advanced information technology, which was intended to increase the competitiveness of the United Kingdom IT industry in world markets by doubling the level of IT research in the United Kingdom over five years and by meeting a series of detailed technical targets.

3. The program is funded jointly by government (HMG) and industry and is managed by a small unit—the Alvey Directorate (AD)—within the Department of Trade and Industry (DTI), but the Ministry of Defence (MoD) and the Science and Engineering Research Council (SERC) also participate mainly through staff seconded to the AD. The IT industry also second staff to the AD. Government expenditure to March 1987 amounted to £98 million.

4. The report's main findings and conclusions are summarized below.

Administration and Financial Control of the Program

5. The government's decision that administrative responsibility for the complex collaborative projects under this major program should be split between three departments meant that there was a vital need for strong central administrative and fi-

nancial supervision to hold the program on course. External evaluations of the program's effectiveness, commissioned by the AD and running parallel with the program itself, were expected to help identify improvements. The NAO found that there had been material weaknesses in administrative areas. The main ones were:

(a) The involvement of three departments gave rise to problems in contracting, financial control, and funding of projects.

(b) The AD did not initially establish central management and financial information systems so that provision of program data was slower, more labor-intensive, and less comprehensive and reliable than it should have been for a complex program of this sort. An integrated computerized system was not introduced until mid-1987—four years after expenditure on the program started.

(c) External evaluations had some influence on the direction of the program but this was limited, mainly because they arrived late in the program's life. The AD stated that they had not expected evaluations to influence the present program much but they would influence decisions on any future IT program.

(d) Project appraisals were thorough but the appraisal process caused delays. In eight of the forty-two cases examined, nine months or more elapsed between receipt of the final proposals and issue of offers to the contractors.

(e) Departmental monitoring of projects varied in standard and approach. But it was necessary, in the AD's view, to strike a balance between standardization and giving reasonable autonomy to technology directors.

6. However, in spite of these weaknesses—which may have been partly caused by a lack of resources—the program succeeded in drawing up detailed strategies within fourteen months and in getting 300 projects underway by March 1987.

Collaboration and Participation

7. The Alvey Committee regarded collaboration involving industry, academics, and research organizations as fundamental to securing the best use of the nation's scarce resources. It also considered that there should be maximum access to the program, which was seen as particularly relevant to small firms. The NAO found that the program had generated a substantial

amount of cooperation. The 187 full collaborative projects extant in 1986 had on average four partners, typically two or three firms and one or two universities. Seventy-two percent of academic groups and 58 percent of the industrial firms had not previously worked with their Alvey partners. However, NAO also noted that:

(a) Difficulties in establishing collaborative agreements had caused significant delays as well as withdrawals from the program, and most project managements considered that the AD should have done more to help.

(b) Participation in projects was dominated by large firms: 5 such firms accounted for 209 of a total of 428 industrial "participations" and the 35 small firms, who were participating, had only 51 "participations" between them.

(c) The Alvey Board decided to spend more on academic research and on program administration and infrastructure than was originally intended. As a result, some £35 million less will be spent by government and, under matching arrangements, also by industry on industry's research work under collaborative projects.

Exploitation of the Alvey-Funded Research

8. The Alvey Programme is designed to give U.K. industry the technological base to meet the needs of the world IT market in the 1990s, but the Alvey Committee considered that exploitation of research would start at an early stage and continue throughout the program and beyond. They saw software engineering (SE) as providing the greatest exploitation expectations and dissemination of the results of the research as the key to exploitation. The AD established arrangements aimed at maximizing such dissemination and at encouraging commercial exploitation. The program is not yet complete but the NAO found that:

(a) A 1987 achievements paper by the AD showed that 10 out of approximately 200 industrial projects in the program had put products on the market or had improved existing production processes and a further 77 projects had products at the prototype stage. The products already being exploited were predominantly in the Very Large-Scale Integration/Computer Aided Design (VLSI/CAD) area from which the Alvey committee had not expected many early exploitable products. In SE, however, there were no products yet being marketed although 16 were at the prototype stage. The AD consider that evidence of exploitable results emerging from nearly half the 200 industrial projects at this stage in the program was highly encouraging.

(b) Under the framework which governed intellectual property rights (IPR), participants are allowed three years to exploit the Alvey results before they are required to make them available under license for exploitation. This is in line with practice on other DTI programs but the AD has recognized that any worthwhile exploitation in IT areas should take place within a year.

Skills Shortages

9. The Alvey committee considered that the then current output of IT graduates was wholly inadequate and recognized the need for a detailed and wide-ranging program of action. It thought that there was sufficient manpower to launch the program but that more would be needed to carry it through and exploit the results. The NAO found that:

(a) There was considerable evidence of continuing IT skills shortages generally and for the Alvey Programme. The NAO's case examination revealed that manpower and staffing difficulties had been reported in over 50 percent of the projects examined. This had contributed to delays (some substantial) or the need for extensions on nine projects; to withdrawal of partners on five projects; and the need to employ foreign experts or an overseas university on three other projects.

(b) The government had instituted two major measures to increase the supply of graduates in IT and other engineering and technology disciplines. The first—the IT in Higher Education Initiative of December 1982–roughly maintained the level of IT graduate output from universities in the face of reductions in university funding in 1981–82. It also helped to increase graduate output from the polytechnic sector. It was too early to judge the success of the second initiative—the Engineering and Technology Programme of March 1985—but its targets for graduate output were less than DTI and MSC suggested in initial discussions and were determined with resource consequences and relevant demographic factors in mind.

(c) The government have decided not to establish a national body to monitor manpower demand and supply but the DTI have set up a new section to collect data on demand and supply for skilled IT manpower and the AD has also contributed substantially to the formulation and execution of central initiatives in this field.

Other Information Technology Schemes

10. In addition to the Alvey Programme there are national and European-funded IT schemes which could duplicate or overlap it and which might enable participants to be funded from more than one source. And the IT86 Committee recommended a successor to the Alvey Programme. The NAO found that:

(a) The organizational arrangements and the controls over Alvey Programme applications were such that it was unlikely that there would be duplication of work between Alvey and other IT programs or double funding from two of these sources.

(b) The government's recent White Paper "DTI—The Department for Enterprise" includes the government's response to the IT86 Committee recommendations. The White Paper indicates that collaborative research programs are to play an increasingly important part in the government's future policies for research and development. But for IT most of the funds available will be channeled toward European programs—mainly ESPRIT— with more limited DTI and SERC resources devoted to a national initiative complementary to ESPRIT within the framework of the overall national collaborative research program. There will be no specific national program of support for applications in IT.

General

11. It will probably be some years before it is possible to make a measured judgment of the impact of the Alvey Programme on the U.K.'s competitiveness in the field of IT. It is clear that a substantial amount has been achieved in terms of new research commissioned and projects supported and of closer cooperation within and between industry and academic institutions.

12. However, in the NAO's view, the rate of exploitation of Alvey-funded research appears lower than the Alvey Committee expected. And there have been other indications that the program might have been more effective given more staff and

better management information systems at the outset and if the balance of program expenditure between work in industry and SERC-funded work in universities and higher education institutions had been closer to that originally envisaged by the Alvey Committee. The AD could also have taken a more positive role in securing more prompt and effective collaboration; and the framework which governed exploitation of IPR by participants could have recognized the special nature of IT development and required results to be made available under licence earlier than for other DTI programs. It will clearly be important for departments to bear these points in mind in the new collaborative programs which will also have to cope with the continuing effects of skill shortages in IT.

Abbreviations

ABRC	Advisory Board for the Research Councils
ACARD	Advisory Council for Applied Research and Development
AD	Alvey Directorate
AI	Artificial Intelligence
AIAI	Artificial Intelligence Applications Institute
AMT	Active Memory Technology
ANSA	Advanced Networked Systems Architecture
ARE	Admiralty Research Establishment
ARPA	Advanced Research Projects Agency
ASWE	Admiralty Surface Weapons Establishment
AWSAP	Advanced Workstation and System Architecture Project
BCS	British Computer Society
BT	British Telecom
CAD	Computer-Aided Design
CARDS	Conceptual and Relational Database Server
CBI	Confederation of British Industry
CCA	Central Computer Agency
CCSC	Computing and Communications Subcommittee
CDI	Collector Diffusion Isolator
CERN	European Centre for Nuclear Research
CMOS	Complementary Metal Oxide Semiconductor
CPRS	Central Policy Review Staff
CSA	Computing Services Association

Abbreviations

CVD	(see DCVD)
DARPA	Defense Advanced Research Projects Agency
DCVD	Directorate of Components, Valves, and Devices
DCS	Distributed Computing Systems
DEC	Digital Equipment Corporation
DES	Department of Education and Science
DoI	Department of Industry (to June 1983)
DTI	Department of Trade and Industry (from June 1983)
EARB	Electronics and Avionics Requirements Board
ECRC	European Computer Industry Research Centre
EEC	European Economic Community
EFTPOS	Electronic Funds Transfer at Point of Sale
ESPRIT	European Strategic Programme for Research and development in Information Technology
ETL	Electro-Technical Laboratory
GEC	General Electric Company
GPT	GEC Plessey Telecommunications
HCI	Human/Computer Interaction
HEI	Higher Education Institution
HI	Human Interface
HMG	Her Majesty's Government
HMSO	Her Majesty's Stationery Office
HUSAT	Human Sciences Advanced Technology
IBM	International Business Machines
I&C	Infrastructure and Communications
ICL	International Computers Ltd
ICOT	Institute for New Generation Computer Technology
IEC	Information Engineering Committee
IED	Information Engineering Directorate
IEE	Institution of Electrical Engineers
IKBS	Intelligent Knowledge-Based Systems
IPR	Intellectual Property Rights

IPSE	Integrated Project Support Environment
IT	Information Technology
ITAP	Information Technology Advisory Panel
JIPDEC	Japan Information Processing Development Centre
JOERS	Joint Opto-Electronics Research Scheme
KBM	Knowledge Base Machine
LPI	Logic Programming Initiative
MCC	Marylebone Cricket Club
MCC	Microelectronics and Computer Technology Corporation
mips	Millions of instructions per second
MIT	Massachusetts Institute of Technology
MITI	Ministry of International Trade and Industry
MMI	Man/Machine Interface
MoD	Ministry of Defence
MRC	Medical Research Council
MSC	Manpower Services Commission
NAO	National Audit Office
NCC	National Computing Centre
NEC	Nippon Electric Company
NEDO	National Economic Development Office
NEL	National Engineering Laboratory
NSF	National Science Foundation
NTT	Nippon Telephone and Telegraph
OTS	Orbital Test Satellite
PAC	Public Accounts Committee
PIM	Parallel Inference Machine
PISA	Persistent Information Space Architecture
PITCOM	Parliamentary Information Technology Committee
PERA	Production Engineering Research Association
PREST	Programme of Policy Research in Engineering, Science, and Technology
PSI	Personal Sequential Inference Machine

RA	Research Assistant
RA	Research Association
RACE	Research and Development in Advanced Communications Technologies in Europe
RAL	Rutherford Appleton Laboratory
R & D	Research and Development
RISC	Reduced Instruction Set Computing
RSRE	Royal Signals and Radar Establishment
SCI	Strategic Computing Initiative
SDI	Strategic Defense Initiative
SE	Software Engineering
SERC	Science and Engineering Research Council (from April 1981)
SIGAI	Special Interest Group in Artificial Intelligence
SIRA	Scientific Instrument Research Association
SME	Small or Medium-size Enterprise
SPP	Specially Promoted Programme
SPRU	Science Policy Research Unit
SRC	Semiconductor Research Cooperative
SRC	Science Research Council (to April 1981)
SSPDC	Solid-State Physics and Devices Committee
STAR	Software Technology Advanced Research
STI	Software Technology Initiative
TIP	Technology Integration Project
UGC	University Grants Committee
UMIST	University of Manchester Institute of Science and Technology
VHPIC	Very High-Performance Integrated Circuit
VHSIC	Very High-Speed Integrated Circuit
VLSI	Very Large-Scale Integration

References

1. D. A. Duce, ed., *Distributed Computing Systems Programme*. (Peter Peregrinus, 1984).
2. Science Research Council, *Proposed New Initiatives in Computing and Computer Applications* (SRC, March 1979).
3. ACARD, *Information Technology* (HMSO, September 1980).
4. DoI, *The Government Response to the ACARD Report on Information Technology* (DoI, September 1981).
5. K. Owen, "Computers Get Brighter . . . and We Have Seen Nothing Yet," *The Times*, London, 9 February 1981, p. 9.
6. Science Research Council, *Artificial Intelligence: A Paper Symposium* (SRC, April 1973).
7. K. Owen, "Michie, the pioneer, Starts Again at 60," *The Times*, London, 14 February 1984, p. 21.
8. B. Randell, "Japanese Fifth Generation Computer Project," 27 October 1981.
9. C. Cookson. "Tapping Britain for Talent," *The Times*, London, 20 November 1981, p. 18.
10. Alvey Committee, *A Programme for Advanced Information Technology: The Report of the Alvey Committee* (HMSO, 1982) (see appendix 1).
11. P. Swinnerton-Dyer and R. Needham, *Artificial Intelligence Research in the UK* (October 1982).
12. SERC/DoI IKBS Architecture Study, *Intelligent Knowledge-Based Systems: a Programme for Action in the UK*, 3 vols. (IEE, June 1983).
13. A. Sloman, Letter to Margaret Thatcher MP, 10 September 1984.
14. A. Sloman, Letter to Sir Austin Bide, (undated) 1986.
15. E. Feigenbaum and P. McCorduck, *The Fifth Generation: Artificial Intelligence and Japan's Computer Challenge to the World* (Addison-Wesley, 1983).
16. K. Owen, "In search of a 'Techno-Hero,'" *The Times*, London, 25 October 1983, p. 16.
17. E. A. Ash, *Higher Education, Industry and Government: New Rules for a Menage à Trois* (IEE, 1 October 1987).

18. K. Owen, "The Exiles of Silicon Valley," *The Times*, London, 8 November 1983, p. 19.

19. Alvey Directorate, *Alvey VLSI: a User's Guide to New Silicon Technology* (Alvey Directorate, July 1987).

20. Alvey Directorate, *Alvey Achievements: Products and Processes Stemming from the National Programme in Information Technology* (Alvey Directorate, June 1987).

21. PREST/SPRU, *Evaluation of the Alvey Programme: Interim Report* (HMSO, October 1987) (see appendix 5).

22. National Audit Office, *Department of Trade and Industry: the Alvey Programme for Advanced Information Technology* (HMSO, March 1988) (see appendix 7).

23. Committee of Public Accounts, *The Alvey Programme for Advanced Information Technology: Minutes of Evidence, 4 May 1988* (HMSO, 1988).

24. ESPRIT Review Board, *The Mid-Term Review of ESPRIT* (Commission of the European Communities, October 1985).

25. K. Hoselitz, *VLSI: A Personal Appraisal* (SPRU, 1985).

26. E. Arnold, *A Review of the Alvey IKBS Programme* (SPRU, July 1988).

27. F. Land, "Completing a National Strategy for Information Technology," *Information Technology and Public Policy* 2, no. 3 (May 1984).

28. Alvey IT Users Panel, *Final Report* (NCC, April 1988).

29. L. Keliher, "Policy-making in Information Technology: A Decisional Analysis of the Alvey Programme," Ph.D. diss., London University, 1988.

30. SERC, *After the Alvey Programme: Academic Research in Information Technology* (SERC, March 1986) (see appendix 3).

31. IT86 Committee, *Information Technology—A Plan for Concerted Action: The Report of the IT86 Committee* (HMSO, 1986) (see appendix 4).

32. DTI, *DTI—the Department for Enterprise* (HMSO, January 1988) (see appendix 6).

33. K. Owen, "In Search of a 'Techno-Hero'" (reference 16).

34. IED, *Silicon towards 2000. Devices: A National Research Programme in Silicon VLSI and CAD* (DTI, June 1988).

35. IED, *Systems Architecture. A Strategy for Research in Parallel Architecture, Distributed Systems, Vision and Speech Technologies* (DTI, June 1988).

36. IED, *Systems Engineering. Improved Design and Construction of Complex IT Systems* (DTI, June 1988).

Further Reading

Fifth-Generation Program Background

Computerization Committee. *The Plan for Information Society—A National Goal toward Year 2000*. Japan Computer Usage Development Institute, 1972.

JIPDEC. *Interim Report on Study and Research on Fifth-Generation Computers (Outline)*. JIPDEC, August 1980.

JIPDEC. *Research and Development Proposals for the Fifth Generation of Computers*. JIPDEC, March 1981.

JIPDEC. *Preliminary Report on Study and Research on Fifth-Generation Computers 1979–1980*. JIPDEC, Fall 1981.

JIPDEC. *Minutes of International Conference on Fifth-Generation Computer Systems*. JIPDEC, March 1982.

T. Moto-oka, ed. *Fifth-Generation Computer Systems: Proceedings of the International Conference on Fifth-Generation Computer Systems, Tokyo, Japan, 19–22 October 1981*. North-Holland Publishing Company, 1982.

ICOT. *Proceedings of the International Conference on Fifth-Generation Computer Systems, 1984*. ICOT, 1984.

ICOT, ed. *ICOT Journal* (quarterly, from June 1983). Tokyo: ICOT.

Alvey Programme Background (Alvey Directorate/IED Publications)

News and Features:
Alvey News, no. 1 (September 1983) then bimonthly from no. 2 (December 1983) to no. 32 (December 1988). IEE.

Progress Reports, Overall and by Technologies:
Alvey Programme Annual Report. IEE: 1984, 1985 (including conference report), 1986, 1987, 1988.

Progress Reports on all Projects:
Alvey Programme Annual Report Poster Supplement. IEE: 1985, 1986, 1987, 1988.

Conference Reports:

Alvey Conference Report. IEE: 1986, 1987.

UK IT 88 Conference Publication. IEE: 1988.

ESPRIT Background

House of Lords Select Committee on the European Communities. *Session 1984–85, Eighth Report: ESPRIT.* HMSO, 1985.

J. Roukens and J. F. Renuart, eds. *ESPRIT '84: Status Report of Ongoing Work.* North-Holland, 1985.

European Commission, ed. *ESPRIT '85: Status Report of Continuing Work.* 2 pts. North-Holland, 1986.

European Commission DG13, ed. *ESPRIT '86: Results and Achievements.* North-Holland, 1987.

European Commission DG Telecommunications, Information Industries and Innovation, eds. *ESPRIT '87: Achievements and Impact.* 2 pts. North-Holland, 1987.

European Commission. *ESPRIT 1987 Annual Report.* Office for Official Publications of the European Communities, 1988.

General IT Background

IT Sector Working Party. *Policy for the UK Information Technology Industry.* NEDO, 1982.

IT Economic Development Committee. *Crisis Facing UK Information Technology.* NEDO, 1984.

ACARD. *Software: A Vital Key to UK Competitiveness.* HMSO, 1986.

E. Arnold and K. Guy. *Parallel Convergence: National Strategies in IT.* London: Frances Pinter, 1986.

Logica. *International Information Policy: From Participation to Regulation.* Logica, July 1988.

Name Index

Allen, Sir Geoffrey, 66, 118
Alvey, John, 3, 34, 35, 42, 43, 51
Aris, John, 206
Arnold, Erik, 204–205
Ash, Eric, 73, 93, 128, 129, 132, 170–171, 183, 230, 232, 237–238, 248
Ashworth, John, 52–53, 236
Atkinson, Reay, 12, 16, 17, 18, 19, 30, 32, 250

Bagshaw, Alan, 82, 147–149
Baker, Kenneth, 10–12, 16, 18, 31–32, 33, 51, 52, 53, 57–58, 60, 61, 118, 185
Barber, Derek, 74–75, 114, 185
Barron, Iann, 7–8, 9, 34, 38, 39, 41, 78, 128, 250, 279
Barrow, Chris, 37, 75, 76, 86, 140–141, 149, 162, 163, 166, 186
Bartlett, Keith, 115, 186, 189, 254
Benjamin, Alan, 9, 13
Benn, Tony, 292
Bevan, Nigel, 140
Bide, Sir Austin, 157–158, 165, 233, 236, 245–247
Bird, Richard, 59
Blackburn, Harold, 152
Brady, Michael, 161–162, 184
Broers, Alec, 184, 203–204
Brown, Vivian, 191
Butcher, John, 117, 255
Butler, Adam, 12

Cadiou, Jean-Marie, 30, 238
Cheetham, Chris, 254
Chorley, Dick, 140
Clarke, Kenneth, 241–242
Clarke, Laurence, 14, 19–20, 27, 28, 68, 87, 120, 149–151, 158, 186, 229, 234, 250, 253–254
Cohen, Ivor, 53
Colbert, Jean-Baptiste, 266
Cooper, Ron, 65, 66–67, 69
Croft, Roy, 53, 93, 129
Cross, Geoffrey, 158

Davies, Hywel, 35, 42
Davignon, Vicomte Etienne, 52, 221
Dignan, Tony, 137
Duff, Michael, 166–167

Egginton, Tony, 10, 93, 182–183, 249, 254, 262–263
Elmore, John, 238

Fairclough, John, 191, 207–209, 259–260
Fawcett, Bill, 71–73, 79, 115, 133–136, 186
Feigenbaum, Edward, 161–162, 168, 249
Fielding, Sir Colin, 71, 93, 129, 178, 230
Fox, Alan, 16
Foxall, Clive, 32
Fuchi, Kazuhiro, 44, 223

Gibson, Mark, 254
Gosling, William, 154
Gray, Peter, 207
Gregson, Lord, 230, 236
Griggs, Arthur, 142
Guy, Ken, 200–202

Haley, Colin, 9, 34, 35, 37, 162
Harrison, Don, 13
Hauser, Herman, 280

Hayes, Sir Brian, 65, 69, 122, 196–200, 254
Herbert, Andrew, 179
Hilsum, Cyril, 230
Hird, Roger, 70, 185, 188–189
Hoare, Tony, 279
Holmes, Geoffrey, 131
Holmes, John, 84, 140
Horne, Nigel, 175, 234, 236, 241, 247–248, 256, 257
Hoselitz, Kurt, 203
Hoskyns, Sir John, 233
Howe, Jim, 159, 172–173
Hughes, Philip, 9, 10, 16, 35, 36, 38, 40, 44, 46, 74, 129, 131, 250
Hüncke, Horst, 238

Jenkin, Patrick, 54
Joseph, Sir Keith, 12, 58–60

Kay, Nigel, 189
Keliher, Leo, 209–210
Kilburn, Tom, 8
Kingman, John, 64, 66
Kowalski, Robert, 15, 45

Land, Frank, 205
Laver, John, 152–154, 169–170
Lavington, Simon, 147
Leighfield, John, 129
Lighthill, Sir James, 15
Lingard, Robin, 13, 26
Lord, Gwen, 68
Low, Cameron, 236, 237, 248–249

Macdonald, Alastair, 26, 30, 35, 43, 45, 65, 66, 93, 112, 133, 253–254, 256
Major, John, 35
Maller, Vic, 37, 162
Marshall, F. Graham, 17, 235
Merriman, James, 31, 32–33
Michie, Donald, 15, 17, 167
Mitchell, Bill, 255
Morgan, David, 186, 187, 254
Morland, Robert, 186–187, 248, 254
Moto-oka, Tohru, 223

Needham, Roger, 16, 32, 35, 37, 44, 49–51, 127, 150, 168, 171–172, 230
Norman, Adrian, 55
Nudd, Graham, 184
Nuttall, Brian, 254

Oakley, Brian, 19, 26, 35, 54, 152–153, 156–157, 229, 250, 253, 256–258
Owen, Kenneth, 115

Pannenborg, A. E., 202
Parkinson, Cecil, 129
Pattie, Geoffrey, 62, 232, 241, 251–253
Prior, Linda, 115

Randell, Brian, 16, 20, 21, 32, 101, 202
Raymont, Patrick, 206
Read, Charles, 16, 35, 37, 45, 53
Roberts, Derek, 9–10, 35, 36, 39, 41, 42, 46, 69, 158–159, 176–177, 250–251
Roberts, Larry, 63
Rogers, Mike, 16
Roith, Oscar, 93, 191, 230

Schwarz, Peter, 154–155
Shackel, Brian, 85, 140, 162–164, 249
Sharpe, Bill, 139
Shorter, David, 160, 186, 188
Sleeman, Derek, 184
Sleep, Ronan, 82, 147–148
Sloman, Aaron, 157–158, 165–166
Solomon, Jonathon, 13
Southgate, Colin, 129, 132
Sparck Jones, Karen, 37, 45
Speake, David, 131, 236
Swinnerton-Dyer, Sir Peter, 49–51, 60

Talbot, Bill, 179–180
Talbot, David, 73, 80, 87, 136–138, 186, 202, 249–250
Tanner, David, 59
Tate, Austin, 167
Taylor, John, 15, 32, 78, 138–139, 157
Tebbit, Norman, 62
Telford, Sir Robert, 19, 33, 93–95, 97, 115, 129–131, 182, 233
Thatcher, Margaret, 10, 52, 53–54, 57, 61, 89, 130, 157–158, 229, 241, 249, 250, 259
Thomas, David, 26, 28, 32, 72–73, 92, 117, 138–139, 149, 180, 186, 230
Thynne, John, 13

Trenchard, Lord, 13
Tucker, Jeremy, 36

Underwood, Mike, 37, 140

Walker, Timothy, 69, 70, 77, 112,
    143–146, 185, 253–254, 255,
    260–262
Wallard, Andrew, 254
Warboys, Brian, 37
Warren, David, 184–185
Warren, Keith, 35, 129, 154–156
Watson, Mike, 173–175
Weinstock, Sir Arnold, 94
Wheldon, Adrian, 188
Whittle, Frank, 252
Wilkins, Mark, 230, 254
Wilmot, Robb, 16, 18
Witty, Rob, 8, 10, 36–37, 73, 100,
    136, 157, 160, 186
Worden, Robert, 36, 180
Worsnip, David, 26, 164

Yoshikawa, Shiro, 16, 18
Young of Graffham, Lord, 241, 255

Subject Index

ACARD, 12
Acorn, 280
Active Memory Technology, 281–282
Advisory Board for Research Councils, 106
Airbus Industrie, 278
Alvey Administration, 143–146
  director's views on, 143–146, 188–189
Alvey Committee, 34–48
  choice of technologies, 38
  extent of direction, 40–41
  members, 34, 45
  nature of program, 42–45
  program cost, 43
  public support, 40
  small companies, 40–41
  two groups, 41
Alvey Conferences, 112, 115, 186, 189, 232, 241
Alvey Directorate, 65, 278
  administrator, 69–70
  board meetings, 86–87
  delegation, 76
  deputy director, 68–69
  directors from MoD and SERC, 71–73
  management information system, 188, 200, 210
  preparation of strategies, 76–78
  secondments from industry, 71
  Xionics system, 142
Alvey Infrastructure and Communications, 141–143
  director's views on, 141–143, 189
Alvey IT User Panel, 206, 237
Alvey Mail, 114, 142
Alvey News, 75, 98, 112, 114, 142

Alvey Programme, 3–6
  academic contribution, 171
  achievement, 6
  advisory committees, 77, 91–92, 134
  allocation of funds, 132–133, 195
  choice of director, 63–67
  collaboration, 4, 91, 97–99, 149, 169–172, 176
  collaboration agreements, 109–110, 144, 154, 166
  collaboration with ESPRIT, 112–113
  communications, 113–115
  community, 6, 245, 262, 263
  controversy, 5
  cultural revolution, 5
  data communications research, 75
  ethos, 209–210
  evaluation, 96, 119–123, 190–192, 202
  expenditure, 194
  follow-on developments, 182
  funding problems, 103–107
  high-speed network, 114, 142, 189
  industrial benefits, 175
  industrial views, 173–177
  infrastructure, 74, 107–108, 113, 157, 160, 189
  innovation, 4, 178–181, 182
  interim report, 191–192, 198
  investment, 5
  large firms, 135
  lessons, 293–294
  level of government support, 61
  Logic Programming Initiative, 82
  NAO report, 193–202
  origins, 7–21
  post-Alvey workshop, 234–235

334 Subject Index

Alvey Programme—(cont.)
  precompetitive research, 3, 98, 208, 259, 268
  publicity, 118–119
  purchase of computers, 107–109, 156–160
  responsibility, 102–103
  scale of program, 268–269
  small firms, 110–111, 199, 257
  speech technology, 290–292
  start of program, 68
  successor program, 229–230, 233, 234–235
Alvey Programme Steering Committee, 92–97, 129–133, 203, 229, 256
Alvey projects
  Admiral, 14, 142, 189
  ANSA, 113, 148, 149, 179
  AWSAP, 179
  CARDS, 148
  evaluation of proposals, 88–91
  exploitation, 88, 109, 113, 144, 187–189, 195, 198, 201
  firms' withdrawals, 177
  Flagship, 148, 151, 277–279
  large demonstrators, 87, 132, 149–151
  management, 90, 109, 144
  monitoring, 119–123
  Parsifal, 83
  PISA, 148
  "Uncle" projects, 100, 103, 173
  Unison, 14, 142, 189
  Universe, 13–15, 114, 172
Alvey Report, 46–48
  CBI comments, 52
  collaborative program proposed, 46
  DoI consultation, 51–54, 57
  IT Fellowship proposed, 48
  program approved, 54, 60
  program directorate, 48, 54
  report published, 51
Alvey technologies. See Architectures; IKBS; MMI; Software engineering; VLSI
Apple Macintosh, 271
Architectures, 38, 80–81, 82, 139, 147–149
  parallel architectures in UK, 275–279
  RISC, 274

small firms, 279–282
Warwick meeting, 147
Arthur Andersen consultants, 203
Artificial intelligence, 15, 172–173, 217, 294. See also IKBS
  expert systems, 270
  human interface, 270–273
  Lighthill Report, 15, 49, 51, 161–162
  progress toward goal, 269–270
  Swinnerton-Dyer and Needham Report, 49–51

Bide Committee. See IT86 Committee
British Aerospace, 180, 253
British Computer Society, 207
British Telecom, 14, 180, 186
  Research Laboratories, 14
Bull, 277

Cabinet Office, 207
  IT Unit, 53
Cambridge University Computer Laboratory, 14
CLIP system, 166
Confederation of British Industry, 52
  CBI Education Foundation, 118
Cray, 273

Defence, Ministry of, 42, 178
  CVD, 78, 105
  influence on VLSI, 135
  RSRE, 64, 78
Design-to-product demonstrator, 150
DHSS demonstrator, 150, 151
Dick, A. B., 158
Digital Equipment Corporation
  DEC-10 computer, 156–157
  VAX computer, 108, 157, 160
Distance-learning courses, 117

East Anglia University, 277
Edinburgh University, 79, 104, 291
  Artificial Intelligence Applications Institute, 167
  Crystal Computer Architecture Laboratory, 274
  Regional Computing Centre, 156
  Speech Technology Research Centre, 152

Education and Science, 58–60, 106
  IT conversion courses, 59
  "new blood" appointments, 60
ESPRIT, 30, 36, 37, 39, 47, 52, 70, 77, 101, 110, 141, 145, 148, 277–278
  comparison with Alvey, 221–222
  Management Committee, 112
  mid-term review, 202
  Technology Integration Projects, 222
Eureka, 246
  COSINE project, 189
Europe. *See also* ESPRIT; Eureka
European Computer Industry Research Centre, 224, 277
European Informatics Network, 142
European Space Agency, 14
Framework program, 251
space consortia, 278
Experimental Aircraft Programme, 253

Ferranti, 36, 99, 186
Fujitsu, 36, 223
  link with ICL, 16, 18

GEC, 14, 36, 41, 68, 90, 93–94, 111, 150, 153, 155, 156–160, 176–177, 186, 253, 291
  Marconi, 93, 153
  Marconi Research Centre, 14
  Series 63 computer, 108, 143, 156–160

Harwell (AERE), 44
Hewlett-Packard, 180
Hitachi, 36, 223

IBM, 24, 207, 273, 278–279
ICL, 16, 71, 73, 87, 150, 180, 276–279, 287
  Digital Array Processor, 281–282
  link with Fujitsu, 16, 18
IKBS, 15, 28–29, 35, 37, 43, 45, 46–47, 72, 77–78, 92, 99, 116. *See also* Artificial intelligence
  Architecture Study, 138
  awareness campaign, 181, 282–283
  community, 108, 138, 160, 172
  director's views on, 138–139, 188
  evaluation, 204–205

expert-system clubs, 181, 188
  Journeyman scheme, 117, 168
  market penetration, 282–284
  Research Area Review Meeting, 138
  strategy, 81–83
Imperial College (London), 117, 152–153, 168, 171, 277
  ALICE machine, 9, 279
Industrial property rights. *See* Intellectual property rights
Industry, Department of, 12. *See also* Trade and Industry, Department of
  anti-ESPRIT, 39
  Electronics and Avionics Requirements Board, 48, 129, 130–131
  industry meeting, 28, 30–33
  IT Division, 12
  Japan mission, 16–18
  mission report, 19, 22–26, 30–32
Inference computing, 227, 270
Information technology
  education and training, 62, 116–118
  industry/academia cooperation, 27, 31
Information Technology Advisory Panel, 53–54
  interdepartmental committee, 53
  IT Skills Agency, 118
  micros in schools, 58
  Minister for, 11, 12, 16, 53, 57, 232, 251
  skill shortages, 116–118, 195–196
  users' views, 205–207
Inmos, 7, 39, 78, 135–136, 285
  Occam language, 279
  transputer, 279–280
INRIA, 223, 277
Intellectual property rights, 28, 52, 109–110, 145, 176, 187, 199
IT82, 13, 58
  Downing Street seminar, 21
  final conference, 52
IT86 Committee, 81, 97, 119, 165, 233
  research and applications, 235–238
  terms of reference, 233–234
IT86 Report, 238–241
  applications scheme, 240
  government response, 242–244

IT86 Report—(cont.)
 research effort, 240
 views on government response, 245–253

Japan
 Agency of Industrial Science and Technology, 23
 collaboration with UK, 16–18, 20, 21, 23, 24, 25, 26, 30, 47
 DoI mission, 16–18, 19, 22–26
 ETL, 17, 23, 215, 223
 Fifth Generation Computer Systems program, 4, 17, 22–26, 223–228, 271–273
 fifth-generation conference, 16, 25, 215–216
 fifth-generation machines and languages, 225–226
 ICOT, 44, 74, 223–228, 277
 JIPDEC, 17, 23
 MITI, 16, 17, 22, 24–25, 36, 223
 natural-language processing, 226
 NTT, 223
 object-oriented language, 227
 parallel architecture work, 273–275
 Project Promotion Committee, 223
 silicon IC initiative, 215
 supercomputer program, 214–215
 VLSI strength, 24
JOERS, 128

Lisp, 226, 274
Logic, guarded horn clause, 275
Logica, 10, 14, 74, 111
London Business School, 121
 Centre for Business Strategy, 190
Loughborough University, 14
 HUSAT, 152–153

Manchester University, 99, 277
 Dataflow system, 9
 PREST, 96, 121, 190, 200, 208
Matsushita, 223
Medical Research Council
 Applied Psychology Unit, 85
Millbank Tower, 68, 71
Mitsubishi, 223
MMI, 35, 37, 38, 46–47, 76, 97, 162–164
 advisory committees, 140
 director's views on, 140–141
 displays, 84, 89

human factors, 84–85, 140–141, 163, 249, 283
 strategy, 83–85
Mobile information systems demonstrator, 150, 151

National Audit Office, 107, 122, 289
 report on Alvey, 193–196
 views on report, 196–200, 200–202
National Computing Centre, 206
National Physical Laboratory, 40
NEC, 223

OKI, 223
Olivetti, 180, 280
Open University, 117

PA consultants, 138
Philips, 180
PITCOM, 205
Plessey, 36, 75, 150, 152–156, 176–177, 186, 253, 277, 285, 291
Prime Minister. *See* Thatcher, Margaret
Prolog, 225–226, 274
Public Accounts Committee, 122, 166, 197

Racal, 103, 150
Research
 cooperative, 213–215
 evaluation of, 265–268
Research and development
 public support for, 292–293
Research assistants, 105–106
Research Associations, 213–214, 257

Science and Engineering Research Council, 7, 42, 105–106, 182–183
 after-Alvey committee, 230
 after-Alvey report, 230–232
 Cosener's House, 20, 26–28
 Engineering Board, 10, 14, 19, 230
 Information Engineering Committee, 7–8, 14, 77, 163–164, 183
 IT87, 28–30, 31
 Janet network, 113
 joint framework for IT research, 255–256, 258, 261–263
 Polymer Engineering Directorate, 10
 Rutherford Appleton Laboratory, 8, 14, 44, 114, 142

Software Technology Initiative, 37
Specially promoted programs, 15, 37
support for IT86 proposals, 249
told of Alvey director change, 254
Science Research Council, 7, 9, 64.
 See also Science and Engineering Research Council
Computing Science Committee, 7
Distributed Computing Systems Programme, 7–9, 275
Roberts Panel, 9–10
Sharp, 223
Shell Research, 180
Siemens, 277
Software engineering, 35, 46, 288–290
 director's views on, 136–138, 187
 IKBS techniques applied to, 137
 Information systems factories, 46, 137
 IPSEs, 90, 136
 strategy, 80–81
Southampton University, 79, 104
Speech-input demonstrator, 150, 151–156, 291–292
SRI International, 180
 Cambridge Laboratory, 180
Starwest, 200
Sussex University
 SPRU, 96, 121, 190, 200, 208

Technology, Ministry of, 64
The Times (London), 26
Thorn-EMI, 279
Toshiba, 223
Trade and Industry, Department of
 Information Engineering Directorate, 69, 114, 223, 253–256, 260–262
 IT Division, 187
 joint framework for IT research, 255–256, 258, 261–263
 LA Division, 140, 261
 Link schemes, 251–252, 258
 post-Alvey strategies, 255
 repackaging, 242–243
 tension between LA Division and Alvey, 261
 White Paper, 243–244
Treasury, 66
Turing Institute, 117, 167–168

United Kingdom
 collaboration with Japan, 16–18, 20, 21, 23, 24, 25, 26, 30, 47
 expatriates return, 184–185
 need for fifth-generation strategy, 19
 possible IT research program, 27
 UK IT88 conference, 204, 263
United States
 Arpanet, 40, 152
 DARPA, 40–41, 105, 216–218
 MCC, 74, 216, 218–221
 National Science Foundation, 216, 223
 response to fifth-generation program, 216–218
 Sematech, 220
 Semiconductor Research Cooperative, 219, 220
 STAR program, 288
 Strategic Computing Initiative, 216–218
University College (London), 14
University Grants Committee, 60, 171
Unix, 83, 156, 158, 160

VLSI, 29, 35, 36, 38, 43, 46–47, 72, 96, 98, 103
 academic contribution, 104–105, 136
 achievement in, 284–287
 brochure, 187
 CAD for, 79, 134, 287–288
 director's views, 133–136, 186–187
 evaluation, 202–204
 instrument industry, 288
 large firms' attitudes, 285–286
 small firms' contribution, 136
 strategy, 78–80, 132
 VHPIC program, 36, 134
 VHSIC program, 36, 203

Xerox PARC, 271, 273